FAMILIES WE NEED

FAMILIES WE NEED

Disability, Abandonment, and Foster Care's Resistance in Contemporary China

ERIN RAFFETY

RUTGERS UNIVERSITY PRESS
New Brunswick, Camden, and Newark, New Jersey, and London

978-1-9788-2930-5 (cloth)
978-1-9788-2929-9 (paper)
978-1-9788-2931-2 (epub)

Cataloging-in-publication data is available from the Library of Congress.
LCCN 2022008511

A British Cataloging-in-Publication record for this book is available from the British Library.

References to internet websites (URLs) were accurate at the time of writing. Neither the author nor Rutgers University Press is responsible for URLs that may have expired or changed since the manuscript was prepared.

♾ The paper used in this publication meets the requirements of the American National Standard for Information Sciences—Permanence of Paper for Printed Library Materials, ANSI Z39.48-1992.

www.rutgersuniversitypress.org

Manufactured in the United States of America

For Isabelle Clark-Deces, who loved me so well,
and for the foster families, who have taught me so much

PROLOGUE

When I married my husband just prior to entering graduate school, and as I got to know the professors and other graduate students in my department, I learned that anthropological fieldwork could be particularly hard on relationships. If I was going to drag this person halfway across the world with me, I might as well ask him where he would be willing to go. It turned out my husband had spent two summers in Xi'an, China, during college, and they had stuck with him. He picked up enough Mandarin during those brief stays to communicate, and he had spent enough time doing missionary work under the guise of teaching English to know that he wanted to get to know Chinese people without the subterfuge.

It was somewhere in the throes of these newlywed conversations and planning for graduate school in 2008 that I also caught a glimpse of Allan Myers's documentary *China's Lost Girls* (2005). The documentary followed prospective American adoptive parents to China, detailing how the "one-child policy" had put pressure on Chinese parents with traditional attitudes to prefer boys to girls beginning nearly forty years ago.[1] From the 1990s into the present, around 150,000 children have been adopted from China to Western countries, and 81,600 of those children were adopted to the United States, according to the U.S. Department of State. Hovering in the background of the documentary, barely visible, yet painfully wiping away their tears as they let their children go to America to be adopted, were Chinese foster mothers. How could they do this heartbreaking work of fostering child after child, only to have them move across the world and never be able to see them again? Who were these women who hovered in the background of both Chinese birth mothers and Western adoptive mothers? If I could somehow talk with them, what would they tell me?

I enrolled in first-year Chinese at Princeton University with twelve or so college freshmen, the majority of them young men hoping to pursue a career in international finance. Alongside my regular PhD load of graduate courses in anthropology, I spent nearly fifteen hours each week that first year, drilling tones in Mandarin, meeting one-on-one with my teacher, and taking weekly quizzes. I was shocked to find out that whereas language learning was highly regimented and disciplined, the art of doing fieldwork—especially, perhaps, in China—was anything but. My husband and I secured tourist visas and through a host of friend-of-a-friend-of-a-friend connections, cobbled together a rough itinerary for a six-week pre-fieldwork trip in the summer of 2009, which began in Nanning, Guangxi, and ended in Beijing. I remember sitting with my Chinese professor in his office at Princeton explaining my intent to go to Southwest China to study foster families. When he heard the name Guangxi his ears pricked up, and he bellowed a guttural laugh, *"I don't even understand a thing they say there. Ha! Good luck!"*

I remember not only the cacophony of languages and accents upon touching down in Nanning but the pervasive smell of mildew, the sea of e-bikes stretching across the broad avenues, the oppressive heat and the way sweat clandestinely slipped down my spine as I braced myself on crowded buses, and my first for-ays through neighborhood markets searching for foster mothers alongside an acquaintance who swore they could be found. Much like those in the documen-tary, however, in that first summer foster mothers and foster families remained hidden from view: it would take me nearly eight months in 2010 to make contact with Mercy Care, the international nongovernmental organization (INGO) that worked with the Nanning Social Welfare Institute, to be invited to meet the fami-lies, so great was their suspicion of foreigners and their intentions.

Yet during that first summer in 2009, I visited private orphanages taking care of children with disabilities outside Beijing and chatted casually with American couples waiting to adopt infants in the grand White Swan Hotel on desolate Sha'mian Island nearby the American consulate in Guangzhou. Little did I know that those two seemingly disconnected and frustrating experiences—given that I was eager to connect with foster families and not disabled, institutionalized children or international adoptive parents—would provide context and clues to not only the history of foster care in China but its present practice, betwixt and between state care and the markets of international adoption. That nearly all the foster children I met between 2010 and 2012 in my fieldwork in Guangxi, as well as a few other provinces, were disabled, and that the foster mothers who reared them were older and disenfranchised, were startling ethnographic surprises.

After taking so much time to even meet foster families, I was shocked by the secrets people confided in me (illegitimate children, illegal adoptions, and infertil-ity) and sudden expressions of emotion I encountered—how women clung to me so briefly and then even physically pushed me away. So powerful and yet fleeting were these displays of emotion that I often wondered whether I imagined them, or if they did occur, and what it was inside of me or between us that elicited such raw-ness, even as I relished the intimacy. Given that foster families were of low status, they often did not know when or where a child would be given or removed from their care. One afternoon I showed up to find that one of my informants had sim-ply vanished, the remaining family huddled together in a puddle of tears.

The fieldwork was unsettling, difficult, and complicated in ways I had not pre-dicted. I was childless and in my late twenties, and I had not expected to become so involved in my informants' families and lives. To say that now sounds callous and trite, but too many ethnographies are written without much attention to emotional privilege, how thinking can be a shield for feeling—a shield we're too often congratulated for. I found out the hard way, of course, that I could not *not* hold babies when they were thrust into my arms, dry tears when they were presented to me, mourn a child who was dying, grieve a child who was leaving, or withhold information about my own relationships if I was going to grow in relationship with the people I studied.

When my grandfather became very sick back in the United States, foster care workers Huilan, Luli, Suling, and Xiao Wang sympathetically told me not to worry, but I became furious with them, feeling that they had no idea what it was like to be in one place and have your family suffering in another. But when he died and I could not afford the time to go back for the funeral, Huilan told me about preparing her grandmother's body for burial, and I felt oddly comforted. Although we would never be equals—after all, I was studying her life, and she was not studying mine—the sinking, slithery uneasiness of withholding my life from her did dissipate in those moments. When I finally left in 2012, it felt like a triumph that people on the street thought I must be Uighur (an ethnic minority) because I seemed to fit in yet I was too pale to be Han Chinese; Suling and Teacher Liu let me sleep with them on the floor in the orphanage one night because they were too tired to navigate the complex process of checking just me, a foreigner, into a hotel; and everyone I knew was mad at me because they could not conceive why I would ever leave China, so seemingly permanent did my life there seem to them.

But, of course, their lives went on very much without me, and have for nearly a decade since I left. And since that time so much has also changed in China—perhaps most notably the government's relaxation of the "one-child policy" in 2016, now permitting all couples to have two children, and, in May 2021, the government introducing a three-child policy (McDonell 2021). Alongside these developments, changes to China's first ever Civil Code suggest that conservatism in Chinese family life is shifting. Specifically, a relaxation in the requirements for domestic adoption—suspending the requirements that couples be childless, allowing parents with one child to adopt a second, and extending adoption of children up through age eighteen—make it possible for more Chinese couples to adopt (*Economist* 2020). The government is also planning to raise the mandatory retirement age in order to account for a declining workforce (Ming 2021).

And in the last few years, due to friction with the administration of U.S. President Donald Trump and Chinese President Xi Jinping's desire to make China more self-sustainable, restrictions on INGOs have all but caused organizations such as Mercy Care to pull out of China, as well as limited international adoption agencies' operations. The COVID-19 pandemic put a halt to foreign adoptions from China, which were already on a dramatically downward trajectory: adoptions were on hold in 2021, and American families finalized just 202 adoptions from China in 2020—down 75 percent, from 819 in fiscal year 2019, and a far cry from their peak of 7,903 in 2005 (Crary 2019; Tan 2021).

Yet despite these substantial changes, this book will show that many of the trends that I identified during my fieldwork have remained steady, if not become more pronounced. Chinese couples are more readily adopting typically developing children from Chinese orphanages, yet disabled children are still more frequently abandoned into institutions. Intercountry adoptions (ICAs) now only process adoptions of disabled children from China. Although ICAs from China have been temporarily paused due to COVID-19, if they reopen, they are likely to continue exclusively for children with disabilities, especially as older children are now readily adoptable in China with the changes to the Civil Code. China remains the top sending country for ICAs to the United States, and the United States accounts for nearly half of all ICAs. Of course, the future of foster care, which has always been unstable due to shallow government commitment, the uncertain needs of older women and disabled children in China, and now COVID-19, remains to be seen.

But if my fieldwork points to just one enduring truth, it is that families in China, just as families across the world, are not islands. Indeed, the COVID-19 pandemic has exposed the fragility of social welfare safety nets everywhere, and once again families, in all shapes, forms, and conglomerates, have had to step in to fill the breach. Foster care in China has certainly become more difficult under the conditions of COVID-19, but it is in no way obsolete. It is perhaps more vital than ever, as more children are orphaned; children and adults are left with lifelong, disabling conditions due to the virus; elders have been further isolated and ignored; and we, as a society, must learn to live with all our fragilities and vulnerabilities more fully in view.

It is not lost on me that when I went to China in 2009 and again in 2010–2012, I was able to often hold my own family and my own vulnerabilities at a distance from my informants. But if my fieldwork with foster families has taught me anything it is that such distance is not only impossible but undesirable. Seeing the way foster mothers loved ravenously, even with disjuncture and departure looming in their futures, changed me. Becoming witness to the meaningful friction of intergenerational discord and the complicated inequalities, politics, and need displayed in ICA, unnerved me. And getting to know disabled people a world away made me realize that I had been missing out on so much of life, both personally and professionally.

I hope the nearly ten years it has taken to publish this book have actually lent even more perspective to these complexities. It is truly these foster families, even in their seemingly fleeting forms, who made me believe in family making for myself. And, while I was in the field, it was these stories, these families, and these people who planted the seeds for me to start to see myself more clearly, to start to see that I could and would have a life apart from China, and yet it would be a life so deeply indebted to who I knew and who I became there that I would never, ever, be the same.

———————

NOTE ON CHINESE NAMES: The treatment of Chinese names varies in different contexts; often, in Western publishing, the names are transposed, with the family name coming last whereas in the traditional Chinese style, the family names come first. In this book I will cite authors as they are credited in the original works: generally (though there are exceptions), for those published in the West, family names will come second; for those published in China, the family names will come first. For informants, their names will be listed with the family name first as they were referred to in the field.

GLOSSARY OF PEOPLE, PLACES, AND CONCEPTS

PEOPLE OF FOSTER CARE

Main Informants

Auntie Huang	Dengrong's foster mother
Auntie Li	Pei Pei and Yuping's foster mother, Kaili's biological mother
Auntie Ma	Meili's foster mother
Dengrong	eight-year-old foster child of Auntie Huang in Daling
Huilan	foster care monitor from the Nanning Social Welfare Institute
Lin En	My pseudonym
Meili	eleven-year-old, typically developing foster child to Auntie Ma
Mercy Care	American nongovernmental organization that supported state-sponsored foster care in Guangxi and several other provinces in China from 2004 to 2021
Pei Pei	ten-year-old foster child with cleft palate to Auntie Li
Suling	Mercy Care foster monitor
Teacher Liu	Chinese director and board member of Mercy Care

Other Informants

Auntie Luo	Ren Ren's foster mother
Auntie Qin	Wei Wei's foster mother
Deng Pufang	son of former vice premier Deng Xiaoping, injured during the Cultural Revolution, who became a disability advocate
Hengwei	Daling foster child (male)
Honghuan	Neighbor foster child to Xiaoyuan who is soon to be adopted to America
Hongmei	eight-year-old foster child with limited vision and intellectual disabilities who had been moved to Daling because of prior abuse in urban foster placements
Mrs. Hu	younger sister-in-law to Auntie Li
Jiaqi	Teenage foster child who was sent back from Daling village to the Nanning Social Welfare Institute

Kaili	Auntie Li's biological daughter
Lili	Jiaqi's autistic foster sister
Luli	Mercy Care foster monitor
Older Sister Mo	physical therapist from Nanning orphanage who accompanied us on trips to Daling
Pengfei	eight-year-old blind and deaf foster child living in Nanning with foster family
Ren Ren	foster daughter (who has cerebral palsy) to Auntie Luo
Director Wang	foster care director of the Nanning Social Welfare Institute
Wei Wei	two-year-old biological grandson of foster mother Auntie Qin
Xiaoyuan	foster child with cleft palate whose birth parents showed up at the orphanage (see also *chuxian*)
Xiao Wang	Mercy Care foster monitor (male, nickname, "Little Wang")
Older Sister Yang	Daling Village Monitor, appointed by the Nanning Social Welfare Institute
Yuping	Pei Pei's toddler foster sister, Auntie Li's foster daughter, who was eventually adopted domestically
Director Zhou	deputy director of the Nanning Social Welfare Institute

PLACES

Daling	pseudonym for foster village three hours drive from Nanning into which twenty-four disabled children from a municipal orphanage were placed with private foster families
Longzhou	where Auntie Ma was sent, close to the Vietnam border, during the Cultural Revolution
Nanning	capital city of the Guangxi Autonomous Region
Nanning SWI	the Nanning Social Welfare Institute, also locally referred to as the Nanning municipal orphanage; a government welfare center for capital city and surrounding regions providing state care to elders, disabled persons, and orphans

KEY CONCEPTS AND ABBREVIATIONS

| abandonment | being relinquished, either for a child or an older person, from family ties that form the ultimate network of social support and social personhood in China |

ayi	Mandarin term for "auntie"; also a generic term of respect for older women
baba	Mandarin term for "father"
baby hatches	holding places for infants, often with incubators, established in 2014 by orphanages to offer families safe ways to relinquish (disabled) children
baihua	local Cantonese dialect spoken in Guangxi
baomu	Mandarin term for "domestic servant" or "maid"
caifangren	official terminology for disabled persons (also *canji* and *canjiren*)
chuxian	literally, "appear"; a phenomenon where birth parents show up to check on abandoned children at an orphanage and the child is not adopted out because the parents are known to be alive
Cultural Revolution	the sociopolitical movement from 1966 to 1976, led by Mao Zedong, to rid China of capitalist leadership as well as to influence, preserve, and advance Chinese communism
CWI	Child Welfare Institute, a state orphanage in China that offers care to orphaned children; CWIs are usually in urban areas and commonly referred to as orphanage (*fuliyuan*)
familism	Confucian belief that patrilineal kinship is an organizing principle for Chinese social life
fuliyuan	orphanage
gongxian	act of service or civil duty
Great Leap Forward	implementation of agrarian collectivization under communism that resulted in poor output and massive famine, 1958–1962
guanjiao	Chinese parenting concept that integrates discipline and care
guoji	kin adoption (usually informal) of a (male) relative
hukou; also *huji*	household registration system established in 1958 to control internal immigration; it has contributed to furthering urban/rural inequalities
ICA	intercountry adoption: adoption of Chinese children to Western countries, beginning in 1992
jihua shengyu	birth planning policies
jiating jiyang	state-sponsored foster family
Meiguo mama	"American mama," euphemism for prospective adoptive parent
maodun	conflict, as relates to parenting

nai nai	paternal grandmother
nengli	ability
"one-child policy"	government restriction implemented in the 1980s to limit births to one child per couple, but considerable variations existed by region
overquota birth	child whose birth exceeded birth planning regulations; also known as an out-of-plan child
patrilocal residence	living with the father's side of the family
personhood	a contextual state of sociocultural recognition
PRC	People's Republic of China
renming	fate; *kuming* is bad fate
sending countries	developing countries that send children for international adoption placements; contrasted with Western receiving countries
shishi shouyang	de facto or actual, yet usually unregistered, domestic adoptions, many of which took place during the 1990s as birth planning policies created a surplus of abandoned infant girls and Chinese families arranged to adopt them
special needs	euphemism for children in the Waiting Child Program who were over the age of fourteen or disabled and thus prioritized for intercountry adoption from China beginning in 2000
SWI	Social Welfare Institute, a state facility in China that offers care to older people, disabled people, and children; SWIs are usually in urban areas
suzhi	Chinese word for "quality"; rhetoric introduced in the government's modernization campaign in the 1990s to raise population quality
waipo	maternal grandmother
Waiting Child Program	special government program begun in 2000 to expedite intercountry adoptions of children over age fourteen and children with disabilities and medical complexities deemed unlikely to be adopted domestically
"Wo bu li ni"	threat uttered by Chinese parents to children, meaning, "I refuse to acknowledge you" or "I don't care"
Zhuang people	dominant minority group in the Guangxi Autonomous Region and the largest of fifty-six ethnic groups in China; the Zhuang language has multiple dialects

FAMILIES WE NEED

INTRODUCTION
Needy Kinship

Early one morning in October 2011, with the air crisp and the sun still rising, I crouched on the steps of the central bus terminal in the already humming capital city of Nanning, Guangxi, waiting. Men smoking feverishly and women bundled in puffy coats approached the travelers exiting the station, offering rides in unmarked cars to nearby towns, as passengers toting misshapen parcels on their backs or overflowing bags in their hands scurried into the nondescript foyer of the station.

Suddenly a cab squeaked to a halt just outside the metal gates. Huilan, the orphanage monitor with the ruddy face and kind smile, and the physical therapist whom we called Older Sister Mo, leaped onto the street, unpacking huge bags of medicine and a tiny walker for a small child. They waved eagerly at me. "Hurry, Lin En!" they called as they ran toward me, pointing in the direction of the ticket window. "We've got to hurry if we're going to make the next bus to Daling!"

MAPPING THE FIELD

Once aboard, our precious cargo stored in the bowels of the bus, Huilan and Older Sister Mo slipped into a deep sleep, while I pressed my face to the smudged window. As the bus rumbled out of the station, the capital city of Nanning, Guangxi, which had been my home for over a year, began to peel back its layers as we sped toward the countryside. We passed the daily commercial activities cramped in the old, tattered quarters of the central city, noodle shops with steam rising from their cauldrons, small tailor and mechanical outfits pressed up against one another, their sewing machines and grease stains spilling onto the brick sidewalks. Finally the bus exited onto the broad, modern thoroughfares adorned with socialist street signs like Minority Avenue and People's Way and littered with e-bikes that weaved, with shrill pulses of their horns, past taxicabs and pedestrians. As the bus pushed through the congestion, it made its way to the outskirts of Nanning, past the large glass-fronted car dealerships, cement university gates, and soaring housing complexes that quietly, yet expansively, mark the way to the ring road.

Butted up against these empty residential skyscrapers were patchwork farms dotted with men and women dipping to their knees to weed the fluorescent green rice fields. While the financial crisis of 2008 had slowed migration, leaving these modern concrete buildings empty, the farmland, which crept not only up to the ring road but lined the railroad station, the banks of the Yong River, and the edges of municipal dumps, attested to a city of reluctant migrants. True to Chinese sociologist Fei Xiaotong's midcentury proclamation, the permanent dirt under city dwellers' fingernails, their calloused hands, their propensity to uncontrollably mix Mandarin with the local dialect, and their willingness to name allegiance to any number of small towns before the capital city all suggest that Guangxi people were firmly "of the soil" (Fei 1992).[1]

In Guangxi, people spoke in heavily accented Mandarin, spat on the sidewalk, held their children to pee over the gutter, cut in line, pushed and shoved their way through crowds, and boasted browned skin from years of farming in the sun. Even my husband's colleagues at the local teaching college, and the professors from the Guangxi Minorities University who invited us to dine with them at an elegant dim sum restaurant, all bemoaned that they, along with Guangxi itself, were "backward" and "uncivilized." It was at once a sincere humility and a deep connection to the countryside and their minority roots that compelled them to speak this way, and also a profound sense of inferiority that Nanning, despite its fecundity, could not compete with modern Beijing, Shanghai, or even Shenzhen.

Beyond the ring road, these humilities contrasted even more starkly with the extravagant beauty of the Guangxi landscape. Farms of banana trees, with their red, green, and yellow fruits, stretched to the horizon. Majestic karst domes rose up to nestle towns that consisted of a few garage storefronts and one solitary street. Along that street, men and women cradled babies in their laps as they squatted, drinking tea, cracking walnuts, and chatting in the sing-songy cantor of the local *baihua*, or the exotic lilt of the Zhuang dialect. Farmers with reed hats bent over the shimmering rice paddies and guided water buffalo along terraced fields that cohabited with the mountainous features. During the tomb sweeping festival, graves were marked with brightly colored paper and streamers, dotting the edges of the countryside with dignity and simplicity.

Approximately three and a half hours beyond the capital city, the women from the orphanage and I exited the bus onto a dusty two-lane highway. Toting the bags of medicine and supplies and the tiny walker, we made our way along the back roads to a small village, tucked up against a stream laden with garbage, the sounds of chickens clucking and the smell of sour and hot peppers wafting toward our noses in the hot sun. We found the villagers laying out their livelihood, the brilliant red peppers, to dry as they chattered leisurely to one another in the local language. Young boys sat on a bench, snickering to one another; babies were strapped to parents' backs in brightly colored hand-woven fabrics, and children and parents alike worked alongside one another.

But despite first glances, this was no ordinary village, just as these were no ordinary parents or children. As we drew closer, I noticed the curved backs and wrinkled hands of the parents, marking them as seasoned and aged. Gradually it became clear to me that these were not parents in the expected, traditional sense, but rather older foster parents rearing China's young in the countryside. Likewise, I noted that many of the children walked with limps characteristic of cerebral palsy or displayed a downcast gaze indicative of autism. The older boys' wide faces and smiles revealed Down syndrome, while still others were hard of hearing, blind, or weakened from disease.

Suddenly, Hongmei, an eight-year-old girl with limited vision and intellectual disabilities who had been removed from a problematic foster placement in Nanning city a few months earlier, came running out of one of the houses, greeting us each eagerly with "Ayi hao, jiejie hao!" (Hello, Auntie, big sister!).

"Hongmei!" Huilan exclaimed excitedly. "How are you doing? Which one is your house?" Hongmei proudly led us over to a steep concrete step, introducing us to her new grandmother and her foster sister.

"My mother's out back, harvesting peppers," she told us.

"Do you like your new home?" Older Sister Mo asked.

"Yes," Hongmei chirped.

We circled the rest of the homes on the two wide streets that made up the main thoroughfare, poking our heads in and greeting children and foster parents who were busying about their days. Huilan came alive with each child she greeted, and Older Sister Mo poked and prodded at the children with palsied legs, admonishing or congratulating the parents on their progress doing physical therapy within the home.

These children with disabilities from the Nanning Municipal Orphanage had been placed in private foster homes in the countryside, just as hundreds of others had been placed in the city, and many waited hopefully to be adopted abroad.[2] Indeed, as we visited families, it was not unusual to hear foster parents trace their previous children's foreign trajectories. "I've had three that have gone to Holland," one mother chirped. "And two to Spain and two to the United States," her husband added. They scooped the children into their laps, asking them where they would like to go someday, to meet their parents. The children, puzzled and fearful, buried their heads into the foster parents' legs, while the old men and women chuckled, their eyes twinkling.

But when the children ran off to play again, the foster parents would inquire about whether the children had been matched with foreign families, and how long it would be until they would face another departure and eventually open their home to yet another child in need.[3] I should have known in those moments, given their hushed voices and their downcast eyes, that the seeming ease and commonplace of this placid life, the months and months that bled into years, was temporary at best. Eventually these women would cling desperately to their foster children as they were ripped from their arms, the state orphanage monitors struggling without success to quiet them and whisk the children away to their adoptive "forever" families.[4] Eventually these relationships would end in heartache, distance, and disjuncture.

If these foster families, disabled children and older women left behind by their biological kin,[5] were being built from the residue of broken families and formed out of desperation, could they create culturally viable kin relationships? If the foster children were destined for foreign countries and foreign families, and if the care that these foster parents provided could seemingly be superseded by the welcoming of another child or the fate of a foreign family, what are we to make of these temporary, makeshift, and presumably replaceable forms of kinship? I began to wonder—alongside the orphanage monitors, care workers, and even the foster mothers themselves—if these Chinese foster families, so disruptive to traditional family ideologies, the Chinese state, and intercountry adoption (ICA), had something important to teach us.

A BRIEF HISTORY OF BIRTH PLANNING AND ORPHAN CARE IN CHINA

The opening pages of this book offer the reader a geographic and cultural introduction to my field site. I came to the sprawling city of seven million, Nanning, the capital city of the Guangxi Autonomous Region, for the first time in 2009, and returned in the summer of 2010 to conduct approximately eighteen months of fieldwork with disabled children in government-sponsored foster care. The bulk of my days from 2010 to 2012 were spent hopping on buses to visit foster families scattered across Nanning and its outskirts. Yet, once a month from October 2011 until the time I left in July 2012, I took another bus to the village of just a few hundred people that I call Daling,[6] where the Nanning municipal orphanage had also placed twenty-four children, two per family, with rural foster families. In addition to these weekly urban and monthly rural visiting patterns, I made several annual trips with an international nongovernmental organization (INGO), which I call Mercy Care,[7] to visit other provinces in China—namely, Hubei and Anhui. I also traveled with Mercy Care American board members and Chinese staff to several other cities in Guangxi to study government-sponsored foster care.

Although it took nearly eight months, in March 2011 my search for foster families finally brought me to an unassuming concrete office in the middle of the capital city, where Mercy Care staff, headed by the soft-spoken Teacher Liu, assembled and told me that they supported hundreds of foster families in Nanning and thousands outside of the region who took orphaned and abandoned children into their homes. Yet that afternoon as Teacher Liu and her staff sat with me in their chilly office, she also began to reference something else that I could hardly have anticipated before coming to China to study foster care. The banners of the faces of healthy girls that hung on Mercy Care's office walls, their white board members, and the photo albums of adopted families strewn about were but faded relics of the past. China's orphanages are no longer crowded with infant girls waiting to be adopted to the West. Instead today those same orphanages and the foster families who take care of them are home to disabled children, presumably abandoned because of their physical and mental disabilities.

Disabled children are also being fostered by older women in their fifties, sixties, and seventies and increasingly being adopted abroad. Indeed, a soaring older adult population in China (13.3 percent of the present population but projected to be 30 percent of the total population by 2050, according to the 2010 Chinese Census) presents challenges to the Chinese state as the decreasing size of families under the modern birth planning policies and the waning notion of filial piety render China's oldest—not unlike its youngest—particularly socially vulnerable. Despite the Chinese government's insistence that elders must be cared for and its bolstering of legal statues or repercussions for such care, it provides little institutional support for elders and effectively undermines their utility by requiring early retirement and incentivizing youthful enterprise and nuclear families. Thus, Chinese foster families, in their peculiar demographic makeup, their needy members, and their surprising utility, exemplify both marginality and resistance in contemporary China.

Yet in order to understand foster care in China, one also needs to understand the intertwined history of the implementation of the birth planning policies of the 1980s alongside the promotion of ICA and the suppression of domestic adoption that began in the 1990s. Although orphans and orphan care in China certainly go back much further than the communist era (beginning in 1949), before that orphans were generally cared for by relatives or neighbors; only a small number of private and missionary orphanages provided for them. Under communism, the Chinese central government began to construct large social welfare and children's welfare institutions—Child Welfare Institutes (CWIs) and Social Welfare Institutes (SWIs)—in urban centers to provide for the care of older adults, disabled persons, and orphans.[8] By the 1980s, however, when China shifted away from a planned economy toward free markets and foreign investment, funding for social welfare began to dry up. Although social welfare institutions remained in operation, they were increasingly strained by growing populations, lack of funds, and their uneven distribution. Whereas major municipalities had ample facilities, small county orphanages were stressed and, in particularly rural areas, residential facilities were not available for an increasing number of orphans.

The reason for the increase in the orphan population was directly tied to the birth planning policies, which the central government implemented in 1978, at the tail end of communism, to control the soaring population. The government began with campaigns incentivizing "later, longer, fewer" births, offering financial bonuses to couples willing to delay marriage or births, space births apart, and ultimately give birth to fewer children. By the 1980s, however, the government turned to more stringent methods of control, including fines, seizure or damage of property, forced abortions, sterilizations, and even seizure of infants. By 1980 the single child policy, now famous the world over, had been implemented in most areas throughout the People's Republic of China (PRC). Yet resistance to the policy, especially from rural villagers needing to rely on sons as not only a form of prestige but also for farm labor and pension, was significant. By 1984 the government relaxed the policy in most rural areas to allow for couples with a first-born daughter to try for a son, and in large municipalities, the government eventually allowed for couples who were only children themselves to have two children. Finally, for minority populations (though notably not for the Zhuang minority population in the Guangxi Autonomous Region where I did my fieldwork), and for families who gave birth to a disabled child, a second birth was often permitted.

There are, however, several important clarifications to be made about the birth planning policies, especially given the infamy with which the "one-child policy" has come to be known. First, over the thirty-five years of its implementation, the "one-child policy" took on many variations, not only in content and implementation but in enforcement, which varied regionally. Therefore, generalizations about the policy or even a characterization of the policy as the "one child-policy" are misleading. Because of these variations, Chinese people generally do not use the term; rather, they use the more encompassing term *jihua shengyu* (birth planning) to discuss the varying policies.

Second, the policies were experienced differently in rural and urban areas, emphasizing and highlighting the increasing divide and stratification between rural and urban peoples in modern China. Rural villagers, who lacked corporate pensions and often economic resources, relied on children—and particularly sons—to farm the land, inherit property, and care for elders. Furthermore, owing to a passport registration system implemented in 1958—the *huji* or, more commonly, the *hukou* system—migration, especially from rural to urban areas, was highly restricted. Therefore, even as the modernization period of reform and "opening up" in the 1980s saw increased migration by rural villagers to the cities for jobs and prosperity, these villagers remained disadvantaged, because they were unable to work legally, settle permanently, or even send their children to school in urban areas due to their rural *hukou* restrictions.

The disproportionate strain birth planning put on rural families, coupled with these migration restrictions, has also been exacerbated by a national shift from a focus on restricting population quantity (*jihua shengyu*) to raising population quality (*suzhi jiaoyu*) from the 1990s to the present. State cadres were intimately involved in monitoring women's menstrual cycles and dispensing birth control, and the government began emphasizing *yousheng youyu* (excellent births, excellent rearing) in the 1990s, impressing on mothers the monitoring of diet and pregnancy in the service of producing "high-quality," rather than defective, children. Although the discourse of *suzhi* (quality) and *suzhi jiaoyu* (quality education) purportedly emphasize the practical work of cultivating and raising human potential and development through effort and education, an emphasis on *suzhi* is often used to justify racial, demographic, and social hierarchies, further entrenching especially the rural-urban divide in modern China (see, for instance, Anagnost 1997, 2004; Bakken 2000; Friedman 2006; Greenhalgh 2010; Jacka 2009; Murphy 2004; Sigley 2009; and Wang 2016).

Finally, and most important for understanding the relationship between the birth planning policies and the development of Chinese foster care, it is noteworthy that the seemingly straightforward rural preference for sons, resulting in the abandonment of infant girls, was not a mere illustration of cultural prejudice but rather a reflection of the clash between cultural values and coercive government policy. In *Wanting a Daughter, Needing a Son*, Kay Ann Johnson (2004) illustrates the Chinese ideal of the two-child family (a boy and a girl) and shows that even under the birth planning restrictions, couples rarely abandoned first-born girls. Rather, out of poverty and desperation, couples consistently abandoned second-, third-, and fourth-born girls when all their other options (suffering the fines, going away and hiding the pregnancy, kin adoption, or local adoption) were exhausted. Johnson's detailed ethnographic work helps complicate simplistic explanations for female abandonment in modern China, evidencing the cultural clash between the widespread desire for both genders amid the restrictive birth planning policies.[9]

A BRIEF HISTORY OF FOSTER CARE AND ADOPTION IN CHINA

Without dismissing the importance of this history, this book necessarily focuses in on the period from 1990 to the present, during which the PRC opened up to ICA, implemented foster care as a method for readying children for ICA, and suppressed practices of domestic adoption in order to enforce the birth planning policies. It is vital to consider these three phenomena together in order to dispel the enduring myth about infant girls—that is, that they were fundamentally unwanted in modern China. Documentaries like *The Dying Rooms*, which aired in 1995, and a sequel in 1996 filmed by British filmmakers in state-run orphanages in China, revealed conditions of squalor and neglect for orphans in state institutions to the world. Human Rights Watch Asia's *Death by Default* (1996) charges that death rates for children were alarmingly high in state orphanages, and in some cases food and water were even being withheld from children as they starved to death. Johnson's work is again instructive in complicating these narratives, clarifying that conditions in Chinese orphanages were certainly deplorable, but children were often so sick and orphanages were so overburdened with foundlings in the early 1990s that the children were often on their deathbeds before they even came to the orphanages.

In accordance with Johnson's earlier work, she shows that these infant girls were abandoned not because they were fundamentally unwanted but because of the enforcement of the birth planning laws, as well as increasing restrictions on domestic adoption. In her second book, *China's Hidden Children* (2016), Johnson charges that throughout the 1990s, the Chinese central government actively suppressed domestic adoptions, even as they expressly encouraged ICAs. The national adoption law, passed in 1991, restricted domestic adoption in three ways. First, it made it possible for birth planning officials to punish citizens for using adoption to circumvent birth planning restrictions and hide out-of-plan or over-quota births—those that exceeded the birth planning restrictions. Second, it made it illegal for parents to relinquish a child for adoption except under extraordinary circumstances, thus forcing couples to resort to abandonment. Third, it required domestic adopters to be thirty-five or older (an abnormally culturally advanced age for parenthood in China) and childless, discouraging domestic couples in China from adopting.

As the PRC opened up to ICAs in the 1990s, these domestic restrictions effectively prevented locals from legally adopting Chinese children and funneled abandoned children into foreign families. The PRC reached its peak for ICAs in 2005, with nearly fifteen thousand adoptions, and from the 1990s to the present over 150,000 children have been adopted from China internationally, over eighty thousand of them to the United States alone. Although these numbers do not seem all that statistically significant given that U.S. domestic adoptions total nearly ten times its ICAs, China has remained the top sending country for ICAs from the 1990s into the present, accounting for nearly one-third of all children adopted internationally. Furthermore, although official statistics are hard to come by, it is clear that the number of ICAs processed from China, especially during the heyday of the birth planning policies, represent a tremendous proportion compared to Chinese domestic adoptions. Critically, Johnson's work, which unveils the local stories of birth parents and adoptive parents whose children were seized by the government and sent abroad, points to significant cultural desire among Chinese families to adopt. Indeed, even over the last two decades, domestic adoption has remained steady and is increasing in the PRC, corroborating Johnson's claim that "were it not for actively pursued policies of suppression, nearly all healthy daughters in the 1990s could have found families who wanted them in China, leaving few healthy children available for international adoption" (Johnson 2016, 14).

In the face of centrally administered and locally enforced crackdowns in the enforcements of birth planning policies in the 1980s and 1990s, many rural Chinese orphanages locally and informally fostered or adopted out children whom they could not afford to care for due to a high population of needy infant girls, inadequate staff, and lack of funds (Johnson 2016). Yet informal arrangements quickly turned to formal, contractual ones as orphanages began to process and profit from ICAs in the early 1990s, when a national movement toward decentralization of social welfare coupled with foreign interest and investment in Chinese child welfare paved the way for foster care projects. A British organization, the Save the Child Fund, is widely credited with being the first foreign nongovernmental organization (NGO) to promulgate foster care in China, founded in the early 1990s within the Guangde Children's Welfare Home units, where mothers and teachers reared five children in family-like institutional settings (Shang 2002; Wang et al. 2017). In their review of China's current foster practices, Wen-chi Wang and colleagues name two other models of alternative foster care projects developed in collaboration with foreign NGOs, including both the Beijing and Shanghai models (Wang et al. 2017). In 1992 the Beijing model recruited several village families to rear institutionalized children in private homes; despite the cost saving and efficacy (the government noted that the children's health dramatically improved in foster care) of this method, the Beijing Children's Welfare Home still had to send in doctors and teachers to support these children's health care and education (Wang et al. 2017). Additionally, according to Wang and colleagues, the Shanghai model, a collaboration of community-based foster care by the director of the Shanghai Civil Affairs Bureau and a British NGO, was the first of its kind to have professional foster care placement, childcare, and continuous postplacement supervision and support (Wang et al. 2017).

By the late 1990s foster care was becoming widely credited by both foreign INGOs and the Chinese government with physical and psychological interventions into better readying children for both domestic adoptions and ICAs, though primarily the latter. In 2000 the State Council issued A Notice on Forwarding "the Opinion of Accelerating Socialization of Social Welfare," and in late 2003 the Communist Party promulgated a Temporary Policy on Foster Care that officially mandated the development and participation of state orphanages in foster care projects. Johnson worries that foster care, with its ties to ICA, will become a "substitute for permanent domestic adoption." She warns that

> authorities seem more willing to promote and invest in foster care than to vigorously promote domestic adoption. Because foster care programs do not threaten birth-planning efforts or compete with international adoption, they don't face the opposition that confronts proponents of domestic adoption. Indeed, international adopters prefer foster care to orphanage care, since institutions are widely believed to create "damaged children." Thus the development of foster care dovetails well with the interests of both birth-planning forces and international adoption. That it does so is of course no reason to oppose foster care. But like international adoption, foster care should not be encouraged as a substitute for, or a means of avoiding, the active promotion of permanent legal domestic adoption whenever possible. (Johnson 2004, 151)

Yet in their comprehensive studies of child welfare in China, Xiaoyuan Shang and Karen Fisher write that even as some sixty thousand children were moved out of institutional care and into foster care in the 1990s, government support for foster care in China was shallow and inconsistent (Shang and Fisher 2014, 234). The government actively funded reinstitutionalization in some urban areas in the first years of the new millennium, constructing state-of-the-art institutions—ironically, in an effort to attract foreign investment. In my travels across China with Mercy Care, even orphanage directors who had long supported foster care revealed pressure to keep children in their institutions in order to maintain the appearance that the state was providing top-notch care. As we approached a small county orphanage in Guangxi one afternoon, Teacher Liu, the Mercy Care director, whispered under her breath that this was the one where the director had pulled all the children out of foster care into the orphanage just to impress officials and visitors once on National Children's Day. Even though China's Ministry of Civil Affairs issued new regulations in 2009, 2010, and in 2014 finally issued the Jiating Jiyang Guanli Banfa (Measures for the Management of Family Fosterage) to reduce numbers of foster children per family from three to two and raise requirements for standards of living for foster families and stipends (Xu et al. 2020), my ethnographic studies of state-sponsored foster care in the PRC show that support for foster care, and implementation of regulations, vary substantially by county, city, and region.

The most significant changes for the child welfare landscape in the PRC in the last decade, and most pertinent to foster care, are an increase in the number of registered domestic adoptions, an overall decrease in ICAs, and a dramatic increase in the proportion and overall number of disabled children in state institutions and foster care. Although I cover these interrelated trends in greater depth in chapter 2, alongside the increasing proportion of disabled children who are being adopted abroad from China since around 2005, it is important for readers to know that even as the Chinese government sought to curtail the relinquishment of infant girls by restricting domestic adoptions in the 1990s, they made an exception for the voluntary relinquishment of disabled children (Johnson 2016, 12). Hence, in the context of birth planning and the government's emphasis on "high-quality" births, disabled and medically fragile children presented burdens not only to families but to China's modernization project (Wang 2016, 43–47). Whereas in 2003 the Chinese government implemented a Care for Girls campaign and red letters championing the intrinsic value of girls can still be seen splayed across the stark countryside, in 2011 it opened a series of "baby hatches" into which parents or relatives could place abandoned children, press a button, and alert a nearby orphanage (BBC News 2014). At least thirty of these hatches have opened up across the country since 2011 and, tellingly, all of the children left in them have been disabled.[10]

Of China's estimated one million or more orphans, those in institutional care are overwhelmingly mentally or physically disabled (Shang and Fisher 2017).

Both the overall population of disabled children and the proportion of disabled children to nondisabled children has been increasing in CWIs and SWIs since 2006. In 2015, Nie Lili, one of the founders of Chinese Children Adoption International (CCAI) stated, "Over 98 percent of children in orphanages now are special needs children. Before 2008 the proportion was 20–30 percent" (quoted in *Global Times* 2015). Although the PRC does not release information on the proportion of children with disabilities in CWIs, this over 50 percent increase in the proportion of abandonments of disabled children in Chinese institutions is certainly significant.

Yet whereas the government once curbed domestic adoption while promoting ICA in the 1990s, since 2006 and to the present, ICAs have fallen dramatically (Crary 2019). One clear reason for this is that the majority of typically developing Chinese children adopted from CWIs and SWIs are now adopted domestically (*Economist* 2020; Wang 2016). Certainly the loosening of birth planning restrictions, changes in domestic adoption laws lowering the minimum age for adoptive parents in 1999 and, a decade later, increasing the number of children couples can adopt, has made a difference (*Economist* 2020; W. Zhang 2006). Since 2008, however, stricter regulations introduced by the Hague Convention to pressure sending countries to find homes for children within those countries have dramatically decreased the overall number of foreign children, including children in China, available for ICA. The Chinese government also tightened its own requirements for international adoptive couples: in 2001 it limited the pool of single women adopters to 5 percent and outlawed ICA from China to gay couples, citing these populations as inconsistent with Chinese cultural values (Wang 2016, 68). In 2007 the China Center for Children's Welfare and Adoption stipulated that due to decreasing supply of available children, increased standards for adopters (including sexual orientation), education level, income, and Body Mass Index had been added to the criteria for couples wishing to adopt (Wang 2016, 69).

From the 1990s until 2009, the majority of ICAs from China were of typical infant girls; however, since 2005 these adoptions have radically decreased, while the number of "special needs" ICAs from China have been dramatically increasing. The Chinese government's Waiting Child Program was launched in 2000 to expedite foreign adoptions of older children (ages eight to thirteen) and children with special needs. Thus, the program groups together older children, who up until 2020 were, at age fourteen, no longer adoptable domestically in the PRC, and children with medical issues, diseases, or disabilities such as cleft lips and palates, heart defects, missing or webbed fingers or toes, Down syndrome, cerebral palsy, hepatitis B, and vision or hearing impairments. From 2005 forward, the proportion of special needs ICAs from China began to increase at a steady pace; by 2009, special needs youth made up nearly half of all Chinese international adoptees. According to international adoption agencies, this rapid increase has continued: the agencies no longer process adoptions of typical children from China. Today all ICA from China is of special needs youth and children.[11]

According to statistics from 2018, the PRC reports that there are 343,000 children nationwide residing in child and social welfare institutions (*Economist* 2020). Yet the 343,000 children in institutional care constitutes but a portion of children who are considered orphans in China. Although the government claims there are between five and six hundred thousand orphans in China, many other groups put this number at closer to one million (Ripley 2015; Vanderklippe 2014). Additionally, the population of disabled children is increasing in CWIs and SWIs, with some estimates putting the increase at between thirty and fifty thousand children with disabilities abandoned per year; other estimates argue that the number of abandoned children with disabilities is one hundred thousand per year (Ripley 2015). It is hard to know at what rate, but both the overall population of disabled children and the proportion of disabled Chinese children to nondisabled children has been significantly increasing in CWIs and SWIs since 2005.

In the chapters to follow, I further explore cultural interpretations of disability in China and discuss the complex reasons for the increasing rates of abandonment for disabled children in China today. In a country where children are legally required to care for their parents in old age and where only one child was allowed for many couples, children who may struggle to care for their aging parents present less sociocultural value. They are also expensive, as government support for families with children with disabilities in the PRC is slim; although schools are legally required to accept and support children with disabilities, they are often rejected outright, if not heavily discriminated against by institutions and communities (Shang and Fisher 2016; Shen, McCabe, and Chi 2008). Still, a cultural explanation or even a national political explanation for the increasing number of disabled children residing in institutions and placed into foster care in China cannot be considered apart from the rising rates in ICAs of disabled children from China, something Mercy Care's work and my fieldwork bring into view. Furthermore, static cultural explanations fail to explain this modern uptick in abandonments of disabled children. In chapter 2, I argue that international demand for disabled children must be considered in dialogue with government policies and cultural prejudice as rationale for such an increase.

STUDYING STATE-SPONSORED FOSTER CARE IN NANNING, GUANGXI

This book takes government-sponsored foster care in the PRC—and specifically the capital of Nanning, Guangxi—as its object of study. In government-sponsored foster care, CWIs and SWIs, which are organized by county and municipality, place children into homes with local families who are subcontracted, monitored, and paid by the state to cover costs associated with the children's needs. The Nanning

Social Welfare Unit is affiliated with the Nanning Social Civil Affairs Bureau and offers residential and community care to senior citizens, disabled people, and children. It was established in 1951 and has a total of 789 beds. The child welfare section includes units for babies and children, a rehabilitation exercise center, and a kindergarten. Child welfare takes care of arranging foster care, adoptions, nursing, health care, therapy, education, and parenting support for children in state care. As the only SWI in the capital city of seven million, it possesses responsibility for all children in state care (Shang and Fisher 2017, 47–48).

In 2009 there were 497 children listed as residing in the Nanning SWI. A total of forty-nine of these children were placed for adoption that year, seventeen domestically and thirty-two internationally. The overall total of institutionalized children has decreased since the 1990s (from 649 in 1997), but the proportion of children placed in adoption actually increased in the early 2000s. Indeed, in the Nanning SWI, significantly higher numbers of children were placed internationally (1,114) rather than domestically (622) from 2000 to 2009. These trends demonstrate the force of ICA in the region and likely the shift in institutionalized populations from typically developing to disabled children. As with social welfare institutions across the PRC, nearly all children at the Nanning SWI have disabilities, though I did come across two children in my fieldwork in Nanning City—namely, Meili and Yuping—who had no disabilities, both of whom were eventually adopted. Although the Nanning SWI does not provide official totals of how many children out of the 497 are residing in foster care, it is estimated that at least half, if not two-thirds, of that total are in foster care placements, supported by INGOs such as Holt International and Mercy Care, as well as the central government.

Mercy Care—founded in 2004 by Teacher Liu, who was a former Holt International employee in Guangxi, and a handful of adoptive parents from the United States at the height of ICA from China—had as its mission to get at the root causes of child abandonment in China by moving institutionalized children into private foster homes. By providing foreign sponsorship for institutionalized orphans to go into foster care, Mercy Care sought to incentivize these foster family placements by minimizing the cost to the government orphanage. By annually supporting and visiting thousands of children and their foster families in over three provinces, including the Guangxi Autonomous Region (where the bulk of its placements were), Mercy Care sought to support and encourage the development of a foster care system not unlike that of the United States. Thus, the form of foster care Mercy Care reinforced was not only culturally specific to its American board members but conceived and rooted in a context of ICA.

These children were adopted through official channels, meaning they were first registered with the social welfare unit, most likely fostered, and finally adopted internationally. Foster care emerged in tandem with foreign investment and ICA in the 1990s as a mechanism for readying children for ICA. My assessment in this book is that Chinese foster care maintains a symbiotic relationship with ICA, but the population of children has changed from typical girls to disabled children and youth. Hence, although the overall number of children being fostered in the PRC today is not necessarily a large proportion of the total orphan population, its pipeline to ICA highlights the practice's significance in global family making.

The Temporary Policy on Foster Care issued by the Communist Party in late 2003 specified that foster parents were to have ample space and an income commensurate with the local average, be between the ages of thirty-five and sixty-five, and possess the time and the abilities to care for children (Wu, Han, and Gao 2005). In exchange for their services, foster parents would be paid a monthly stipend commensurate with local standards of living, but children would remain wards of the state until they were returned to the orphanage or adopted. The orphanage was to place no more than three children with any given family and it still remained responsible for the overall social welfare of the children, meaning that orphanage representatives visited the children regularly (every three to six months) and many parents received services, like health checkups or physical therapy for their children, either at the orphanage or in their private homes.

The children I observed in foster care in my fieldwork in Guangxi included infants, toddlers, children, and teens. Given that up until 2020, children over the age of fourteen were ineligible for adoption domestically or internationally, it was unusual to see them in foster care. With the exception of two children, Meili and Yuping, out of hundreds that I met in foster care, all children being fostered were children with disabilities. The most frequently occurring disabilities were facial and bodily deformities, cerebral palsy, autism, Down syndrome, and undiagnosed developmental delays. Children in urban placements made frequent visits to the Nanning SWI for health checkups, therapy, and, in some cases, even attended school at the orphanage. Foster care monitors from the Nanning SWI made quarterly visits to urban foster families and Daling village. In addition to the quarterly visits to Daling, the Nanning SWI appointed a village monitor who reported by phone regarding concerns for the children's welfare. She even kept a scale in her home with which monitors and therapists would weigh children during quarterly visits. On occasion Director Wang, who was in charge of foster care, or other municipal officials would accompany foster care monitors on their visits.

The wages for foster parents varied considerably, especially since they were not standardized until 2009–2010, when the Ministry of Central Affairs issued two sets of regulations that required that children living with extended family or guardians receive a minimum standard of living at 600 yuan per child, while the subsidy for orphans in child welfare agencies was set at 1,000 yuan (Xu et al. 2020). In Guangxi, where moderate incomes measured around 1,000 yuan per month (roughly the equivalent of US$165) the stipends of 700 yuan for healthy children and 800 yuan for children with disabilities paid by the orphanage (and in part by Mercy Care) were comparable salaries with the median incomes of other professionals, and commensurate or greater than many state pensions. Yet, according to Mercy Care, state orphanages were often reticent to engage in foster care because they felt they could save money by providing institutional care to orphans rather than paying out these stipends to foster families. Although these stipends are considered benefits for children, and the orphanage required accounting for its expenses, both orphanage officials and foster mothers recognized that there was some wiggle room as to how the expenses were accounted (see chapter 3).

In a 2001 survey of eight SWIs across the country, Shang and Fisher (2014) found that all had some foster care services and around two-thirds of all institutionalized children were in foster care. Most children stayed fewer than a few weeks in the institution before being placed with foster parents, the majority of whom belonged to low-income households in the area. As Yanfeng Xu and colleagues (2020) note in their scoping review on family foster care and child welfare in China in 2020, foster families now consist of older parents fostering primarily children with disabilities, with the hope—albeit not always realistic—that many of these children will be adopted abroad (2020). In their study of foster care in urban Nanjing, Xu and colleagues note that foster parents were predominantly middle-aged (between forty and sixty) with a middle school or high school education, but I found that there were very few parents in their forties fostering in Guangxi. Instead, most foster parents I met were in their fifties and sixties (though some were in their seventies), because women's retirement (mandated by the government at age fifty for blue-collar female workers and at fifty-five for white-collar women) and the lack of a grandchild were two prominent reasons couples cited for why they were taking in foster children. Although Shang and Fisher (2016) found in a survey of a rural foster care project that parents were between forty and fifty years of age, they also reported that companionship for one's own children was ranked lowest among the list of motivations to foster. Even though the average age of foster parents in Guangxi is a bit more advanced than ages of foster parents in other research, foster parents there were always significantly older than the CWI and SWI workers and Mercy Care staff who monitored the foster care placements. Owing to their advanced age, foster parents had few children of their own in the household (Auntie Li was a notable exception), though many took care of grandchildren, either occasionally or permanently, alongside foster children.

Therefore, in this book I refer to foster parents as *seniors, elders,* and older adults and SWI and Mercy Care workers as primarily *middle-aged,* even though a few of them were in their twenties. As I detail throughout, the advanced age of foster parents has to do with significant demographic shifts in the PRC that have both delayed marriage and children for young couples but also somewhat alienated young people from their aging parents. In his early work on the effects of postcommunist family life, anthropologist Yunxiang Yan (2003) has noted the rise of the conjugal unit and private life under socialism. Yan (2011a, 2011b) also notes an increasing incivility among young couples who demanded resources and support from their aging parents without offering the same care in return. However, he has argued (2018) that Chinese familism, the Confucian emphasis on patrilineal relations and family as the center for all social life, retains much of its features in modernity, now shifting toward neofamilism, which is marked by increasing focus on children versus elders, increased intimacy in family life, materialism, and tension between individual and family interests.

The age gap, with foster parents being in their fifties to seventies and orphanage and Mercy Care workers in their midtwenties to midforties, was significant because it broke down along distinct generational experiences in China. As readers will glean, foster mothers Auntie Huang, Auntie Li, and Auntie Ma were born in the 1940s and 1950s, experienced the communist revolution and Cultural Revolution as young people, and then gave birth to children during, just prior to, or at the beginning of China's birth planning policies, starting in 1978. They had navigated the shift in China's industrializing, modernizing, and privatizing economy while raising families and retired, if they were lucky, with modest state pensions or little at all. They often felt out of step with the pace of changes in Chinese modern life. Given Guangxi's decidedly rural character, their child-rearing had taken place in much more primitive, simpler conditions.

By contrast, orphanage and Mercy Care workers were of the generation that came after the 1970s and 1980s; born during the height of the birth planning policies, they likely grew up with few siblings or none, entered a hypercompetitive academic and cultural environment given the population boom, and found themselves increasingly disillusioned with the way modern pressures, such as obtaining a college education, working full-time and earning enough to make ends meet, clashed with priorities on family life and care. This generation, in accordance with the government's shift from population quantity to quality, was increasingly pressured with raising children who could compete in a cutthroat, even immoral landscape (see, for instance, Kuan 2015; Xu 2017; and Yan 2011a, 2011b). By the time I arrived in Guangxi, the country was beset by poisoned milk and rice, controversies over counterfeit goods, Good Samaritan extortion scandals, and cheating allegations on major entrance exams to college; the word on the street was that China was experiencing a moral crisis. Hence, child-rearing, with its decidedly moral overtones, was of public concern.

But for young people in Nanning, Guangxi, there was also a desire to prove their class value. Their families having migrated from the countryside to the city in the 1950s, they were legally urban residents now, in contradistinction to recent migrants who had struggled to eke out a living in factories, rent an apartment without a *hukou*, or even send their children to school. But that did not mean that life was easy: they made their only children's upward trajectory—complete with upper-class education, English training classes, talent development classes, and testing assistance—top priority. Testing into an elite university was their ticket out, and would be assurance for their parents that they had done their jobs. Both Teresa Kuan (2015) and Jing Xu (2017) profile the management by middle-class mothers of their children's activities and behaviors in modern China and the conflict they feel about trying to give their children freedom and autonomy while making sure that they also do not become disobedient. Indeed, like Kuan and Xu, my work with respect to middle-aged INGO and orphanage workers raising their young families also demonstrates the strenuous, stressful nature of modern motherhood in China, as well as the extent to which women still remain responsible for so much of the work of moral caregiving.

But Chinese INGO and orphanage monitors also found themselves conflicted parents amid class struggle: they wanted to attract young women to foster children, yet they themselves would never have taken in disabled children, so focused were they on cultivating their own children's futures. Therefore, they had to rely on older foster parents, whose loneliness led them to foster, but whose low income and lower-class modes of parenting were often deemed inappropriate and problematic. For instance, Huilan, a thirty-year-old orphanage foster care monitor with one child of her own, often complained that it was difficult to find good young couples who wanted to foster. Yet she, too, relied on her own live-in parents-in-law to care for her daughter when she was off visiting foster families. As Teacher Liu, the director of Mercy Care with one child of her own, once declared, "It takes at least three people to raise a child; two just won't cut it."

I remember that then, as a newly married childless woman in my late twenties, I felt a bit disdainful of Teacher Liu's proclamation and a bit torn between the younger generation's criticisms of the foster mothers' backward ways of child-rearing and the significant pressures the women in my age cohorts were naming. Initially, despite the importance of these institutional relationships to my research, I resented the presence of state foster care monitors, especially the formalities they introduced to my research, their unsolicited commentary, and their personal ramblings regarding their own family relationships in the field. Yet gradually I began to see not only the significance of these criticisms of foster mothers and the way they indexed some of the challenges of modern Chinese life but the double-edged nature of their claims. As I argue in this book, despite their efforts to control and monitor the relationships of foster mothers and foster children, state and INGO foster care workers presented their own family struggles in dialogue with these seemingly marginal families, often coming to envy the very bonds of foster care that they also undermined.

In this book, Suling, a young foster care monitor in her midtwenties, single and living away from her family back in the countryside, and Teacher Liu, the forty-five-year-old director and founding board member of Mercy Care, are the two primary informants who represent the organization. I would often travel with Suling to conduct routine visits every few months to foster homes in Nanning that mirrored the visits the state orphanage also conducted. Meanwhile,

Director Wang, a woman of about fifty who supervised the foster care program at the Nanning Municipal Orphanage; Huilan, the foster care monitor in her thirties; and Older Sister Mo, the thirty-year old physical therapist, serve as the primary informants from the state orphanage. Becoming acquainted with Mercy Care in spring 2011 was an invaluable asset to my fieldwork, as shortly thereafter staff members introduced me under their wing to the higher staff at the Nanning SWI and granted me access to all the foster families with whom they worked in Guangxi and several other provinces. With Mercy Care's help, I then formed my own relationships with Director Wang, Huilan, and Older Sister Mo, with whom I traveled to the rural foster project in Daling monthly during the last eight months of my fieldwork, from the fall of 2011 to the summer of 2012. Suling accompanied us on a few of these trips also, but Mercy Care had just a few children under its sponsorship placed in Daling. The majority of those twenty-four children were foster care placements initiated by the Nanning SWI.

Although the relationship between Mercy Care and the Nanning SWI was good, there was skepticism on both sides: Mercy Care worried that the SWI was only motivated to do foster care because of foreign funding, was not eager to facilitate ICAs for kids with disabilities, and generally did not care much about disabled children. Mercy Care American board members and Chinese staff were motivated by their shared Christian faith to offer foster care to orphans (particularly, disabled children) and were highly skeptical that ordinary Chinese people could understand or appreciate the self-worth of such children. Although Mercy Care was neither registered as a religious INGO nor publicly referenced its Christian faith, its work often blended American nationalism and Christian values, drawing on private donations to invest in foster care but also regularly working relationships with local and national officials to expedite ICAs for couples in the United States that Mercy Care knew were looking to adopt children with disabilities or medical conditions it deemed urgent. Mercy Care's service work in China, regardless of its seldom mentioned Christian motivations, was also precarious. Despite concerted efforts, it had been denied official registration as a charity in China, so it had pursued various circumspect routes to operate and pay its staff, including once registering them all as bakers through a relative's local bakery. With donations from the United States supporting stipends for foster families and six to seven Chinese staff members across Guangxi, Mercy Care's influx of cash, and its yearly trips that brought Americans and American board members to tour Chinese orphanages and foster homes, were subject to tremendous government scrutiny. The organization frequently had trouble obtaining visas for the visits and was often followed and questioned by security police in its travels.

For these reasons, public orphanage officials had an ambivalent relationship with Mercy Care. Encouraged and pressed to cultivate lucrative international partnerships through any means possible in the 1990s and early 2000s, officials were eager to accept foreign money but not always motivated to put that money toward foster placements, continue foster placements at significant effort or cost, or allow Mercy Care uninhibited access to state children and foster families. Although Mercy Care's Suling and I conducted most our visits alone and she contacted the families directly, the children belonged exclusively to the SWI, and Suling often struggled to get accurate information about the children's futures from state staff. As will be evident in several chapters of the book, whereas Mercy Care advocated for alternative family care for all orphans, the state favored a mixed social welfare approach that included both residential and foster care, allowing for children with "more severe" disabilities to receive care in a more controlled environment. As chapter 4 notes, the Daling rural foster care project seemed purposed toward providing more permanent placements for disabled children who had not fared well in urban foster care or were unlikely, due to the severity of their disabilities, to be adopted abroad. Daling, in fact, can be taken as evidence that attitudes toward foster care and disability were in flux in China: even as most people I spoke with, INGOs, orphanage staff, and foster mothers imagined a better future for disabled children through ICA to Western countries, it was also clear that foster parents were forming indelible bonds with disabled children.

For my part, after struggling to gain access to the state orphanage for months due to suspicions around Westerners, the relationship with Mercy Care was a godsend. I was able to gain the organization's trust primarily because I am a Presbyterian pastor with a seminary degree, and after disclosing this, Mercy Care was eager to share its work with me and also to take advantage of my seminary training in having me lead devotionals and marriage retreats with its staff from time to time. I was very concerned and cautious around these exchanges, especially because Mercy Care staff participated in underground, illegal house churches in China and my affiliation with them could have drawn further suspicion, gotten them in trouble with the authorities, or compromised my research. Yet because Mercy Care was offering me so much access to its foster families, help in navigating the landscape of social welfare, and general cultural guidance, I felt I could hardly refuse to assist with some of its religious programming. Mercy Care staff members did not disclose to state officials that they were Christians, and neither did I, so this secrecy was a constant feature of challenge and stress in conducting my fieldwork.

However stressful it may have been for me, it was far worse for Chinese Mercy Care staff, who knew that their faith affiliations to the Western Christian INGO put them in real danger. On numerous occasions (not while I was there), their office was ransacked by police, staff were interrogated, and their work was complicated or stymied by police surveillance. As I traveled with American board members and Chinese staff to orphanages in other provinces, state staff and officials were not always warm to our presence. Much of this suspicion of Westerners was left over from the bad press for Chinese orphanages in the 1990s, but also reflected increasing tightening of regulations and standards for Western INGOs operating in China. As Leslie Wang (2016) observes about her fieldwork during the same time period, roughly 2006–2014, most orphanage facilities were still quite poor. In Yulin Orphanage in Guangxi, for instance, we were let into an enormous baby room with approximately fifty cribs, laid out in rows, to which just a few nursing staff attended. There were volunteers who came to hold the babies in the hallways, but we were whisked in and out decidedly quickly and asked not to take pictures. I kept a notebook with me throughout my fieldwork in which I scrawled jottings, but I could tell such note-taking was merely tolerated and at times expressly discouraged. Even though I always disclosed my researcher status, I was never allowed into state institutions alone; I was always accompanied by state or Mercy Care officials.

Eventually I went on visits to see Auntie Ma, Meili, as well as Auntie Li and Pei Pei, on my own in their homes; in fact, Mercy Care was thrilled for me to cover the quarterly visit and even write up the report in English, as it needed to be mailed to sponsors in the United States. All of my visits to Daling foster homes were, however, supervised by Huilan, and sometimes Older Sister Mo, or Suling from Mercy Care. During such times I played a more observatory role given the official nature of the visit. When I was able to visit on my own, foster mothers openly complained to me that the orphanage failed to provide them information about the pasts or futures of the children they fostered. They seemed at once frustrated by the intrusion of the orphanage into their private lives and also palpably lonely for connection and companionship. On such occasions I tried to remain deferential to the orphanage, given its critical support for my research project, but I also felt privileged to really hear out these women's concerns. Therefore, my fieldwork consists of two conflicting registers (between these official supervised visits and unofficial visits) and was punctuated by periodic events hosted by the orphanage and Mercy Care for families, such as picnics in the park or parenting seminars.

I was never able to use audio or video recording due to the sensitivity of the relationships, so I was left to transcribe my jottings more thoroughly as I road home on the bus and to type them up when I had time. I did not conduct any formal interviews, but rather used participant observation to enter into the lives of my informants as much as possible. Foster mothers thrust their babies into my arms, insisted that they were headed out to the market and I may as well tag along, and asked me to help a child totter about the living room while they caught up on the dishes in the kitchen. Some foster parents were glad to see me and curious about what I was doing in China; others were far more reserved or even embarrassed that a Western visitor had come to their home unannounced (Suling did not usually tell them I was coming along). During trips across the country, out to Daling, or even from one corner of Nanning to the other, I had ample time to ask Huilan or Suling questions not only about foster care in China but also their daily lives. I relished the closeness of these relationships, as well as those with the families who are the main informants in this book. When it came time to leave the field in 2012, I did not want to go because I felt so connected, even indebted, to my informants.

And yet the work was also emotionally challenging. During the winter and spring of 2011–2012 in Daling, several children fell so ill they had to return to the orphanage. In the south of China, people typically do not have heat, but winters are damp and cold. Children were snuggled up under heavy comforters, but the air was so damp that mildew grew everywhere in the cinder block buildings. I saw children coughing and gasping for breath, and foster parents struggling to keep them comfortable or to feed them when they were clearly aspirating on the food, so weak had they become. Conditions of some foster homes were so meager that I worried for children's care and safety. Whereas in the United States such children would receive feeding tubes to prevent aspiration; splints and surgeries to make sure their bones grew properly if they could not walk; and standers, wheelchairs, and equipment suited to their bodies, in China I saw few of those supports provided for disabled, orphaned children.

Additionally, the fieldwork was emotionally intense. People spoke openly about disability and abandonment in ways that were troubling to me as a Westerner, even as the West was often falsely idealized for its assumed benevolence, parenting, and wealth. The class differences between foster mothers and orphanage and Mercy Care staff were certainly palpable, and foster parents were emotionally invested in the children they cared for. Some placements did not work out and there was hardship there, yet even when a placement did work out—a child was adopted domestically or internationally—it was bittersweet, even painful. When I was in the field, there was not a concerted effort for orphanage or INGO staff to provide training to foster parents regarding childhood trauma; therefore, many of the parenting techniques seemed inappropriate or callous. Finally, vocabulary and treatment of disability in China differed considerably from Western contexts. These cultural clashes were far more difficult in practice than I sometimes realized. For instance, I struggled for years to even write about Jiaqi's removal from her foster home, so painful was it to experience. Even though the book makes clear that foster care creates families from those who need them most, it is incredibly painstaking work, and I felt emotionally implicated in that work, too.

Furthermore, the suspicion around INGOs in China, Mercy Care's Christian affiliation, and my research in general kept me worried and anxious. Even getting my visa was a long, drawn-out process, because despite my efforts to cultivate relationships and affiliate as a visiting scholar with a local university, I was never able to obtain this status. Instead I registered under a student visa and took local Mandarin classes at the teaching college where my husband taught English. We had to make an emergency trip out to Hong Kong a couple of times during my fieldwork due to visa issues, and each time we went to submit our paperwork in Nanning, we had to press through crowds and were told to come back with additional paperwork. Nothing ever seemed clear or certain about our status in China, and I had nightmares about the police seizing my fieldwork, something happening to my informants, or getting kicked out of the country. Given that there were just a couple hundred Americans and Europeans in Nanning, my husband and I were highly visible, and to make matters more complicated, many of the foreigners, several in my English class, were actually undercover missionaries. Even though I was legitimately in Nanning doing research and my husband was actually teaching English, it would not have been surprising for the government to suspect otherwise. Still, the period in which we lived and studied in China, 2010–2012, was a relatively free time for INGOs and for Christians. We generally enjoyed a high degree of autonomy and freedom, even if I felt like we were living with the specter of danger.

FOSTER CARE: A "NEEDY KINSHIP"

This book makes an ethnographic contribution to contemporary studies of the Chinese family and the state, but it also explores experiences of disability and practices of foster care through the overlapping lenses of kinship, inequality, and global politics. In assessing child and elder abandonment, I contextualize Chinese notions of disability and use them to further cultural and theoretical nuance in disability studies by demonstrating how personhood finds mutual recognition and rehabilitation on the margins of society. By detailing how personhood among poor, older foster mothers and children with disabilities emerges in relationships of need, I complement disability studies' critiques of caregiving and dependency and highlight how need can be surprisingly resistive, disruptive, and creative. Finally, by unearthing exclusive and pejorative subtleties in the uplifting of foster mothers and their children as "special" and "extraordinary," I give ethnographic credence to the ways in which compulsory able-bodiedness undermines and controls certain forms of difference, even as it touts to liberate (McRuer 2006; Qian 2014).

Although state-sponsored foster care of disabled children, emerging alongside Deng Xiaoping's reform and opening period after the 1980s, is a narrow, novel object of study, the futures of such children have also become significantly intertwined with the market for international adoption. Today the majority of children adopted from China are children with disabilities, a fact that many take to highlight both the embrace of people with disabilities in the West and the persistent exclusion against persons with disabilities in the East (as well as the Global South). Yet, building on the work of Kristen Cheney, David Eng, Kay Ann Johnson, Leslie Wang, and Barbara Yngvesson, I trouble this one directional flow of children and resources in the international adoption market with particular respect to Western demand. In both foregrounding the ethnography of Chinese foster mothers who readily provide needed care to Chinese orphans with disabilities and demystifying the deep-seated need that underlies Western desire and adoption of Chinese children, I show how Chinese foster families simultaneously undergird yet complicate inequalities and hierarchies of modern family making. By demonstrating how disabled children are rehabilitated through Western, heteronormative, ICA, I confront a persistent ableism inherent in the processes, structures, and demand for such children that slights and erases the contribution and kinship of foster families from view.[12]

As an anthropologist of family and social life, I am most interested in how an ethnography of contemporary foster care can contribute to the emergent body of literature that takes extrabiological forms of family seriously in further mapping and understanding human kinship. New studies have powerfully highlighted the ways in which kinship can be formed through substances other than biological ones (food, land, hearths, or houses; Carsten 1996, 2004; Weismantel 1989), thus foregrounding the importance of social relationships in creating kinship (see, for instance, Franklin and McKinnon 2002; Modell 1994; Ragone 1994; and Wozniak 2002). As so many anthropologists have aptly pointed out, the opposition between biology and culture is a false dichotomy and naturalization (Schneider 1980, 1984; Strathern 1992; Weston 1991). Therefore, we do well to pay attention to both the slow work of kinning—namely, care, nurturance, feeding, exchange, and choice (Howell 2006; Weismantel 1989; Weston 1991)—and the transformations in the ways we think about kinship offered by new reproductive technologies and global forms of kinship, including ICA (Franklin 2013; Franklin and McKinnon 2002; Howell 2006; Leinaweaver 2008; Strathern 1992; Yngvesson 2010).

What is so provocative and intriguing about state-sponsored foster families in China is the way they hover between modern and postmodern (or post-Schneiderian?) studies of kinship. Despite persistent local practices of adoption, adoption by strangers and even kin in China is often kept secret, perpetuating the myth that Chinese families are homogeneous, efficient, extended, and harmonious biological entities (see Johnson 2004, 2016; Shang, Saldov, and Fisher 2011; Waltner 1990; and Watson 1975). Even though anthropologists of China such as Fei Xiaotong (1992), Sulamith Heins Potter and Jack Potter (1990), Arthur Wolf (1980), Margery Wolf (1968), and Yunxiang Yan (2003) have done much to trouble this paradigmatic Chinese family form, the self-sustaining biological unit remains the much-sought-after modern, familial ideal, from urban elite to migrant laborers.

Yet what I also encountered among state-sponsored foster families and state orphanage monitors was a self-conscious recognition that their families were deeply embedded in the global reproduction of primarily Western families by way of the international adoptive market. Despite the Chinese penchant for biological kinship, these families, seemingly out of necessity and social poverty, reared children that provided a much-sought-after global alternative. Thus, in pressing the boundaries of idealized Chinese family forms these foster families, and the orphanage monitors who surveilled them, were deeply aware of both the costs and the creativity of their marginality.

Somewhat surprisingly, returning to Kath Weston's work on gay kinship helped me work through this elusive puzzle that had emerged for me in the field—the seeming paradox that even as foster families remained subordinate to other family forms, necessarily both biological Chinese ones and international adoptive ones—they somehow also surmounted a formidable resistance to them. Indeed, for Weston, gay families, or the "families we choose," assert their resistance in a kind of sleight of hand: they construct a false opposition between biology and choice that simultaneously brings them to paramount status with biologically created families. Yet gay families also probe at this constructed opposition, thus failing to be constrained by "procreation's status as a master term imagined to provide the template for all possible kinship relations" (Weston 1991, 213). This is why Weston's *Families We Choose* is both an apt and a fraught title: choice is consistently undermined by its false opposition and its false construction. As Weston puts it, "descriptively speaking, the categories of gay kinship might better be labeled families we struggle to create, struggle to choose, struggle to legitimate, and—in the case of blood or adoptive family—struggle to keep" (1991, 212).

At first glance, foster families seem to do work similar to that of gay families in that they—as well as adoptive families—mirror blood relations, furthering the false dichotomy of choice as a powerful alternative to biology. But what Weston has helped me to realize is that Chinese foster families' sleight of hand comes in their presumed dispensability, their palpable impermanence. Indeed, foster families hardly substantively oppose even our socially constructed hegemonic forms, such as nuclear, biological, or even chosen families, because their extinction, rather than their preservation, appears a common goal. Foster families represent a liminal, undesired form in the developmental schema of family creation rather than a viable alternative, because their existence is predicated upon their brief temporality; their desired goal remains their expulsion, extinction, and extermination. Of course, ethnographic accounts such as Esther Goody's (1982) and Danielle Wozniak's (2002) have rightfully complicated the subordination of foster care's efficacy, impact, or affect based upon these temporal limitations. Indeed, one central claim of my own ethnography concerns the "contractual excess" emotion of such relationships that dramatically transcends their temporal bounds, muddying and complicating the presumed bounds of families—foster or otherwise.

But following the ethnographic questions with which this chapter begins, my work must still query whether kinship, robbed of its orientation, its goal, and its relationship to permanency, ceases to matter. Hence, even as the new studies of kinship have powerfully and readily contextualized the socially constructed nature of kinship, they tend to presume permanency as a given, unspoken, desired effect of viable families. As Judith Modell writes, "Permanency is as strong a core of kinship as the genealogical principle with which it is intertwined. But permanence, like genealogy, is a cultural convention, not a fact of nature" (1994, 234). So what might foster families offer to the study of contemporary kinship given their radical impermanence, and how might that opposition clarify persistent unintended boundaries around modern families and their evolution?

My ethnography demonstrates that the bonds formed in foster care often exceed their temporary contracts, making more desirable forms of (Chinese) biological kinship (the nuclear family enforced through birth planning, the suppression of domestic adoption, and the elevation of "high-quality" families), bolstered by state control, vulnerable to their emotion. Even as foster relationships are often (but not always) temporary, I show that such relationships are not replaceable, as is the presumption; instead they radiate emotion that practically exceeds many Chinese families' traditional bonds of kinship. It is the (often) "unselfconscious resistance" of these poor, older foster mothers (Modell 1994; Wozniak 2002) to middle-class, educated Chinese state actors that flies in the face of their seemingly marginal, disempowered character.[13] Thus, I demonstrate that in foster care, disempowered, defamiliarized older women's and orphaned, disabled children's desperation for one another transforms into conviction, advocacy, and affection that confronts Chinese state power and policies in startling ways. As these disempowered women begin to demand rights, rewards, and recognition of their temporary families from state officials, they trouble local policy and cultural convention about what actually constitutes family. Their emotional pleas and actions also powerfully complicate the young state orphanage workers' biological and hierarchical notions of the modern family, revealing these young people's fundamental ambivalence and discontent with their own modern lives and social roles.

Therefore, rather than finding themselves subordinated to "procreation's status as a master term" or permanency's presumed paradigmatic end goal in postmodern kinship studies, foster families offer new, compelling, affective and liberating challenges to middle-class orphanage monitors to reconceptualize parent-child relationships (Modell 1999, 61). Indeed, such resistance transcends its limited local context not just in threatening state orphanage monitors' notions of family but also in jeopardizing international adoption processes. As foster parents in Guangxi demanded more compensation, lobbied to keep their foster children rather than give them up, or refused to continue to foster following the relinquishment of a precious, irreplaceable foster child, they contended with the power of the Chinese state and threatened to stymie the chains of ICA that rested so firmly upon the backs of their hidden, temporary character.

And yet, in scholarly work regarding the politics and proliferation of ICA (L. Briggs 2009, 2012; Dorow 2006; Howell 2006; Marre and Briggs 2012; Yngvesson 2010) and also in popular media (Evans 2008; Myers 2005; Xinran 2011), foster families, who are numerous and instrumental in preparing foreign children for ICA, remain strikingly absent from discourse and from public view.

Popular and scholarly studies feature with prominence and provocation the transitions adoptees make from birth mothers to adopted mothers, and from birth families to "forever" families, not only powerfully foregrounding and favoring the permanence and hierarchy of such family transitions (Yngvesson 2010, 93–94) but eclipsing and sublimating the work of foster mothers and foster families that makes possible such exchanges. Meanwhile, scholarly studies and popular discourse in both China and Western countries affirm the importance and viability of private foster care as a psychologically superior alternative to orphanage care and group homes (Wang et al. 2017); however, as Wozniak writes, "the image of the 'bad' foster mother is not a reality but a cultural archetype that exists to sustain the emotional and economic exploitation of women" (2002, 215). Thus, the narrative of ICA both expunges real foster mothers from the validity of such social reproduction while also invoking the threat of their subordinate character.

Hence, when I write that foster families (and particularly state-sponsored Chinese foster families rearing disabled children who are eventually adopted to the West) are *families we need*, I do so with a double entendre in mind. Foster families and their children with disabilities are needed to expand white, heteronormative, and able-bodied (adoptive) families as they absorb, contain, and make invisible foster mothers and their children with disabilities. But such foster families also expose the needy underbelly of kinship, disrupt the sham of permanence in studies and paradigms of kinship, and make visible and compulsory need itself, by "invok[ing] . . . the inadequate resolutions that compulsory heterosexuality and compulsory able-bodiedness offers" (McRuer 2006, 31). By making visible such foster families, this book unearths constructed hierarchies of family the world over by undermining hegemonies of care and uplifting the critical category of need.

This is why I have titled this book *Families We Need* and why I argue that the everyday resistance of foster families does not merely challenge other Chinese families or the Chinese state but the very ideological notion of both the "natural" biological family and its permanent, singular, "choice-based" (adoptive) viable alternative. I find that, however unintentional, the ideological notion of choice-based kinship had indeed stripped the scrappy, struggling kinship of gay families, open adoption families, and especially foster families of their subversive, constrained qualities. What we see is that choice-based families (gay families, adoptive families, surrogate and in vitro fertilization families, etc.) only become viable when they are viewed as analogous to biological families by the state, which reinforces both their sublimation to the biological and their false opposition to other "deviant forms" (Butler 2004).

I argue, however, that in their temporary, plural—but especially "incomplete," needy, and unruly—forms, foster families do not so much oppose this hierarchy of family forms but draw attention to the common disruptive need for relationship that undergirds all of human kinship. In a sense I am trying to "naturalize" need as it highlights a real struggle for kinship that reshuffles and unsettles assumptions that kinship is either biologically granted or emphatically chosen. What is so provocative about these foster families, then, is not the way in which they exist apart from some permanent, singular, chosen family as viable alternative family forms, but the way in which their very features complicate the distance that middle-class orphanage care workers and the Chinese state seek to create and maintain from them. In putting forth this notion of the disruptive foster family, I am arguing that such families are disruptive not primarily because of their difference but because of their similarity to all families: they are fundamentally intertwined with the production and the maintenance of the modern, elite, adoptive family in the West, both complicating such distinctions and revealing our human existence as deeply needy individuals.

Whereas many have identified the need parents have for children (alongside the need children undoubtedly have for parents), I want to suggest—as I do in the book's title—that families also need one another, that we in the West and state orphanage monitors in China and "average families" *need* foster families because of what they reveal about our collective deep desire for social belonging and kinship. I contend that foster families have been sublimated within the chains of international adoption, China's national narrative, and new studies of kinship (Carsten 2000; Franklin and McKinnon 2002) because their visibility poses a challenge to the apolitical ideal of the modern family. Yet foster families suggest that kinship is not only slow, messy, and man-made but also deeply needy, and that powerful need for human relationship is often disruptive, disorderly, excessive, and unruly to even those who have had a hand in creating and sustaining it.

AN OUTLINE OF THE BOOK

Families We Need traces the movement of three primary Chinese foster children, Dengrong, Pei Pei, and Meili, from the state orphanage system into the respective humble homes of foster mothers Auntie Huang, Auntie Li, and Auntie Ma. Throughout this ethnography I demonstrate how these families' relationships and their interactions with orphanage and INGO care workers resist state control, shift societal roles, and call into question normative ideals of family in China, anthropology, and beyond. The introduction and conclusion that buttress the narrative, ethnographic chapters aim to present a broad, yet bold argument that contends with challenges in contemporary kinship studies and suggests new avenues for analysis and understanding. Meanwhile, the ethnographic chapters engulf the reader in the emotional politics of family making, love, and loss in everyday China.

In chapter 1, "Abandonment, Affinity, and Social Vulnerability," I describe the parallel abandonment of Dengrong, Pei Pei, and Meili and their foster mothers, Auntie Huang, Auntie Li, and Auntie Ma by their biological families amid the complex Chinese history of kinship, family, adoption, foster care, and disability.

Detailing the ways in which the Chinese state is often complicit in these children's and older women's abandonment by placing primary responsibility for the care of older and disabled persons on absent family members, I illustrate the social vulnerability and marginality of foster families in contemporary China. Readers will note that although one foster child at the center of this book, Meili, is not disabled, her story is included to emphasize the critical effects of social abandonment by family members for children and elders in China today.

Chapter 2, "Fostering (Whose) Family?" takes a brief pause from the narratives of foster families to contextualize the way in which foster care in China has come to support and sustain the market for ICA and query the increasing, disproportionate abandonment and adoption of children with disabilities beginning in 2005. Readers concerned with historical and structural shifts within Chinese social welfare, its relationship to the state, and ICA will appreciate the additional global context this lends to the book's central arguments on kinship and family.

Chapter 3, "Needy Alliances," explores the affective processes of caregiving whereby foster children move from being "ugly children" to beloved foster sons and daughters. Whereas foster parents are initially critical of their foster children and unaccepting of their disabilities and limitations, they gradually become experts in their care and advocates on their behalf. Additionally, I show how, in the raising of these children, foster parents are somewhat rehabilitated in the eyes of the state and society as they find purpose and respect in the commitment to raising a child. Although foster parents' social vulnerability may be positioned as a weakness in the eyes of society and the state, I show how foster parents draw upon this vulnerability as a resource in framing their reserves and abilities as effective parents.

Chapter 4, "Envying Kinship," highlights the ambivalence of the state orphanage and Mercy Care workers who facilitate these contractual foster care relationships as they both admire and undermine these older women's ability to provide care. I show how state orphanage and Mercy Care workers' family relationships mingle with those of the foster families to question their normative ideals of family, thus revealing their own social vulnerability. These middle-aged women, who leave their own children in the care of their own parents during the workday, displace their own concerns and insecurities onto the foster mothers, causing friction and conflict. Yet I also demonstrate how the orphanage and INGO workers, despite their efforts to reform these families, eventually come to envy them. As they speak wistfully about the deep affection these foster mothers have for their disabled children, they reveal their unfulfilled desire for intimacy in their own family lives, suggesting that the boundaries among biological families, foster families, and adoptive families are not so hard and fast as they seem, despite their efforts to solidify them.

Chapter 5, "Replaceable Families?," queries to what extent the exceptionalism afforded to children with disabilities in Chinese foster families actually serves to marginalize and stigmatize such children and families. This chapter also picks up on some of the structural challenges raised in chapter 2 with respect to the participation of foster families in the market of international adoption and their contribution to the maintenance of normative, racialized, and ableist family hierarchies. The question of foster families' liminality and marginality is raised with respect to their global import and impact.

Chapter 6, "Disruptive Families," details the differing fates of the three foster children and their foster parents. Following the fates of the foster mothers and foster care monitors, the chapter also demonstrates the (often unselfconscious) resistance foster mothers' emotion and affection present to the state, as their feelings transcend and transgress the boundaries of temporary kinship. I show that despite its investment in the emotional quality of these foster relationships, the state is ultimately vulnerable to such emotions, as they disturb and disrupt the patterns and contracts of fosterage that provide care to marginal children and facilitate lucrative and high-profile ICAs. Given that the orphanage officials represent the state in these interactions but exhibit ambivalence, they illustrate an emotional quality to state relations that is not often associated with modernity or the Chinese state. I argue that the emotional indictment of the state at the hands of foster parents renders the state surprisingly vulnerable to alternative, "marginal" forms of kinship.

Finally, the conclusion, "Families We Need," reflects on the critical resistance foster kinship raises to normative categories of kinship not only within anthropology but also in China and the West. While discussions of ICA often foreground birth mothers and adoptive mothers, I argue that foster mothers remain absent and subordinated not merely because of the temporary quality of foster kinship (after all, birth mothers are quite temporary mothers) but also because of the presumed "replaceability" of their care. Instead, my ethnography demonstrates that foster care provides transformative effects not only for foster children but also for foster mothers and middle-aged state orphanage care workers. Such evidence reminds us that foster families are hardly replaceable within modern constellations of family even as they are noticeably expunged from ICA narratives. Indeed, what this book illustrates is that kinship is not only surprisingly alive and central to modern nations with strong states but deeply desired and needed by those on both the margins and at the center of social life.

1 · ABANDONMENT, AFFINITY, AND SOCIAL VULNERABILITY

One afternoon, a year into my fieldwork, I sat talking with two of the Mercy Care foster family monitors, Luli and Xiao Wang, a woman and a man, both in their late twenties. They confided in me that despite the fact that they had each had trouble conceiving with their spouses, their parents would never allow them to adopt. When I asked them why, Luli and Xiao Wang let on that they would never have asked their parents outright, but to their aging parents, an adopted child would not be considered their own child, and beyond that their parents would not need to provide another reason.

Xiao Wang mused that if you adopted and then gave birth to a child of your own at some point you would have to split the assets, or the inheritance, and he wondered aloud how one would make such a decision, and whether the birth child would not always resent the adopted child. Luli said that a woman at her church who had a biological child had adopted because she wanted her child to have a sibling and admitted that she had trouble truly accepting this child as her own. Both Luli and Xiao Wang admitted that they wondered, too, if they could ever accept an adopted child as their own.

I was shocked to hear them talk so openly about their reticence to adopt when their daily lives were spent encouraging foster parents to form bonds with foster children. I had spent a year getting to know these young people, I thought I knew them well, and I felt foolish that they seemed to be explaining something so obvious about their lives and beliefs that I somehow had completely missed it.

"It just goes against our traditional culture to adopt," Luli and Xiao Wang protested. Puzzled, I pointed out my knowledge of how adoption had actually happened a lot, historically, in China (Waltner 1990; Watson 1975), and Xiao Wang retorted that that was way back when people had "tons of kids." But then I pointed to kin adoptions, which I knew were also still quite commonplace in China (Shang, Saldov, and Fisher 2011).

"Oh, those don't happen much anymore," Xiao Wang responded dismissively.

"I believe they do in the countryside," I replied, and then I shared some stories I had heard from local friends in Guangxi about people who had passed an overquota birth child onto their sister to be raised as her own, or who out of poverty needed to pass their last born off to a relative.

"Actually my father was *guoji*," Xiao Wang blurted out suddenly. "Yeah, it was due to poverty, kind of like some of the orphans, I guess. My grandfather gave my father to his brother's family when he was ten to care for, because he was the youngest and his brother and his wife didn't have any children." Then Xiao Wang went onto describe how at age twenty-three his father had come back to live with his birth family, and though his relationship is amicable with the uncle who raised him during his teenage years, it remains understandably strained with his birth father.

GUOJI

It took nearly a year in the field, but that afternoon I learned that *guoji* (kin adoption)—from *guo*, which means to cross or pass on, and *ji*, which means to inherit, continue, or succeed—was so woven into the fabric of local life in Guangxi that it was hardly detectable, let alone recognizable as a form of adoption or foster care, even to people who facilitate foster care placements and adoptions for a living. Although Luli and Xiao Wang eventually acknowledged the parallel between *guoji* and adopting an orphan, they struggled to articulate precisely why prospective parents and grandparents did not consider the personhood of orphans commensurate with those of biological children. Local kinship practices like *guoji* are so deeply embedded in the cultural consciousness that they are unconsciously, if not morally, distinguished from practices of formal, government-sponsored, foster care and adoption.

Some of the reasons these local practices go overlooked is because they so seamlessly integrate children without homes, and parents or families without means to care for children, into Chinese society and, as Xiao Wang also suggests, they are often kept a secret from the children themselves. James Watson describes both the historic preference for *kuochi* (*guoji*), agnatic adoption, among powerful lineages in Hong Kong, and the surprising prevalence of adoption of outsiders, which served to avoid intralineage conflict and shore up the bond between father and son (1975). The perception that outsiders disrupt the family line, or that even insiders' loyalties might be tested if they knew their origins, is one reason families would opt to keep an adoption secret.

As Kay Ann Johnson (2016, 12) points out, although international adopters often place a virtue on openness, Chinese adopters of Chinese children can easily pass as biological parents, and openness thus becomes a choice. Johnson identifies that in about half of the cases of domestic adoption she and her team of researchers studied in the south central region of China over several decades, the adoption was kept a secret from the children. She outlines a myriad of reasons why people might keep adoptions secret and shows that, by the 1990s, the practice of domestic adoption in China was fraught with difficulties, putting families and children at great risk of fines, separation, and even seizure of the child by the government (2016, 30). Although this present volume focuses neither on domestic adoption nor the birth parents that relinquish adopted children, Johnson's work powerfully illustrates why birth parents and adoptive parents may be benevolently motivated to choose secrecy yet also struggle with that choice.

As Xiaoyuan Shang, Morris Saldov, and Karen Fisher (2011) emphasize in their work on child welfare in China, apart from the increasing number of domestic adoptions of unrelated children through informal and formal channels, the vast majority of orphans in China are still informally adopted or fostered within familial circles. Johnson (2016) shows that even at the height of the birth planning crises in the People's Republic of China (PRC), the priority for would-be relinquishers of overquota children or would-be adopters was a kin or a neighbor relationship, such that the family could be sure of the fate of the child and could often watch, secretly, from afar. Johnson argues that the "overcrowding of orphanages and creation of a pool of children available for international adoption was closely related to, if not wholly caused by, active government suppression of customary adoption practices" (2016, 57). She refers to these local adoptions as *shishi shouyang*, best translated as de facto or actual (not informal) adoption, given that despite being unregistered with the government these were clearly permanent arrangements that fully incorporated children into the adoptive family.

Infamous cases in which children are abandoned in busy marketplaces, outside the door of orphanages, or even in the increasingly common baby hatches (Wang 2016, 40) were shown to be desperate, last-ditch attempts to preserve the life of the children in the face of no options for a local adoption in which birth parents knew, or at least knew of, the adoptive parents. Yet, once children were recovered by the orphanage system, they became wards of the state, not just literally but culturally and symbolically. Children were given an approximate birth date and a last name. Sometimes, all of the foundlings recovered in the same year are given names that reflect the Chinese zodiac sign for that year. Up until 2012, when the practice was outlawed, many were given surnames such as Dang (Party) or Guo (Country) to mark their indebtedness to the nation (*Economist* 2020). Practically, because they are from nowhere, a child abandoned at an orphanage is also given a *hukou*, a household registration, that literally resides in the orphanage. Notoriously difficult to alter, even for people with financial means and prestige, these registrations both limit transport and employment for orphans but, perhaps most important, they mark them as orphans for life as they grow, no matter what opportunities they may achieve or seek.

Hence, what I discovered over my eighteen months of fieldwork in Guangxi is that, for a Chinese child, being abandoned into an orphanage constituted somewhat of a social break or even a social death that was not easily culturally rehabili-tated. This is because in Chinese society, to be without family is to be without personhood, and those who have passed through the orphanage have become detached from family in a way that marks them for life. This is, of course, not an ultimate distinction; there are exceptions to every cultural rule. One exception is domestic adoption, another is intercountry adoption (ICA), and the third, my object of study, is government-sponsored foster care, which oscillates between the two. This chapter argues, however, that the cultural stigma around child abandon-ment in China, coupled with the increasing participation of the PRC in ICA, which also practically suppressed opportunities for domestic adoption, furthered the social rejection of children abandoned into orphanages from the 1990s to the present.[1] This explains how foster care monitors like Luli and Xiao Wang could believe in ICA and foster care as the only options for disabled orphans, because children who were *guoji* would never darken the door of a Chinese orphanage.

Yet lingering in the background of this chapter, and what will become more prominent throughout the book, are a parallel group of people in China, who being without grandchildren—and sometimes even without children, or without financial and political means—also find themselves increasingly socially obsolete. Indeed, I open with the stories of Luli's and Xiao Wang's hesitancy to adopt to make a clear distinction between elders like Luli's and Xiao Wang's parents who have grandchildren or the means to make demands on their biological children to have grandchildren and those who do not. Many scholars have noted the signifi-cant vulnerability for Asia's rapidly growing older populations given shifting cul-tural practices, increasing economic pressures, and scant state welfare.[2] Perhaps nowhere else in the Asian world has social change been as dramatic for older people as in China, where nearly sixty million people who came of age during the Cultural Revolution toiled in the countryside, lived and breathed socialist rhetoric, and quickly found themselves struggling to catch up with modern edu-cation, entrepreneurship, and open markets (Yan 2011b). Indeed, older people were unable to take advantage of the economic reforms of the 1980s because they were implemented after or just as they retired.

Meanwhile, the disintegration of the collective economy that made old age support almost entirely the responsibility of family members, the collapse of supporting structures for the institution of filial piety, and the lack of effective intervention mechanisms for parental neglect makes older people in con-temporary China particularly vulnerable (H. Zhang 2004, 84). For rural seniors especially, the lack of pension for farmers makes them almost entirely reliant on family members for care in old age. For all seniors, early mandatory retirement ages in China (age fifty for female blue-collar workers, fifty-five for white-collar women, and sixty for most men) often rob them of their earning abilities and their social status in family decisions, as well as the wider society. According to the 2020 Chinese Census, at 264 million, today's seniors over the age of sixty make up 18.7 percent of the population, but they are projected to make up nearly 30 percent of China's total population by 2050.

This chapter describes the social abandonment of three primary informants and their families, acquainting the reader with cultural perceptions of child abandonment and family in China while also explaining that this abandonment must be considered in relationship with a constellation of government policies that have made care for vulnerable children and older people both state and local crises. The reader can see how foster care offers one such solution to these crises, but foster families still remain culturally liminal due to the subordinate status of abandoned children, children with disabilities, and elders without strong family ties. Furthermore, as was mentioned in the introduction, foster parents are ineligible to adopt foster children. In chapter 2, I reexamine the practice of foster care in the context of ICA and the increasing rates of adoption of children with disabilities through ICA from China since 2005. But, to begin, here I situate foster families, and the disabled children and older women who make them up, within both the shifting demographics of modern China and the prevailing cultural claims on family making and personhood.

I use the term *abandonment* (a term often rejected by adoptive families and other adoption communities) not because it represents the intentions of birth mothers or birth families;[3] indeed, the present study does not include birth mothers or birth families. But the term highlights an important and isolating social experience for both orphaned children (especially those with disabilities) and older persons in China. In her work on kinship, Marilyn Strathern draws a distinction between alienation and detachment, the former being a state of social ostracization and the latter a potential liminal state that "crafts an object whose value exists *both* in respect to its origin *and* in being caused or elicited by another" (1992, 181, emphasis in the original). What is critical, then, in using the term *abandonment* for orphaned, disabled children or older persons is that they are not being released from their families with the expectation of finding value through or among other social relationships. In fact, as I show in this chapter, abandonment communicates a fundamentally devalued state of personhood that renders them perhaps more socially vulnerable than their actual or perceived disabilities.

AUNTIE MA'S STORY

Auntie Ma, the foster mother of eleven-year-old Meili, was also the mother of an only daughter who had recently married, moved in with her in-laws, and begun the process of starting a family of her own.[4] Although Auntie Ma's biological daughter also lived in the capital city, she saw her infrequently, and she was unlikely to provide her any practical or physical support in old age given Guangxi's traditional patterns of patrilocal residence.[5] Auntie Ma was a widow who received a small monthly pension from the state and lived alone in a seventh-story apartment; her extended family lived many hours away in the countryside. Hence, like many seniors in China, she was vulnerable due to her relative familial and social alienation and her limited finances and social networks.

Over the course of my fieldwork, however, I discovered that despite her frequent and humble self-critique of her own simple background and uneducated status, Auntie Ma did not represent herself as a victim of her circumstances. She spoke openly, even brazenly about hardships during the Cultural Revolution.[6] Although she bemoaned how her youth was taken away from her when she was sent to the rice paddies in Longzhou, close to the Vietnam and Yunnan borders, and mourned the early death of her husband, she, like many other foster mothers, was remarkably generous, resourceful, and kind.

Yet Auntie Ma also clasped my hands awkwardly and tightly when I would come for a visit, running her hands over my arms, drinking me in with what seemed to be desperation. She was also anxious and doting—in a way that was not endearing but rather obsessive. She wondered aloud, and with indignation, as to how I had crossed the highway to her apartment on my own, even though I was a grown woman, and she crossed the highway alone nearly every single day to go to the market. She seemed desperate for company, alternatively brash and then awkwardly brimming with tears. Her apartment was dark and cold during the winter, with just a space heater for warmth, and stifling in the oppressive heat of the summer. Auntie Ma made the best of it—she was scrappy, for sure—but she was also palpably lonely. When I would come and ask what she had been up to, the answer was always "Nothing"; she was a simple woman, she would say, and there was nothing she did worth noting.

The last time I saw Auntie Ma she shoved a bulging bag of peanuts she had brought back from the countryside into my purse and insisted on walking me, as she always did, across the six-lane highway to the bus stop. She began to talk about how she felt quite lucky in the life she had been given: how poor she had grown up, as one of five children with only one pair of shoes to share; what had happened during the Cultural Revolution and the Great Leap Forward; and all those who had died or now had no insurance or pension. I remember very clearly as we stood by the side of the crowded road, with traffic rushing by and exhaust pouring out of the noisy buses, that she looked quite content when she said that she knew from experience that she was living in the best times in China and she did not take it for granted.

MEILI'S STORY

Meili was a shy eleven-year-old when I first met her at Auntie Ma's seventh-story apartment with the Mercy Care monitor Suling one afternoon. Unlike almost all the children I visited in foster care, Meili showed no signs of physical or mental disability, and at eleven, she was nearly a young woman. I wondered what it would be like to talk with a child who might remember her abandonment and who would be able to more clearly articulate her own opinions and feelings.

As with the younger children, however, Meili's foster mother did most of the talking; Auntie Ma eagerly grasped at my pudgy arms, commenting on how lovely and fat I was, especially in comparison to her skinny frame. She mentioned her own digestive illnesses that sucked the life out of her and left her gaunt and weak. And she indulged herself and Meili, her foster daughter, in daydreaming aloud of what life might be like in America.

In comparison, Meili was reserved, pensive, and aloof. Although she asked the occasional pointed question about my background, she was clearly embarrassed by her foster mother's scurrying around to make her guests comfortable, her forward questions, and the way Auntie Ma seemed starved for attention. When Suling began the usual interview she does with foster kids, trying to glean the relationship between foster mother and child through a series of questions about schoolwork, hobbies, friendship, and behavior, Meili compliantly and sparingly answered the questions, while Auntie Ma interrupted frequently to provide clarification: She might like math, but that does not mean she is good at it. The reason Meili does not do much on weekends is because her foster mother is fearful of strangers, and Meili is becoming a little rebellious as she gets older. To this Meili began to protest.

"What about the bathroom door?" Suling asked Meili. "At the orphanage," she continued, referencing a recent health checkup when Meili had presumably misbehaved. "Why did you go into the bathroom and lock the door? Didn't you do that?"

"No," Meili replied, bewildered.

By now I had become accustomed to (though not completely comfortable with) these inquisitions by foster care monitors, both from international nongovernmental organizations (INGOs) and the government, not only with older children but also with children as young as two or three. Children were not being consulted for information but rather tested for cultural understanding. Did they understand that they were to be obedient to their parents at all costs? Did they understand the ways in which that obedience was communicated? If not, sometimes the questions would turn to scolding and shaming; other times they would lighten toward questions in which the children themselves would choose fictitious options or consequences (see chapter 3). In this case, Auntie Ma came to her aid: "No, she wouldn't do something like that," she said.

"Hmm, must be a mistake," Suling said as she scrawled in her notebook. When Suling asked Meili if she remembered her friends at the orphanage or the orphanage itself, she looked equally bewildered.

"She was too young," Auntie Ma said quickly. "She doesn't remember much, she was only five or six when she was abandoned." Were it not for these words, Meili might pass for just another eleven-year-old girl growing up in a cramped apartment with an overbearing mother. But when I came back by myself on the cusp of the monthlong break for the Chinese New Year to visit Auntie Ma and Meili, excitement over red envelopes and games of badminton shifted abruptly to questions from Auntie Ma about whether I was going to be Meili's new mother. "I've told the orphanage I want you to be, because you're kind," she said. I did not know how to respond, glancing awkwardly at Meili and then back at the wide grin of Auntie Ma. This was not the first time I had been bluntly asked to adopt kids and take them home with me. But whereas the comments were usually directed playfully, with mischievous smiles or as warnings to misbehaving children, I sensed the desperation in Auntie Ma's voice and worried that this request was for real.

"Oh, Meili is wonderful, but you know, I'm still doing my doctorate. I'm really in no position to raise a child; I'm too busy studying." I repeated this excuse several times throughout the conversation as Auntie Ma jubilantly referred to me as *Meiguo mama* (American mama). Finally Meili interrupted and corrected her. "Not mother, older sister!" she said. I sighed a bit, thankful for her intrusion.

It was during that same, expansive, dizzying conversation that Auntie Ma began to whisper her abandonment story to me, even though Meili was sitting right there, chomping away on some of the candy I had brought her. "Well, she really wasn't at the orphanage very long," she said in a hushed tone. "She was around five or six when she was abandoned, and she remembers a bit. Her mother and father had divorced and so the mother had no choice but to leave her, and then it was a bad situation with the stepmother, and they had a new baby boy, and it was the stepmom who beat her on the head, I think she still has a scar." Auntie Ma brushed Meili's hair from her forehead, and Meili turned away. "So, eventually she abandoned her to the orphanage. I keep thinking her birth mother must wonder about her, wonder what happened to her. I tell her that sometimes, and I think about putting up an announcement and maybe she would come after her. But if she could be adopted to America that would really be best, because Americans have money and it's a developed country, and they could really take care of her permanently," Auntie Ma reasoned.

Meili barely looked up from the book cradled in her lap. She was an avid reader. She seemed to use reading as an escape from the harshness of her past life and from the uncertainty of her future. Despite how removed she appeared, and despite hardly a flinch in facial expression in the very room where Auntie Ma told how Meili had been cruelly misled to believe her stepmother was just running to the market to buy something but instead left her in the back seat of the cab, I knew there was much beneath her stoic expression.

I knew because Meili had remembered these circumstances when Auntie Ma had taken her home—at first, reluctantly (Auntie Ma recalled how sickly and dirty she was, and with the deep gash on her forehead, no one wanted her). So much so that every time Meili saw a police officer, for years afterward, she would chime in, "There's the car that brought me to the orphanage." Whether she hid these experiences from herself, she could not hide the feelings. Additionally, Meili's abandonment would have taken place in 2005, roughly the peak year for ICAs from China, so the orphanage had eagerly begun her paperwork. But when they questioned Meili nearly a year after she had come to live with Auntie Ma, she had said she did not want to be adopted, and she did not want to go to America. The orphanage staff worried she would run away and try to find the family that had abandoned her, so they stopped pushing. They stopped her paperwork for ICA.

Meili and her story of abandonment continued to fascinate me in the field, because even though she was not physically or mentally disabled, she had been ostracized from her birth family and had ended up in the orphanage. Yet the fact that Meili was left behind by her birth mother following divorce is actually quite common today in China. In her work on child welfare, Xiaoyuan Shang (2008a) shows that, in accordance with the Chinese tradition of patrilocal residency and the bride leaving her natal family, many children who are considered orphans are actually children absorbed by the husband's family and, in most cases, the husband's brothers' families. In rural China, Shang (2008a, 205) finds that the definition of *orphan* varied based on sociocultural assumptions: an urban definition meant that the child had lost both parents; a patriarchal definition meant that the child's father had died and the mother had left to remarry; only the orphans who fell into the government category of the "three nos" (no parents, no capability of looking after themselves, or no other relatives who were legally responsible to care for them) were entitled to formal state benefits.[7] In fact, in her numerous surveys of over fifty-six counties in China, Shang (2010, 82–92) finds that the most common reason for children becoming orphans is the death of a father and the departure of a mother. Especially in divorces decided outside of court, women are often forced to leave children with their husband's family due to social conventions and pressure; or, knowing that they will face much discrimination and financial difficulty if they try to remarry and already have a child, or try to raise children as a single mother, they leave children behind reluctantly.

Historically, however, in most families an abundance of siblings, children, and extended family created a climate where kin adoption was not only prominent but also amply possible. Yet the fact that Meili could not be absorbed into a larger family network on her father's side, as would be the traditional patrilocal responsibility, suggests that decreasing family size, increasing economic costs of child-rearing, and a social policy that permitted only one child per couple coalesced to create a disincentive regarding kin adoption for families caring for children of divorce (Shang 2008a; Shang, Saldov, and Fisher 2011). Given the enforcement of the birth planning policies beginning roughly in the 1980s, Meili's father, likely born during that time period, may not have had any siblings to help care for her. If Meili's birth family practiced patrilocal residence, like most families in Guangxi, Meili's father's parents would have lived with them and likely had little resources or say over whether they could provide care to Meili. With the birth of a new son to Meili's father and her stepmother, Meili's fate was sealed. There was simply no place for her any longer in the family that she was born into, and no role for her to play in the new one.

Meili's abandonment helps identify some of the ways in which cultural beliefs and practices—for instance, patrilocal residence—clashed with modern governance and changing demographics, such as birth planning policies and the shrinking size of the Chinese family. The fact that Meili had not been adopted locally or internationally was somewhat due to her own stated preferences, but it was also reinforced by Chinese cultural reverence for the biological family. She did, indeed, still have a father somewhere, whom she remembered, and the orphanage reasoned that he could come to collect her or she might run back to him at anytime. Thus the government did not process her paperwork for ICA.

Here the orphanage's reticence to process Meili's paperwork is evocative of what Linliang Qian terms "a familist ideology," a Confucian belief that patrilineal kinship forms the organizing principle of all social life (Qian 2014, 255; see also Fei 1992). Although familism provides an ideal rather than a real-life model for family life,[8] contemporary anthropological studies have confirmed its enduring, yet shifting salience (see, for instance, Brandtstadter and Santos 2011; Davis and Harrell 1993; Oxfeld 2010; Y. Yan 2003, 2011a, 2011b, 2018). Additionally, many scholars stress the relational sense of the Chinese self (Fei 1992; Guo and Kleinman 2011; and Tu 1985). As Qian puts it, persons "embedded in family-based social obligations and attached responsibilities . . . cannot be defined outside this matrix" (Qian 2014). This chapter will further explore the relationship between familism and abandonment for children, elders, and disabled children.

Meili found herself in the liminal space of foster care: no matter how much Auntie Ma came to love her as her own, she could never adopt her, both due to regulations with respect to birth planning and the domestic adoption law and to state preferences for younger, more suitable parents. Additionally, Auntie Ma had been conditioned to believe that Meili was better off in America. Not only did Meili not belong to her, but she did not belong to a family in China, so it made sense that Meili's predicament could not be resolved through any other channels besides ICA.

PEI PEI'S AND XIAOYUAN'S STORIES

The first time I met Pei Pei, it was an early winter weekend morning, and everyone except her foster mom, Auntie Li, was sleeping soundly. "Go in and wake them up," Auntie Li declared cheerfully. I crept reluctantly with Suling into the dark, tiny room, where she tickled and roused Pei Pei and little Yuping from their bunk beds. They trudged with sleep in their eyes and steps into the dark, cramped living room, and it was only then that I noticed the deep scar across Pei Pei's upper lip. Pei Pei took Yuping affectionately into her lap, and as Yuping wiped the sleep from her eyes, Pei Pei slipped a heavy sweater over Yuping's head and fitted it over her delicate arms.

The house slowly came to life as Auntie Li's eldest (and only biological) daughter entered the room, and Suling began to ask about school, sisterhood, and what they normally did on the weekends. As Pei Pei spoke, her sweet, polite words came out halting and garbled, vestiges of a speech defect due to a poor cleft palate repair. Auntie Li complained that she did not raise her hand much in class, despite how smart she was.

"I don't raise my hand because no one can understand me," Pei Pei protested.

"I don't get it," Auntie Li puzzled. "The teacher says she can't understand her, but we can understand her just fine, so that can't be it. I think she gets nervous, and then she doesn't speak clearly and then no one can understand, so I guess it's a waste of time for the teacher to call on her when the class is only forty minutes long," she reasoned. Pei Pei had been picked on at school and beaten up, even though the teacher insisted that the other children did not know she was from the orphanage, so the beatings were random and unrelated to her status as an orphan.

Suling began to take photos of the girls and also scrawled in her notebook. When Pei Pei ran into her room to get one of the books she loves to read, Auntie Li turned to Suling in a hushed voice and asked, "So, tell me what's going on. Is she going to be adopted out? Have they done the paperwork?"

"I don't think so," Suling said, furrowing her brow. "I thought her mother was still around, maybe mentally ill. If she has a mother, she can't be adopted, right?"

"Well, does she have a mother?" Auntie Li asked, exasperated. "The orphanage doesn't tell me anything!"

"I don't know," Suling replied hesitatingly, wondering aloud to me whether she had confused Pei Pei with another foster kid.

"I wasn't going to tell her anything," Auntie Li continued. "I didn't want to confuse her." Suddenly Pei Pei was back with the book, blissfully unaware of the conversation that had just transpired in her living room.

Over the course of subsequent visits, I learned that Pei Pei's mother was indeed alive, yet incarcerated. Beyond that, I was not able to learn many details. Given that she was unavailable to care for Pei Pei, one might imagine that, like that of other abandoned children, Pei Pei's guardianship would be relinquished to the orphanage, she would be placed in foster care, and she would become eligible for adoption. But as I got to know Pei Pei, her foster mother, and her foster family, I discovered that children of the incarcerated occupy some of the most precarious positions in Chinese child welfare. Because these children have legal guardians, they are neither eligible for state welfare nor can they be adopted, and they often end up on the streets if they are not taken in by relatives. Catherine Keyser (2009) describes the interventions of private individuals and INGOs in the 1990s to create the Sunshine Villages, a network of private foster homes for children of the incarcerated, but notes their precarious position given that INGOs are not always welcomed by the Chinese government.

The fact that Pei Pei was in foster care in the first place was a little surprising. In cases such as hers, children were at best doomed to life in an institution and, given that fate, orphanages rarely saw fit to expend time and resources to place them outside in a foster family. In fact, the orphanage began to doubt their investment during the time that I knew Pei Pei, Auntie Li, and her foster family. The orphanage reasoned that it would be more cost effective to send Pei Pei to the local orphanage school rather than continue her foster placement and pay the school fees for a placement out of district. In Pei Pei's case, while she was once abandoned, perhaps in part due to her impairment, she was now doubly abandoned because she was tied to a legal guardian, and yet, an incarcerated one. Even if Pei Pei could be declared legally abandoned and absorbed within the orphanage system, it would be unlikely that anyone would wish to adopt her given the stigma for children of the incarcerated in China (Keyser 2009).

As is true for children who have been trafficked, locals are reticent to adopt children who, like Meili and Pei Pei, technically have families, because they fear one day their birth families will come to reclaim them. The legal requirements for orphanages to post parent-finding ads in the paper and to wait for two months before declaring the child an orphan are quite clear, but the problem of child trafficking is also becoming one of significant proportion in modern China.[9]

The Chinese assumption is, however, that birth families have ultimate claim to children, and this is perhaps best demonstrated by the local phenomenon known as *chuxian*—literally, "to appear." It is a situation in which birth parents show up at the orphanage to check in on, but not to claim, an abandoned child. In the event that this happens, the child in question will likely never be adopted within China or internationally, but instead be confined—and, one might argue, doubly abandoned to life as an orphan and, in many cases, life within an institution. As far as I could tell, there is no national or local policy that specifies how varied abandonment trajectories affect eligibility for adoption, but in practice they certainly held children in administrative limbo.

I have memories of orphanage and Mercy Care workers whispering under their breaths that children were *chuxian*. What a shame it was that their parents had shown up just that one time at the gate of the orphanage; for were it not so, they, like their lucky peers, could be adopted to a warm home in China or even America. I remember walking with Suling down the dark sidewalk one evening as we came home from a visit with a family in the capital city. "Just once," she had said with angst and anger. Just once is all it took for a child's fate to be sealed.

Of course, parents knew not what they did. They would show up years after the abandonment, in some cases surprised and overjoyed to find that a previously unhealthy child had survived; in other cases they had meant to check in on a child without the orphanage knowing that they were the parents, but their odd mannerisms and teary eyes betrayed them. The Mercy Care director remembered one case in which the parents had wanted the child—now eight years old—back. "Of course, the orphanage was infuriated," Teacher Liu told me. "The orphanage staff were the ones who had reared this child, taken care of him all these years at great expense, so they told the family they'd need to pay for those eight years in order to get the child back. And the family wouldn't or couldn't do so, so they left empty-handed."

On my final trip to visit foster families in Guilin (another populous city in Guangxi), we had visited a foster family with a beautiful little girl named Xiaoyuan. Suling and I had walked the narrow paths between the rice paddies to the traditional-style home on the outskirts of the city, where chickens scattered in the courtyard as we pushed open the rusty gate and Xiaoyuan's foster mother came bounding down the stairs to greet us. "Come upstairs," she beckoned. "We'll have some watermelon. Xiaoyuan and her brother are watching television. It's been so long since you were last here; just wait until you see how smart and strong she's grown."

The atmosphere was jubilant as the five of us sat in Xiaoyuan's living room, sweet country air wafting in through the second-floor windows, which overlooked the fields her family farmed for a living. Xiaoyuan sang for us, slurped down watermelon, and even her teenage brother, who slumped moodily against the slope of the wooden sofa playing games on his phone, looked up from time to time and smiled adoringly at her. Xiaoyuan's foster mother brought apples and oranges and added them to the stack of fruit on the coffee table and slipped the child onto her lap as she carved into the fruits, peeling them and handing them to us.

"Does Xiaoyuan want to go to America?" she asked sweetly.

"No!" Xiaoyuan cried out petulantly.

"And why not?" her foster mom said, feigning exasperation.

"What about you, Mom?" Xiaoyuan asked hesitantly.

"You could call me, call me up and say, 'Hi, Mom, I'm in America with my new mommy and daddy.' You could call me anytime!"

"Maybe . . . maybe I could text you," Xiaoyuan stammered, and we all laughed.

Full of fruit and joy, we walked down the steps, through the courtyard, and out the gate, Xiaoyuan's foster mother clinging to our arms and thanking us for coming. She leaned against the gate and began to whisper. "You see how extraordinary she is, how beautiful, how smart. And yet she can't be adopted, can she?" Suling nodded, trying to console Xiaoyuan's mother as the tears began to creep into her eyes. "I just want her to go to a great family," the foster mother continued. "To give her what we can't give her. This isn't a rich household, I'm not a great mother, my own son doesn't even listen to me . . ." her words trailed off as she smiled pleasantly, but the tears were tumbling down her cheeks now.

"No, Ayi, you are her family, you love her, you care for her, the one she should be with," we tried to reassure her. "This is her great family; you are it." But no amount of reassuring would give her solace. Xiaoyuan had been abandoned as a little baby with a cleft palate, now repaired to the point that it was undetectable. Neither Suling nor Xiaoyuan's foster mother knew the whole story, but somewhere along the way her parents had shown up at the orphanage to check in on her, and she would never be adopted because of it.

Down the street we visited Xiaoyuan's neighbor, Honghuan, who also dangled her legs off her foster mother's lap and hesitated when we talked about her going to America. Her siblings and neighbors teased her: "Do you want to go? Will you go? You're so lucky!" Her mother jokingly said, "Yeah, I don't want you anyway!" Honghuan buried her head in her mother's chest, but her fate was sealed as well. Unlike Xiaoyuan, her parents had never returned after abandoning her many years earlier, and her paperwork had already been matched with a family thousands of miles away in a foreign country. "Your new mother will look just like this auntie," her mom said, motioning to me. "Go take a picture with her." Honghuan eyed me suspiciously, and we all laughed.[10]

STATE, SOCIETY, AND SOCIAL ABANDONMENT

Meili's, Pei Pei's, and Xiaoyuan's cases reveal how the state can often be complicit in the abandonment of children by excluding certain individuals from vital familial and societal relationships. By keeping children of the incarcerated, like Pei Pei, and *chuxian* children, like Xiaoyuan, in administrative limbo and binding them to biological families that fail or are unwilling to care for them, the state prevents certain children from being fostered or permanently adopted. By relegating such children to lives in institutions, the state perpetuates and legitimizes the social vulnerability of abandoned children. The very fact that an orphan's household registration resides permanently in the orphanage is yet another signifier of their abandonment, which often results in social vulnerability. Not only are orphans stigmatized by their lack of social connections (recall the teasing Pei Pei endured at school as a result of her known orphan status), but *hukou* designations have also historically classified individuals into distinct, socially stratified, groups (Cohen 1993). Citing the state's *hukou* restrictions against rural laborers and their children, which prevent them from legally relocating to cities in search of jobs or sending their children to urban schools, Guo and Kleinman (2011, 256) argue that social exclusion, though universal, has been fostered by the Chinese government as a powerful means of social control.[11]

Thus, Pei Pei's and Xiaoyuan's cases demonstrate that it was not merely disability but social abandonment (not unlike that of their older foster parents) by family that disenfranchised them. Hence, despite the rather careful monitoring of language in regard to disability within foster care settings, as Shang (2008a, 210) notes in her research with children in kin fosterage, parents often casually referred to the children's bad fate (*ku ming*), or accepting one's fate (*ren ming*), as a result of their abandonment in front of the children. As in the case of Meili,

one will note that Auntie Ma spoke plainly of Meili's abandonment in her presence. Likewise, it was Pei Pei's orphan status, perhaps even more so than her
speech impediment due to a cleft palate, that drew discrimination from her peers
at the public school. Hence I will go on to argue that children with disabilities are
pointed out and pitied (along with their poor, older foster parents) not only
because of their perceived functional limitations but often because of their lack of
social connections, their inability to engage with society, and their lack of obligations to family or others.

DENGRONG'S STORY

On the other hand, cases of abandonment for children like Dengrong—whose
young body, weakened by disease, became too much for her struggling family to
bear—seemed clear cut. My first visit to see Dengrong in her new foster home
came just a few months after she and twenty-four other children with disabilities
had been moved into a tiny hamlet in Daling. Huilan, the orphanage monitor,
whispered to me in hushed tones that Dengrong had been abandoned at the
orphanage at the age of five and still remembers it. Dengrong was now eight and
had spent the last few years of her young life on the "special needs" floor in the
orphanage before being moved to Daling to be granted a foster family.

At Dengrong's house, Huilan and Older Sister Mo, the physical therapist,
deposited the tiny walker they had carted on the bus that morning and eagerly
showed the rather despondent Dengrong how to steer it across the concrete
floor. Dengrong's serious little face intensified as she put every ounce of her
strength into moving the walker from the center of the cold, barren room to
her tiny, wooden chair, where she finally retired. "She's lazy," her new foster
mother, Auntie Huang, said, her eyes twinkling. "I've tried to get her to walk, but
she says she's too tired, it's too hard, she prefers to be carried."

It was hard to tell what import Auntie Huang's comments carried. On the one
hand, children from the orphanage often became dependent on their caregivers
and refused to take responsibilities for themselves if they were moved relatively
late in life into foster homes. On the other hand, Dengrong appeared quite weak.
In addition to her cerebral palsy she struggled with asthma and had contracted
some dangerous upper respiratory infections in the past. Finally, over the course
of my research, I heard many foster mothers refer to their children—those with or
without disabilities, and whom they loved very much—as lazy. It was not always
a serious critique, but a way to demonstrate some control over the unknowns of
such children's conditions, even to familiarize them as ordinary children belonging very much to these foster families.[12] It was certainly disturbing, however,
when the critique was applied to disabled children for whom moving across the
room was not altogether a simple task in everyday life.

Huilan and Older Sister Mo began to explain Dengrong's condition to Auntie Huang, and especially the ways in which cerebral palsy causes the muscles in the arms and legs to tighten, thus making it difficult to move. They implored the new foster mother to encourage rather than critique her; Dengrong had known a lot of hardship in her young life, and she needed to hear that she was loved and wanted within this household. Auntie Huang smiled as she received these comments, but continued to protest that Dengrong was often solemn and quite sullen.

"You have to talk with her," Huilan admonished. Turning to Dengrong, who was slumped in her chair, she asked, "Does Mama tell you she loves you?" Dengrong weakly shook her head. "Do you love your new foster mother?" Huilan continued.

"No," Dengrong chirped.

"What about your father?"

"No."

"And sister?"

"No."

"Dengrong," Huilan cooed, squatting down and placing a hand upon her slight shoulder. "You know you need to try to be good and loving to your new foster family so they will love you back. Do you want to go back to the orphanage?" Dengrong did not respond. "You want to go back to the orphanage? When you have a family here that loves you? C'mon, don't you like it here?" Again Dengrong remained silent.

Huilan stood up and let Older Sister Mo take over, trying to prod Dengrong into speaking while she pointed to Dengrong's confusion, further admonishing Auntie Huang. "She needs to hear that you love her, she needs to be held. Kids like this who have no family, they need to be convinced that their new family really loves them. Tell her you love her."

"Mama loves you," Auntie Huang hollered from across the room.

"Not like that!" Huilan protested. "Go take her in your arms and tell her."

Auntie Huang flashed an embarrassed grin and strode across the room, scooping Dengrong's bony body into her arms. "See, Mama loves you, you know. I tell you, don't I?" she coaxed in a raspy voice. Dengrong turned her head away.

Suddenly there was a screeching noise just outside the door. Dengrong's foster mother cried, "Baba's home from work!" Her husband drove a small taxi cart, transporting people to and from the village to the county seat.

"Hello," Dengrong's foster father said, swatting playfully at Dengrong's foster sister and joining us inside.

"I was just telling your wife that children like Dengrong who have been abandoned need a lot of verbal encouragement," explained Huilan. "Like, they really need to hear you say that you love them. Here, Baba, take Dengrong in your arms and hold her and tell her that you love her." Auntie Huang transferred Dengrong to her foster father, who smiled at her sweetly and said, "There, Dengrong, how's that?"

"Tell Baba you love him," Huilan and Older Sister Mo urged. Dengrong shook her head. "C'mon, Dengrong, Baba goes out every day and works so you can eat. Can't you see he loves you? Don't you want him to love you? You don't want to go back to the orphanage, do you?" Dengrong's beady eyes filled with heavy tears, and as the girls continued to prod, finally she lurched forward, thrusting her arms around her father's neck and screeching, "Baba!" as she let out great, full-body sobs.

Dengrong's foster parents seemed positively embarrassed, but the orphanage monitors were quite satisfied. "See how much it means to her, when you hold her and you show her you care?" asked Huilan, gently stroking Dengrong's back as she burrowed her tears into her father's chest.

Far from the administrative limbo effected by the state for Meili and Pei Pei, Dengrong's case shows just how invested state employees could be in the formation of foster care relationships. Huilan and Older Sister Mo seemed convinced that the bonds of foster care would not congeal without their resolute intervention in displays of affection and proclamations of love—the everyday dynamics of family life.[13] They felt that because Dengrong had been abandoned by her biological parents, it was all the more important that Auntie Huang and her husband articulate their desire to serve as Dengrong's parents and profess their love for her. Yet Dengrong had a role to play, too: as Older Sister Mo and Huilan urged Dengrong to assert her desire to be part of her new family and stay in her new home, they made it clear that the alternative, returning to the orphanage, represented a life without loving relationships—and surely she did not want that.

The underlying emotions bubbling beneath this exchange—Auntie Huang and her husband's reticence to show their affection for Dengrong, Dengrong's own reticence to return it, and the state orphanage's urgency to effect it— illuminate the neediness of being without family in a country that demands family connection. Indeed, the interaction, even in the name of a desired social good, feels decidedly forced and manipulative to both parties. It presumes their desire for connection precisely due to an underlying paucity and lack of social connections and preys on this lack, even as it does critical work to assuage it. In subsequent chapters, I further wrestle with the emotional labor orchestrated by care workers and demanded of foster families and its complicated, critical relationship to the making of foster families.

This lack of social and familial connection brings together abandoned children like Dengrong with poor, disenfranchised foster parents such as Mr. and Mrs. Huang. But for the twenty-four children in Daling who had been abandoned on account of their significant disabilities, as well as the majority of children in Child Welfare Institutes across China, it stands to wonder what cultural perceptions about disability may also have been contributing to increasing abandonment of children with disabilities. In the next section, I further explore how abandonment and personhood are intertwined for disabled children in contemporary China.

DISABILITY, ABANDONMENT, AND
PERSONHOOD IN CHINA

Notably, Chinese cultural notions of disability are not divorced from other beliefs about the centrality of family life and relationships, nor can they be disconnected from the dramatic demographic and social changes in China, mostly initiated by the Chinese state over the past century. Hence, even if discrimination can provide some explanation for abandonment of children with disabilities in China, it is important to note that discriminatory cultural attitudes toward people with disabilities in China fail to explain a *contemporary increase* in the proportion of children with disabilities who are abandoned. This section briefly introduces the concept of disability and disability rights in the PRC, but with the aim of further expanding this definition in the following chapter to take into account not just national but global politics of social welfare, disability, foster care, and adoption.

Modern disability policy in China can be traced to the highly visible advocacy of Deng Xiaoping's son, Deng Pufang, who was paralyzed during the Cultural Revolution and whose advocacy led to dramatic changes for people with disabilities in China in the 1980s (Kohrman 2005). Deng Pufang's work institutionalized disability rights and regulations in China by establishing the China Disabled Persons' Federation, the China Welfare Fund for the Disabled, and the Chinese Rehabilitation and Research Association for the Mentally Disabled in the 1980s. In 1991 legislation was passed in China to recognize mental illness as a disability, and in 2008 China ratified the United Nations Convention on the Rights of Persons with Disabilities (UNCRPD). Since then China has passed and revised numerous pieces of rights-based legislation, including, for instance, the Regulation on the Education of Disabled Persons (first issued in 1994, and revised in 2017) and the Regulation on the Prevention and Rehabilitation of Disabled Persons (first issued in 2017) (Zhao and Zhang 2018). Hence, in China people with disabilities have expansive legal rights to education, healthcare, citizenship, employment, and public transportation.

Yet when the PRC ratified the UNCRPD in 2008, it chose not to accept the United Nations' definition of disability, which moved away from a medical model of disability, or a definition representing individual pathology, toward a more social, relational model. Sui Ming Kwok, Dora Tam, and Roy Hanes (2018, 156) argue that the definition of disability in China—as represented, for instance, in article 2 of the Law on the Protection of Disabled Persons, remains consistent with a definition of individual malfunctioning, and the terms *normal* and *abnormal* are frequently used when evaluating disability in China. They note that this not only has implications for discrimination and poor implementation of disability rights in China but that Chinese definitions of disability also serve to undermine statistics from representing the full number of disabled persons in China today (156–157). According to Kwok, Tam, and Hanes,

> Disability-related legislation is quite inclusive but people with disabilities rely heavily on family supports; state policy promotes a disability rights lens, but in practice, there are limited rights for people with disabilities as government bureaucrats influence over the development of the actual state policy. In brief, while much of the disability legislation as written has many elements of what western disability rights activists would consider a rights based focus, the actual decision-making process pertaining to disability policy is rooted in a hierarchical top down process and, for the most part, provision of care remains a low governmental priority. Disability remains highly stigmatized; prejudicial attitudes toward people with disabilities is widespread; most government, public, and private agencies are inaccessible; and disability rights advocacy organizations and NGOs exist, but these organizations may have minimal influence over the development of disability-related public policy. (2018, 158)

Strikingly, throughout the duration of my fieldwork in China, I never heard government or INGO officials, foster parents, or locals refer to disability or people with disabilities with the official language of disability or disabled persons, *caifang* or *caifangren*. Notably, children with disabilities were referred to primarily through the specific language of their diagnoses, *zibizheng haizi* (autistic children) or *naotan de haizi* (kids with cerebral palsy), or generally as *teshu de haizi* (special needs children) or *you zhili zhang ai de haizi* (literally, children with mental obstacles). This language was certainly conditioned by INGO and orphanage workers who were particularly sensitive and negative toward foster parents who referred to children as *sha* (demented); they often complained and, in fact, facilitated a change of foster households if they heard children referred to this way.[14]

Hence, it was clear that disability was generally understood to be an undesirable deficit. This was apparent through the overt discrimination against children that we will see throughout the book among some foster care monitors and foster parents but also through the language of misfortune, bad fortune, or bad fate. Discriminatory attitudes toward children with disabilities were especially clear in that facial and bodily deformities were some of the least intrusive for the children from a functional standpoint, but these would often be referred to by orphanage staff and foster mothers alike as highly unfortunate and requiring medical attention regardless of their practical limitations (see chapter 3).

The case of a boy I met in the orphanage in Hubei is particularly illustrative of distinctions between physical and mental impairment and social vulnerability.[15] When I traveled with Mercy Care to Qichun, Hubei, in the spring of 2012, I met a young boy who had been abandoned at birth by his parents because he had been born with his bladder outside his body. As the orphanage director and his associates described his condition at length to the Chinese employees and Western board members of Mercy Care, they wondered what results surgery could produce for this child. One of the board members, who had adopted a young girl from China with the same medical condition, repeatedly assured him that with surgery it would be possible for the little boy to lead a relatively normal life. Despite these assurances, the director and his employees hesitated, finally disclosing in hushed voices that their concern was really over whether the boy would ever be able to have children when he grew up. Without this ability, they concluded, no one in China would want to adopt him.

Such an account speaks to the lack of distinction between impairment and disability, as tied to the social construction of personhood in Chinese culture. In this case, as in many others, the boy's impaired condition may or may not have presented functional limitations for his life. Yet the perception that his impairment might prevent his ability to conceive and thus fulfill a fundamental obligation of Chinese personhood to family and society resulted in a presumed social paucity, to which his abandonment was likely tied. Guo and Kleinman argue that the nonpersonhood assigned to individuals with HIV/AIDS or mental illness in Chinese society "is both a telling instance of extreme stigma and a reverse mirror for better understanding what a person is in Chinese culture" (2011, 238). Building on other scholars' assertions (Fei 1992; Potter and Potter 1990) that personhood in Chinese culture is fundamentally social, Guo and Kleinman write,

> In the Chinese view, no one is born a full person. That is to say, no one is born with the right to be a person; instead, one has to learn to be a person and also to act as a person to prove his or her personhood. . . . Being a person implies an obligation to engage appropriately in interpersonal exchange relationships, build social networks, and maintain a moral status (face). . . . Acting as a person is to fulfill his obligation. Whether or not one should be treated as a person with rights is based on whether or not one has fulfilled the obligation of acting as a person. Rights come after obligations. One has to exchange the fulfillment of social obligation for the claim of personhood and the rights of being treated as a person. (2011, 243)

Thus, those who lack the ability to fulfill their distinct social roles lack moral status, belong nowhere, and can be treated as nonpersons (Guo and Kleinman 2011, 243). At least conceptually, then, this status of nonpersonhood helps to explain one reason why parents may abandon their own child. Suggesting that a study of stigma (and here they present multiple cases of individuals whose families are discriminated against because of their illness, or individuals who are abandoned by their very families because of illness) shows that what really matters in Chinese society today is security (2011, 257), Guo and Kleinman help explain how children who are perceived as lacking the ability to care for their parents in old age can be discarded. In a society in which children with disabilities are deemed fundamentally unable to fulfill future social and familial roles, they cannot act as or be understood as social persons.

Yet, as this chapter argues, it is not merely children with disabilities, or even children without them, who can suffer such loss of social personhood through abandonment. Citing familist ideology, wherein the Chinese family serves as the axis of all social relations for persons, Qian describes how philanthropists use *family* as a key marker (rather than *disability*) to distinguish between "normal children in families" and "abnormal children in social welfare institutes" (2014, 255). As Qian puts it, because culturally the family is the "appropriate and the 'normal' place for children to grow up, children who grow up elsewhere are all 'abnormal'" (2014, 256). Therefore, the same complex notion of Chinese personhood used to justify the abandonment of a child with disabilities is the same notion that causes others to perceive a child who has been abandoned as useless, pitiable, and ultimately a nonperson. As Qian concludes, "it is the *presumed unrelatedness* and *isolation from responsibility* (given or received) of the institutionalized children that make visitors label them as the 'abnormal unfortunate'" (2014, 256, emphasis in the original). Their requisite need for personhood denies them personhood in a society in which belonging to family is presumed.

Furthermore, the description of Meili and her foster mother Auntie Ma foreshadows how the fates of foster mothers Auntie Huang, Auntie Li, and Auntie Ma were deeply intertwined with those of their foster children. In fact, often precisely because of their need for one another, these affinities and alliances formed and flourished. Yet this desperate need for family in a society in which such relationships were a prerequisite for personhood further marginalized both the children and their foster parents—quite precisely, in their very struggle for relationship.

Hong Zhang, in her work on elderly abandonment in China (2004, 2005), and Xiaoyuan Shang and Xiaoming Wu, in their work on social welfare (2011), have shown that China's seniors constitute some of the most exposed in contemporary society, because the familial system of generational caregiving is breaking down, especially across increasing distance and failing extended family bonds. To many this is as much evidence of shifting economic and demographic circumstances as it is testament to the waning cultural value elders have in contemporary society. As Yunxiang Yan first argued in *Private Life under Socialism* (2003), since the post–Mao Zedong era the conjugal unit has triumphed, and elders have lost their financial security, familial and social functions, and status. As many older people are no longer operating as heads of households within the family or publicly within the village community, patriarchy in its historical and traditional sense in China has all but disappeared. Indeed, the period between which adult children form their own families and give birth is a particularly trying one for elders, who with scant retirement funds and little to offer their adult children in the way of child care, are left to fend for themselves.

Hence Yan has also been particularly critical of a certain immorality and incivility that he registers ethnographically among China's youth, whose market-driven individualist attitudes cause them to renege on obligations to their elders (2003, 2011a, 2011b). The Chinese government, which in many ways effectively undermined this cultural system of patriarchy and filial piety under socialism (Y. Yan 2003), shirks responsibility for the growing older population, enshrining and prosecuting children's obligation to care for their parents in old age in law.[16] The rise of a form of neofamilism in China that shifts the focus from elders to children can also be seen in the "familialization" of social welfare, in which the state has both championed economic liberalization to stimulate individualization and simultaneously withdrawn its own welfare provisions, making the family the major provider for elder care and care for disabled persons (Y. Yan 2018, 28). Thus, similarly abandoned by their families, orphaned children and older women present a burden to the Chinese state, who displaces that burden back onto the families themselves.

CHAPTER SUMMARY: SOCIAL VULNERABILITY

Meili, unlike Dengrong and Pei Pei, had no physical or mental disabilities. Although Meili was abandoned and declared orphaned, her biological father was probably still living, as was Pei Pei's biological mother and, presumably, Dengrong's. Out of the three, Pei Pei was the only one whose parent was incarcerated. Scholars of child welfare in China traditionally divide vulnerable children into three groups: (1) orphaned or abandoned children; (2) children of prisoners; and (3) street children (High 2013; Keyser 2009; Shang 2008a, 2008b). Even so, I consider Dengrong's, Meili's, and Pei Pei's stories together, because I believe they help us to better understand the collective experiences of social vulnerability that stem primarily from social abandonment in contemporary China.

Meili's story in particular helps support my observations that social vulnerability is a consequence of abandonment rather than a necessary implication of physical or mental impairment. As Guo and Kleinman put it, "stigma follows and results from nonpersonhood in China, and not the other way around as stigma theorists contend" (Guo and Kleinman 2011, 248). In other words, in order to protect personal and familial interests, people exclude certain individuals from family and society, who are thus further stigmatized by their lack of social connections or their nonpersonhood. Hence, "in the Chinese context, stigma breaks down social relationships and reveals the boundary of social networks. The excluded exist beyond the boundary of friendship, kinship, and community" (Guo and Kleinman 2011, 250).

Thus, I argue that the concept of social vulnerability is particularly relevant to understanding the experience both of abandoned children and older adults in China today.[17] For instance, using the case of Ru Lin, a woman with a hunchback who marries Xing, a man with schizophrenia, Matthew Kohrman shows how Ru's social isolation from her natal family, which results from marrying Xing and moving in with his family, coupled with her inability to have children, make her more socially vulnerable than her disabled (mentally ill) husband in the eyes of the villagers. Both her "precarious family situation" and her inability to fulfill her social role by bearing children deem her "abnormal" and "not fit to be a wife" more so than her own physical disability, her hunched back (Kohrman 2005, 158–159).

Anthropologists and other scholars of China have identified a distinct divide between certain individuals—namely, peasants and migrants, who were discriminated against as "low quality" in the government's effort to champion and construct "high-quality" subjects, individuals, and families. Yet despite these individuals' differential treatment within the social imaginary and acknowledged vulnerability within contemporary Chinese society, few scholars have analyzed how the discourse of human quality (*suzhi*) may or may not apply to older persons and persons with disabilities in Chinese society.[18]

Disabled children and seniors are often hidden from view, and given that Chinese systems of social welfare continue to delineate the family as the primary provider for care, they find themselves at the mercy of other family members. Lacking the ability to provide for themselves, forced into mandatory retirement (in the case of seniors), and with real or perceived physical or mental impairments, members of these two groups are perceived as socially deficient. Regarding the important national category and symbol of ability (*nengli*) that emerged in the modern era (and contrasts with the term *quezi*, meaning "crippled" or "lame"), Matthew Kohrman (1999, 894) writes, "The 'lame' (whatever their gender) . . . are not the only persons to whom Chinese today negatively apply the concepts of neng li; there are many (including children and the very elderly)." Relatedly, Leslie Wang argues that the abandonment of disabled children in the present era is demonstrative of the way in which children's value is increasingly market based, as children with disabilities are not only symbolically, but literally, excluded (either sequestered in orphanages or adopted abroad) from China's national populous (Wang 2010a, 40).

Drawing on the cases of Dengrong, Meili, Pei Pei and their foster mothers, I argue that it is not primarily abandoned children's physical or mental ailments, or poor older women's bodily frailty or even perceived inabilities, that immobilize them from participation in society; it is instead the social paucity of being abandoned by their families that forces them to the fringes of Chinese social life. In some cases, children whose impairments prevent them from not only functioning as typical children but also from fulfilling their social obligations to care for their senior parents (like the boy born with his bladder outside his body in Hubei) lose value in the eyes of the parents, potential adopters, and the wider community. Yet, in other cases, children without physical or mental impairments like Meili find themselves on the outskirts of Chinese kinship circles because of increasing trends of pregnancy out of wedlock, divorce, and the diminishing size and influence of extended family units.

Following Devva Kasnitz and Russell Shuttleworth's broad social definition of *disability*—"disability exists when people experience discrimination on the basis of perceived functional limitations" (1999, 4)—I argue that abandonment becomes a perceived functional limitation toward becoming a full Chinese person, thus rendering poor, older foster mothers and their disabled children especially vulnerable. Deprived and removed from the social obligations that make Chinese people human, these children and older women find themselves on the fringes of Chinese society. Hence, I argue that children and seniors who are abandoned by their families, regardless of whether they are physically or mentally disabled, are socially vulnerable in China today.

While many others have chafed at this language of abandonment because it admittedly fails to acknowledge the difficulty of relinquishing a child (particularly in China) or a planned adoption, I maintain it in this chapter precisely because of the effect of vulnerability it registers in the PRC. Poor older women and disabled children may find certain disadvantages in any society, but because of their significant alienation by their biological families in China, they are without the life-giving relationships that convey their very humanity to those whom they encounter.

What I have also aimed to show in this chapter is that, as it is both complicit in these individuals' abandonment and also active in their social restoration, the state plays a contradictory role. As Huilan and Older Sister Mo strive to encourage affective bonding between Auntie Huang and Dengrong, one wonders to what extent foster families, by the very nature of their extrafamilial bonds, can achieve social recognition in the eyes of society. To what extent do foster families stand to resist the practices of the state that may keep children like Pei Pei in administrative limbo, even as the families simultaneously provide for them? And which families is it that the state truly supports in China today if foster families remain marginal due to their extrabiological character? As we shall see in chapter 2, state-sponsored foster care makes pivotal contributions to the market for ICA, a market that is increasingly popular for adopting children with disabilities from China. Therefore, chapter 2 places the social vulnerability of foster mothers and foster children within both national and global contexts, further querying the inequalities and politics of family formation in modernity.

2 · FOSTERING (WHOSE) FAMILY?

Doing my fieldwork in a tropical and sprawling city of seven million Chinese, I was met daily with relentless stares and inquiries, and when I traveled to apartment complexes where families had fostered children for decades, foster mothers always steered the conversation to news of America. They retreated into their apartments to unearth photos of Chinese children with white parents, letters they could not read or understand, and presented these to me, with tears in their eyes, wanting to know how their children were. Nearly every time I went to a village or an apartment complex with Chinese staff members of international nongovernmental organizations (INGOs) or orphanages, foster mothers instantly pushed their foster children toward me, suggesting that I might adopt them. "Which one do you want?" they would ask. "How about this one? Do you want this one?"

I was horrified and embarrassed. I protested that I was a researcher, I was too young, I was not there to adopt, but just to learn; but the foster parents kept insisting. As chapter 1 attests, even time did not seem to heal some of these misunderstandings, as Auntie Ma held out hope for many months that I would still consider becoming Meili's adoptive mother. Everywhere I went, misrecognition that I was a foreign prospective adoptive parent rather than a researcher permeated my fieldwork. My explanations made no difference to them.

"WHICH ONE DO YOU WANT?"

I have had years to think about it, and I realize that what I was really trying to say in those moments of protest was something like, "I'm not like those other white people, though. You can trust me!" I wanted—I *needed*—my informants to trust me in order to do good research. So I tried to create some separation from other foreigners, particularly other Americans. I wanted to convince them that I was different.

But the foster families were making it very clear that they could not trust me, because my whiteness referenced a political economy wherein white foreign families had the power to choose and take home Chinese children. Young children often cowered and hid behind their parents when they first saw me coming. I could not separate myself from that reality with my words, because history and experience had revealed the truth to those families. They could not trust me.

Although I was always embarrassed to stick out in these crowds and to be presumed to only be there to take children home, these interactions also powerfully confirmed the extent to which locals in Guangxi, including Chinese foster parents, assumed that disabled foster children from state orphanages were destined for foreign families. As I argued in chapter 1, the assumption that such children in state orphanages were there because they had been abandoned by their own kin subtly reinforced the divide between children who could be subsumed into Chinese families and children who would be adopted abroad.

In order to offer a fuller interpretation of the increasing number of abandonments of disabled orphans in state institutions in China, I step aside in this chapter from the primary stories of foster children Dengrong, Meili, and Pei Pei and into the large-scale politics of supply and demand when it comes to intercountry adoption (ICA) from China. Anthropological studies of kinship have been attentive to innovative trends in modern family making, global inequalities, and the complicated intersections of supply and demand with respect to ICA, but they have yet to consider the relationship between foster care practices in so-called sending countries like China and how they support and shape ICA and family making in receiving countries. Even within the robust literature on ICA from China (Dorow 2006; Eng 2006; Johnson 2004, 2016; Wang 2016), scholars have yet to identify, describe, or analyze the symbiotic relationship between Chinese foster care and ICA from China. Furthermore, although ICA from China has been thoughtfully scrutinized with respect to economics, race, class, and gender, few scholars have investigated the increasing number of "special needs" adoptions from China in relationship to the abandonments of children with disabilities that I describe in the introduction and chapter 1. Accordingly, very few scholars have applied a disability studies perspective toward interpreting the role that ableism plays in Chinese foster care and ICA.[1]

Thus, this chapter makes three contributions. First, although abandonments of children with disabilities have always taken place in China, this chapter insists that these contemporary trends of abandonment of children with disabilities must be analyzed alongside the increasing numbers of ICAs of disabled children from China. Drawing on Kay Ann Johnson's groundbreaking studies of domestic adoption that undermined simplistic notions of gender bias with respect to contemporary China (2004, 2016), this chapter expands upon the cultural attitudes regarding abandonment and disability explored in chapter 1. I draw a parallel with Johnson's work on gender to suggest that disabled children are not merely unwanted in China due to cultural attitudes, but rather that the unsupportive political and economic environment within China and increasing international demand outside China are further marginalizing Chinese children with disabilities.[2]

Second, the ethnographic, statistical, and scholarly evidence presented in this chapter establishes links between the practice of foster care in China and ICA from China. Even though foster care existed as a domestic practice prior to the establishment of Child Welfare Institutes or ICA, I argue that state-sponsored foster care of disabled children, the focus of this book, makes an important contribution to sustaining ICA from China. This is a fact that is unacknowledged and underdeveloped in the literature and often obscured from public discourse, especially given that ICA from China is now almost exclusively for older children and children with disabilities. Thus, both the relative increase in the number of adoptions of disabled children in ICA from China from 2005 to the present, and the increase in foster care for such children, dovetails with an increasing demand for disabled children through the Waiting Child Program in ICA from China.

Third, because state-sponsored foster care so effectively supports the formation of foreign, primarily white, adoptive families and further discourages or prohibits Chinese foster parents from adopting disabled children, foster families occupy a disruptive, liminal, and marginalized space in contemporary Chinese kinship culture. I argue that just as "child saving" efforts in ICA of healthy children often mask ICA's market dynamics and perpetuation of inequalities (Cheney 2014), Western desire and acceptance of Chinese children with disabilities is not an unparalleled social good but demonstrates covert maintenance of global and moral hierarchies and reveals ableism.

Therefore, in this chapter, I argue that in addition to scrutinizing the role of demand in the making of this upward trend in ICAs of disabled children from China, it is also vital that the market for ICAs be assessed from a disability studies perspective in order that ableism not permeate and undermine what is often construed as the "best interests of children." Indeed, by reviewing this phenomenon of ICAs from China of children with "special needs" through the lens of international demand and a global politics of ableism, we see the way in which ICA contributes to the maintenance and expansion of Western, heteronormative, ableist families. Therefore this chapter queries which families are actually being fostered, promoted, or privileged through the development of foster care in China. This is a question I continue to take up throughout the book, which explores both the resistance and the constraints foster families in China experience today.[3]

UNDERSTANDING CHINESE (SUPPLY SIDE) CULTURAL FACTORS, GOVERNANCE, AND POLITICS

In the introduction to her book *China's Hidden Children* (2016), Johnson confronts the ubiquitous popular discourse that readily interprets the widespread ICA of infant girls in the 1990s and early 2000s to Western countries as confirmation that Chinese culture and Chinese parents despise women and girls. It is impossible to summarize the extensive contribution Johnson and her colleagues' research has made to understanding the complex intersection of birth planning, child abandonment, contemporary domestic adoption, and ICA from China, but this section highlights how her work complicates simplistic notions of son preference, unearths the voices of birth parents and adoptive parents in China, and provides data that shift the cultural narrative regarding the lack of desire for daughters or adoption within China. "While the one-child policy is usually seen as a background factor," Johnson writes, "the question of why there are children available to adopt in China quickly turns to the question of 'why girls?'" (2016, 21)—a query that firmly centers the focus on Chinese culture as the primary, most culpable factor responsible for the pool of children available for ICA. Bringing then what only appears in the background (the one-child policy) into the foreground, Johnson pinpoints the coercive birth planning policies and the Chinese central government's dogged efforts to implement them (rather than son preference or an unwillingness to adopt) as blameworthy for both the large-scale abandonment of infant girls and their ICAs at the turn of the twenty-first century.

In her book *Wanting a Daughter, Needing a Son* (2004), Johnson describes the long-held ideal for Chinese families to have both a boy and a girl that was disrupted by the restrictions of the one-child policy. Furthermore, she and her research team discover that contrary to popular belief, couples were rarely committing infanticide or abandoning their first-born baby girls in favor of sons. Instead, finding the stress too much to bear, families often abandoned second-, third-, or fourth-born baby girls in the countryside, where policies were less stringent. It is most important to note that individuals or couples rarely made these decisions to abort, abandon, or kill a baby, but did so (and continue to do so) in the context of extended families.

In their insightful ethnography of Maoist and post-Maoist China, Sulamith Heins Potter and Jack Potter (1990, 240–243) describe the way in which methods of influence among birth planning officials often involved leveraging one's family members against them. Likewise, in a conversation I had with a Chinese man who helped found an INGO to keep young girls in school in the countryside, he remarked that he did not know a single woman who had made such a decision. "There's always a man, a father, a husband, an uncle, a grandfather behind those decisions," he said gruffly, "but the women are made to suffer the memory of those children for a lifetime." As Potter and Potter note, in Chinese marriage and birth, the private interests of the husband and wife are scarcely relevant. Instead it is the importance of family continuity, or familism, that enables parents and parents-in-law so strong a voice in the reproductive decisions of the household (Potter and Potter 1990, 230).

Johnson (2016) corroborates this complex environment in which infants were abandoned (1980s–early 2000s), making it clear that local families were left with few choices as government officials pursued "out of plan" children and sought to punish their families. Both Johnson and Potter and Potter helpfully document the progression of birth planning policies, which rarely consisted of the infamous one-child policy, but gradually waxed and waned historically and geographically between combinations of incentives, fines, birth planning methods, forced sterilizations, and even forcibly taking children (Johnson 2016; Potter and Potter 1990). Johnson further shows that despite the careful structuring of birth planning and domestic adoption laws that made it nearly impossible to legally relinquish a child (for domestic adoption), both birth families and adoptive families were constantly maneuvering against the government to provide homes for children whose births were considered out of plan.

Similarly, I argue that the role of Chinese culture in the contemporary proliferation of abandonment of disabled children in China must be considered in relationship with domestic birth planning policies, as well as the lack of domestic support for families raising children with disabilities. As chapter 1 established, and Eleanor Holroyd's research among parents caring for children with disabilities in Hong Kong further shows, disability was often experienced as a "disruption to the parent-child order," a threat to the cyclical and reciprocal enactment of caregiving responsibilities that facilitates cultural personhood in a Chinese context (Holroyd 2003, 8, 18). As Guo Jinhua and Arthur Kleinman (2011), building on the work of Chinese sociologist Fei Xiaotong (1992) confirm, being a person in China cannot be understood apart from relationships and fulfilled obligations, upon which rights are contingent. Hence, Chinese familial culture necessarily makes exclusions based on individual's—and especially children's—abilities or inabilities to fulfill their social roles. As Linliang Qian asserts, the familist norm, which idealizes the family as the "axis of all other social relations," causes children who grow up anywhere other than their family to be deemed not just "unfortunate" but "abnormal" (2014, 255, 256).

Guo and Kleinman's, Holroyd's, and Qian's cultural interpretations all offer important background for understanding China's discriminatory cultural attitudes toward children with disabilities, and especially those who reside in state institutions. But their cultural explanations fail to explain the increase of over 50 percent in the proportion of children with disabilities who have been abandoned from 2008 to 2015 (*Global Times* 2015; Vanderklippe 2014). Indeed, despite the relevance of such cultural ideas, culture is not static, and thus it is vital to examine these ideas about personhood in context with shifting practices of domestic adoption, foster care, and social welfare in modern China.

As Xiaoyuan Shang, Karen Fisher, and Jiawen Xie (2011, 299) acknowledge, China's child disability support system, established before the 1990s, is still based on the notion that family and kinship care are the primary providers for the needs of children with disabilities, but significant social, economic and demographic changes since then have reduced family capacity to care for such children. As chapter 1 showed, rising rates of divorce and migration, the decline of extended family households, and a disproportionately large population of older adults in the People's Republic of China (PRC), combined with the government's retreat from social welfare provisions, has left families scrambling to provide for individuals who need extra support. Another alarming trend is that rates of congenital birth defects have skyrocketed in China: there was a 40 percent increase in birth defects in babies born between 2001 and 2006 (Hu 2007). Especially in rural areas, where such defects are suspected to be tied to pollutants, such as those brought about by the burning of coal and pesticides (Demick 2009; Lyn 2011), the financial costs of caring for such children is very hard on families.

Furthermore, healthcare support for disabled children does not extend to the public school system, forcing the burden to be borne by individual families who often report rampant discrimination throughout service provision. In a study in which they employed a broad interview methodology and a smaller case-study approach to understanding the "right to life" of children with disabilities in China, Fisher and Shang report that "parents frequently said that they considered abandoning their children while they were raising them because they did not have access to government support." They conclude that "the social services implications of the research are that China has not yet established an effective system to protect the life of children with disabilities" (2014, 562, 570). Chapter 1 made clear that despite legislative support for rights for disabled people, disabled people in China still experience much difficulty accessing education, employment, and other rights associated with citizenship.

Based on her fieldwork with children with disabilities in Chinese welfare institutions, Leslie Wang alleges that the Chinese government's approach to abandoned, disabled children goes beyond neglect. Even as children with disabilities disrupt the natural order of caregiving and filial piety within traditional Chinese understandings of personhood (Holroyd 2003), Wang argues that "rather than trying to change the larger cultural mindset toward disability, state authorities have tended to blame the situation on the 'backwardness' of rural people" (2015, 135). Alongside Johnson, Wang cites a similar "perfect storm" of political will, market forces, lack of government support, and cultural beliefs that have contributed to the disproportionate abandonment of children with disabilities in modern China. Wang's point, similar to social welfare researchers like Shang and Fisher (2014), is to demonstrate the near total neglect of the Chinese government's provisions following the reform and opening up period of the 1980s with respect to the large population of persons and children with disabilities, in tandem with policies and rhetoric that discriminate against such persons as "burdens."

For instance, in 2011, the Chinese government opened up a series of so-called baby hatches near orphanages, where desperate parents could abandon children into state care. As Wang describes, "Painted in happy pastel colors with cartoon animals adorning the walls, the small spaces are empty, save for an air conditioner, an incubator, and a baby bed. Parents (or other relatives, in some cases) set the baby inside and press a button to alert the nearby orphanage. If all goes to plan, someone from the orphanage will retrieve the child within 10 minutes" (Wang 2016, 39).

Although the Chinese government has set up at least thirty of these facilities over the last decade, one baby hatch in Guangzhou, Guangdong, in January 2014 had to suspend its operation after only two months, because it was so overwhelmed by the 262 disabled children with cerebral palsy, heart disease, and Down syndrome who were rapidly abandoned (*BBC News* 2014). In 2013 a recently opened baby hatch in Nanjing had received over four hundred infants, prompting a representative from the People's Congress to urge the government to close the baby hatches (*Sohu News* 2015). Yet, in the same news article and in an editorial written in 2015 by Chinese researchers Sun Wenjie, Zheng Yumei, and Xie Yiqiong in the journal *Women and Birth*, experts express doubt that closing the baby hatches permanently will decrease the number of infant abandonments and deaths (Sun, Zheng, and Xie 2016). Others argue, however, that the hatches themselves normalize and even promote the abandonment of disabled children, overwhelming social welfare institutes rather than offering support for struggling families and communities. Whereas following the widespread abandonment of infant girls in the 1990s the Chinese government launched a comprehensive national campaign to champion the value of girls in society, no such campaign or effort has been entertained with respect to children with disabilities. Indeed, the baby hatches stand in stark contrast to such an effort.

Johnson blames the Chinese government for its complicity in processing a great number of ICAs while undermining domestic adoptions in China. As she argues, domestic adoptions from Chinese orphanages in the 1990s, though not significant, "certainly exceeded international adoptions at the beginning of the decade." But the 1991 adoption law, which was "heralded for paving the way to international adoption," also limited adoptions of orphans to childless parents over the age of thirty-five, "an unacceptably advanced age to become a first-time parent, according to Chinese social norms and practice, especially in the countryside" (Johnson 2004, 142–143, 145). Thus the law, far from encouraging domestic adoption, made it both more difficult for birth parents to arrange informal adoption for an unwanted or overquota child and more difficult for desiring adoptive parents to adopt even formally from a state orphanage given that they needed to be childless and over the age of thirty-five. As Johnson notes, because of the domestic prohibitions, "foreigners adopted more than 35,000 children" from roughly 1994 to 2004, "though many times that number of adoptable children remained behind in the orphanages" (2004, 146).

Yet even with revisions to the 1991 adoption law in 1999 that lowered the legal age for adopting parents to thirty and allowed families with children to adopt healthy foundlings, because the revisions only applied to children being raised in welfare institutions, "efforts to publicize the new possibilities for legal adoption were local and sporadic" (Johnson 2004, 147), and birth planning authorities often refused to grant approval or readily blocked such adoptions (Johnson 2016). Thus, ICAs continued to flourish, while domestic adoptions dwindled or remained stagnant. As Johnson and others (Dorow 2004; Wang 2016) have noted, the steady and significant fees incurred from foreign adoptions (US$3,000–5,000), which were often prohibitive for domestic adopters, popularized and encouraged ICAs while further discouraging domestic adoption. As Johnson succinctly puts it, "Over the last twenty years, unknown numbers of 'unwanted,' legally certified 'abandoned children' in China's orphanages have been taken directly from the homes of would-be or existing adoptive families" (2016, 165).

Although the situation for domestic adoption of disabled children differs significantly given that the birth planning policy has always presented a loophole for a second child to parents whose first child had a disability, the context of poor social welfare for such families and poor promotion of such freedoms by the government still applies. In my fieldwork, for example, I found that parents who were eligible for such a second birth or an adoption were unaware of this benefit, and many also failed to see the benefit given the cost and care they needed to give to their first child. Even in a context in which domestic adoptions of healthy children have markedly increased in China (see Wang 2016), presumably due to both social discrimination and lack of social welfare, children with disabilities remain largely institutionalized, in foster care, or are adopted internationally rather than domestically. If we take Johnson and Wang's point that culture is just one factor that—in relationship with poor domestic social welfare and governmental promotion of ICA over domestic adoption—has been used by the government against its people, we begin to see a very different picture of the rise in abandonments and ICAs of Chinese children with disabilities.

First, one need only look to the statistics to see that whereas the proportion of children abandoned (seemingly as a result of their disability) is rising, the overall significance of that figure with respect to China's total population is quite low. Although it may seem obvious to point out, it is important to note that most parents in China, even those who have children with disabilities (of which there are approximately five hundred million, Shang and Fisher 2016), *do not abandon their children*. Indeed, even by some of the largest estimates that put Chinese child abandonments at one hundred thousand per year (and one should note that the range in estimates here is extremely concerning given that most scholarly sources would put that number at between thirty thousand and fifty thousand), the percentage in terms of abandonments of disabled children by their parents, even on the most extreme scale, comes to a mere 0.02 percent (for the more modest number of thirty thousand to fifty thousand abandonments, this comes to a miniscule .006 percent to .01 percent of the population). In other words, despite the overwhelming scale of Chinese abandonments of children with disabilities, it is so important to keep in mind that very few parents of disabled children in China abandon their children.

This statistical evidence, along with the increasing proportion of disabled children who are in foster care, also serves to confront simplistic assessments that pin the proportional rise in abandonment of Chinese children with disabilities on Chinese culture. Official statistics are practically impossible to come by, but due to a government mandate in 2003 and financial and social incentives, nearly every orphanage in China today has some version of foster care practices, and these are notably expanding to include (and even prefer, in some circumstances) children with disabilities. As we shall see in subsequent chapters, foster parents cited numerous benefits of foster care to both themselves and the children, including improved psychological, physical, and social welfare, as well as improved social standing and acceptance in Chinese society. Older couples who were previously socially isolated and children who were institutionalized became integrated into Chinese society, and these foster parents became fierce advocates for the needs of their children. Given the above statistics on the number of biological families raising children with disabilities in China and the practice of foster care, as well as the willingness and transformations detailed by foster parents in my research, it is impossible to conclude that children with disabilities are culturally and practically unwanted in contemporary China.

Yet since 2000 the Chinese government has explicitly encouraged ICA of disabled children through the Waiting Child Program. In her book *Outsourced Children*, Leslie Wang explores the Chinese central government's complicity in the exportation of children with disabilities to the West, coining the phenomenon "outsourced intimacy" whereby Westerners absorb devalued children, yet China is portrayed as seemingly keeping their best interests in mind (2016, 134). Wang's research took place in multiple orphanages across the PRC, many of which had foreign funding and partnership. Indeed, her research also focuses on the ways Western INGOs in the PRC help to care for and remake disabled orphans into desirable adoptees, but foster care and foster families are curiously absent from her account. In Wang's cases, the disabled children she studied were also institutionalized because they were so sick that they needed nursing-level care. She mentions throughout the book that few children from among these were actually adopted abroad, but that was still the hope among institutional staff. Children who were adopted seemed to disappear quickly from the institution, so it is not clear whether they were sent to foster homes or directly adopted from the orphanage.

Yet one might argue that foster families are also absent from the visible chain of ICA to the world for the very reason Wang cites—namely, that foster parents, like their foster children, are also considered "low-quality" citizens whom the government deems inappropriate to be visible to Westerners adopting from China. Indeed, while I was researching foster care, several prospective adoptive families, when they learned that their child was being fostered, expressed interest in going to the foster home to meet the child's foster parents. In each case the orphanage care workers persuaded the foster parents to meet the adoptive parents at the hotel at which they were staying and in a highly supervised visit. When I asked why this was the case, both orphanage and INGO workers suggested that foster families might ask the adoptive families for money, and this could be embarrassing for the adoptive families. Yet the change of venue did not seem to have much to do with the explanation offered. Indeed, it seemed more likely that if the adoptive families saw the meager means that foster families lived by, they might feel compelled to offer money or critique that the orphanage was loath to receive.

In the next section, I argue that foster families play an important role in sustaining the global chains of ICA. According to my own fieldwork, and according to major adoption agencies,[4] the vast majority of children who are adopted through ICA are fostered, and ICA relies on foster families to provide critical psychological support for children to move into new, permanent homes. As my research has shown, orphanages and foster homes in China are now homes for disabled children whose presumed and desired trajectory is foreign adoption outside the PRC.

THE WAITING CHILD PROGRAM AND FOSTER CARE

With the Waiting Child Program, established in 2000, and the government's limitation of the supply of healthy girls for ICA, the PRC expressly encouraged the increasing proportion of "special needs" adoptions from China (even in light of a downward trend in ICAs overall). Beginning in 2000, the Chinese government agreed to expedite ICA of children through the Waiting Child Program on the basis that they were less desirable for adoption due to advanced age or more difficult to find adoption placements for due to medical needs or disabilities. While waiting times for prospective international couples for typical children from China stretched to nearly six years, children adopted through the Waiting Child Program came home in a reliable six months to a year and a half (Wang 2016, 140). The official international nomenclature of "special focus" children or "special needs youth" for the program somewhat obscures the population of children, which does include children with disabilities, such as Down syndrome, cerebral palsy, dwarfism, and autism. Yet this population also includes children over the age of fourteen who heretofore could not be adopted within China (*Economist* 2020), as well as children with heart disease, cleft palates, and clubfoot, for whom operations are often strategically procured in Western countries following ICA.

Wang reports that by 2009, "the last year for which figures were published, special needs youth constituted nearly half of all foreign adoptees; this was a huge jump from 2005, when they did not add up to even one-tenth of adoptive placements" (Wang 2015, 140). Although statistics are scarce and ICAs were notably halted due to conflicts between the administration of U.S. President Donald Trump and the PRC, as well as the COVID-19 crisis, most foreign adoption agencies have only been processing Waiting Child Program adoptions over the last decade. This is due to a dramatic increase in domestic adoptions of healthy children in China, incentivized by the government's relaxation of their policies: since 2000, a new policy permits children through age eighteen to be adopted domestically, permits parents to adopt a second child, and permits childless couples to adopt two children (*Economist* 2020).

But the foreign-facing focus of the Waiting Child Program and the central government's simultaneous encouragement of domestic adoption has also created two separate trajectories for disabled children and typical children in China today. Although both prioritize foster care in order that children be well adjusted psychologically for adoption, typical children are adopted within China, whereas disabled children, children with medical conditions, and older children are prioritized for ICA. As Wang (2016) points out, the Chinese government prefers to blame this on the backwardness of its people, arguing that they would not want to adopt children with disabilities. Yet Wang identifies numerous cases in her research of local women who wished to adopt disabled children and, in too many cases for me to count, foster parents also expressed the desire to adopt the children with disabilities that they were raising.

Because of the previous limitations on the number of births and the stringent requirements for domestic adoption, however, most foster parents who had biological children of their own and were of advanced age were told they were not eligible to adopt. Even if they were eligible to adopt, they were often dissuaded from doing so by orphanage officials due to their subordinate social status, low income, or even "backward" habits (see chapters 3 and 4). The extralegality of some of the foster care practices in Guangxi, due to either economic hardship or poor official oversight, actually continued to delimit or undermine the rights of foster parents with respect to the children in their care, but many of these extralegal practices, like allowing foster parents to take in extra children "under the table," were also proffered by government officials.

Meanwhile, the foster care offered to disabled children by Chinese foster parents over the past decade has continued to sustain ICA from China. Furthermore, as with prior entanglements of birth planning policies that limited domestic adoption, restrictions on foster parents continue to funnel children into ICA rather than nurturing a culture that accepts and assimilates them within Chinese families. Hence, in this section, I have shown that the increased proportion of disabled children being abandoned in China and adopted abroad is not just a domestic but an international modern phenomenon. Given the evidence, I think it is fair to conclude that on a grand scale, China's children with disabilities, due to a constellation of complex international and domestic factors, are being exported.

Johnson and Wang notably shift popular and scholarly attention from the pitfalls of Chinese culture to Chinese government failure and coercion, as well as lack of international responsibility and an inequality between international and domestic adoptive parents. This inequality, as well as the relationship between foster care and ICA, is further apparent in the way foster families are systematically utilized by the government and ICA to sustain international families yet prevented from adopting disabled children themselves. Yet both Johnson and Wang stop notably short of considering what role international demand for such children has played in exacerbating, perpetuating, or even igniting these inequalities. Therefore, in the next section, I attempt to expand Johnson's above critique of the international adoption community to consider how the work of scholars who have taken international demand for adoptees into account (see, for instance, L. Briggs 2009, 2012; Cheney 2014; and Joyce 2013) might deepen our understanding of this rise in proportionate abandonment and ICA of children with disabilities from China. In the next section, I argue that we must also consider what role ableism plays in the shifting trends of ICA from China.

UNDERSTANDING THE DEMAND SIDE OF ICA FROM THE PERSPECTIVES OF INTERCOUNTRY ADOPTION AND GLOBAL DISABILITY DISCOURSE

By 2005, when ICAs from China reached their peak, their visibility was notable when considering not only the supply of such children flourishing within China but also the demand for Chinese children around the world. Many scholars, including Kathryn Joyce (2013), Dianne Marre and Lisa Briggs (2009), Jessaca Leinaweaver (2008), and Leslie Wang (2010a, 2010b, 2015, 2016), have queried with respect to China the effect of the market's demand on the supply of children in international adoption, which has led to allegations of Hague Convention violations, abuses, and suspensions of adoption policy, especially in the cases of countries like Ethiopia and Guatemala. China has come under fire for allegations that the government fabricated ages of older children or falsified their orphan status. There are also several reported cases in China of parents with sickly infants being urged by doctors to relinquish the children in order to profit from a foreign adoption, and numerous concerns about and cases of child trafficking documented beginning in 2011.[5]

Thus, while it is nearly impossible to prove, it is reasonable to consider whether a similar dynamic of supply and demand is at play in the increased proportional abandonment of disabled children in China. In my conversations with orphanage personnel (and much in line with Wang's research), I found that the Chinese government, knowing that Western countries will pay for expensive medical procedures, prefers to expedite these adoptions of children with special needs abroad. Indeed, during my fieldwork I often witnessed Mercy Care working with local and national authorities in China to handpick and expedite ICA for children whose medical needs they deemed urgent and threatening. This is significant, especially because even though rights and access for disabled children in China may be poor, there are facilities within the PRC that expressly care for and facilitate such surgeries for children (Wang 2010b, 2016).

When I spoke with a program director for the China Center of Adoption Affairs in Guangzhou in 2011 and pressed her on why children with disabilities were increasingly being adopted abroad, she hedged, slowly replying that their medical needs often exceeded the expertise of Chinese hospitals. Hence the Chinese government participates in, or perhaps even exploits, the same cultural perception that disability (of many varieties) compromises social personhood in proffering these ICAs. Therefore, it is not as simple as the Chinese government falling victim to "backward" notions of social personhood; rather, as Wang notes, in this way the Chinese government also benefits from this process of "outsourcing its intimate labor" both to poor foster mothers inside China (Raffety 2017) and Western adoptive families (Wang 2015, 133).

Scholars of ICA like Kristin Cheney have examined how adoption's "child saving" efforts often "mask both ICA's market dynamics and the crises of social reproduction on the 'demand' side that precipitate ICA" (2014, 247). In reference to the first point, Cheney points out that although the Hague Convention "encourages co-responsibility between states' parties, sending countries are primarily responsible for implementation—often with inadequate resources" (2014, 253). Thus the politics of development that undergird the flow of orphans from the Global South to the Global North perpetuate inequalities, further disadvantaging sending countries while sentimentalizing the service being provided by adopting countries. For instance, Cheney astutely points out that the egregious costs of ICA pale in comparison to the scant costs of keeping children with their birth families (2014, 256). Even in the cases in which sophisticated medical care is required, it is impossible to believe that a country with human and economic resources such as China could not process its own medical operations and procedures with or without limited financial support. Therefore, outsourcing such medical care to the West in support of orphan care and adoption is not only unnecessary and inefficient but arguably undermines the further development of a more supportive, robust Chinese disabled child welfare system.

As Cheney puts it, "ICA is ideally about finding families for children who need them, but due to its marketization in an unequal world, in practice ICA is skewed toward finding children for families who want them" (2014, 255). This gets to Cheney's second point about how Western demand for children fuels the manufacturing and commodification of orphans ripe for Western intervention. Indeed, as I found in my work with Chinese foster families, they had internalized this narrative as they often commented that despite the important role they played in these children's lives, such children would be better off in America or another Western country. Although such families did fight for the rights and care of these children, even struggling to keep them in certain scenarios, they were powerless against the sway of the economic and political power of Western adoptive families and—perhaps even more important—against the internalized construction of "a class-based model of appropriate and 'deserving' parenthood that reinforces middle-class entitlement while pathologizing poor parents" such as Chinese foster parents (Cheney 2014, 257).

Cheney further argues that even with dwindling birth rates and delayed childbirth by women in the West, ICA has become a neoliberal tool of the maintenance and reproduction of the white, middle-class, heteronormative family that perpetuates not just economic and political but also social inequalities (2014, 256). As David Eng puts it, "in the context of transnational adoption, consumptive labor takes the form of a political economy of passion meant to shore up not just the material but, equally important, the psychic boundaries of the white middle-class nuclear family—guaranteeing its social and ideological integrity as well as its affective ideals" (2006, 56–57). Although Wang goes so far as to say this movement of disabled children from China to the West is an example of "outsourced intimacy" on the part of the Chinese government, the eager reception of, facilitation of surgeries for, and processing of adoptions of children with medical needs from China also suggests a "rehabilitative mission" on behalf of the West to such children. As Kathryn Joyce (2013) has observed, the Christian desire to provide for the less fortunate through evangelical adoption actually maintains moral hierarchies between the West and abroad through the marginalizing care of "others."

Yet these global politics of adoption are not new (the very first adoption agencies emerged in the context of providing a Christian home to Korean War orphans) but rather freshly significant in the face of the disproportionate abandonment of children with disabilities and their Western adoption from China. As Joyce points out, "the Christian adoption movement . . . of children with high medical needs has become a distinguished category of its own"—one that, through sacrifice in the hardship of raising these children, Christians prove their love for God (Joyce 2013, 216–217; see also Stryker 2010). Although such accounts are mostly anecdotal, and a full-fledged empirical study of ICA of disabled children and adoptive parents in Western countries has yet to be carried out, the notions of disability tacitly invoked in these practices and comments evoke moral pity, helplessness, and neediness, extending rather than complicating the child saving discourse that contributes to political, economic, and moral hierarchies in ICA.

Therefore, it is necessary to consider how demand and desire for children with disabilities from China harbors and conceals ableism (ironically, through a "rehabilitative mission") that both undermines the personhood of disabled children and maintains moral hierarchies in ICA. In drawing on, for example, Robert McRuer's analysis (2006, 3) of disability in neoliberal discourse, we can see that even as disability may be no longer stigmatized but rather celebrated, ICA of children with disabilities also serves to "produce and secure" compulsory able-bodiedness (and heterosexuality) while containing and absorbing disability (as well as queerness). In quietly rehabilitating and reappropriating disabled children from China to Western countries, Western "progress" is complicit in the exclusion and exportation of such children insofar as it serves to highlight Western morality at the expense of the pitying, subordinating gaze of disability.

As ICA appropriates and absorbs these children into Western heteronormative families, we see the extent to which the expansion and transformation of such families is both contingent upon disabled bodies and also bent upon masking and rehabilitating their difference. In markets where babies have become fetishized as priceless objects of desire, global politics has revealed ICA to be a profiteering venture for sending countries but one that also further entrenches and subordinates them to Western demand (Dorow 2006; Marre and Briggs 2012. Thus, what unbridled reception of children with disabilities from China signals is perhaps not so much an increasing acceptance of children with disabilities in the West but a reassertion of the fetishization of the "underdeveloped" child so in need of Western medicine, development, and progress in the form of the disabled child.

The discourse of ICA of children with disabilities is alarmingly ableist in that it hinges upon the rehabilitative and curative potential to not only rid China of children with disabilities but to reimagine such children's restoration within Western, heteronormative, ableist modern families. Hence, although ICA is often understood as a solution to the problem of disabled child abandonment in China, it is vital to examine how demand for such children may be part and parcel of the problem. With so much sociopolitical change in China regarding the social value of girls and restrictive birth planning policies, it may be hopeful to consider that this present problem of disabled abandonment may be nearing resolution. Yet there is not only a lack of political will for the services people with disabilities and families who care for them need in China but also a seemingly sustainable, income-generating demand for their international exportation. Even though under the birth planning policies families of children with disabilities were permitted to have a second child, this option rarely proved to be comforting given the stigma of their lack of personhood and the financial burden to be born in caring for them for life. Thus, even the two-child policy presents little hope for the resolution of the disproportionate abandonment and exportation of children with disabilities from China given both their inability to be productively and socially incorporated into the modern Chinese family and their presumed fate to be adopted by families abroad.

CHAPTER SUMMARY: FURTHERING THE LIMINAL CHARACTER OF FOSTER FAMILIES IN CONTEMPORARY CHINA

What this chapter has shown is how, from a structural standpoint, foster families remain embedded in practices of ICA and cooperation with INGOs and state actors. Hence, foster care has come to function in a symbiotic relationship with

Western INGOs and ICAs of disabled children from China. The Chinese government furthers the marginalization of children with disabilities by facilitating their abandonments through the establishment of baby hatches, failing to support their needs and welfare by instead offering institutional and family support, and expediting Waiting Child Program adoptions to Western countries rather than encouraging local adoption of disabled children. Yet Western "rehabilitative" desire for such children maintains the flow of the ICA of disabled children from China to the West. Overall, the influential, symbiotic relationship between foster care and ICA obscures the relationship between foster care and commensurate cultural practices of family, further entrenching and ostracizing foster families' liminality in Chinese culture.

And yet, as the subsequent chapters will show, despite the instrumentalization of foster families in practices of international family making and governance, relationships between foster parents and foster children are not merely instrumental. Rather, their affection and emotion often exceed their temporary nature, challenging the relationships of other families around them and complicating seemingly rigid distinctions between family forms. Accordingly, despite the complex political and economic history of how foster families have come to work in collaboration with state and international markets, this ethnography examines how the local practices of family making may transcend their seemingly small spheres of influence.

3 · NEEDY ALLIANCES

Auntie Ma talks about how when she initially saw Meili, a child who had no mental or physical disabilities,[1] she was dissuaded by how sickly, yellow, and dirty she was. When she recalled the great scar that ran across Meili's forehead when she came to live with her, she often shook her head with disgust, remarking on how ugly the gash made the little girl rather than voicing compassion for the suffering she had experienced at the hands of her stepmother prior to being abandoned. Many foster parents expressed similar reactions to orphans both with and without disabilities—children who drooled uncontrollably, children who were dark skinned, or children who could not communicate or communicated through awkward grunts and groans.

When I visited various foster households, foster parents snatched up toddlers who ran in circles to demonstrate and detail their deformities in front of the children and the community. "Look at how ruined his foot is; he can't hardly run!" they would exclaim, despite the fact that the child in question had been blissfully scampering about the courtyard only seconds earlier. Many parents confessed fear or discomfort with the appearances of children with cleft palates. "I could hardly look at them when the orphanage placed them with me. I wanted them to take them back, but they said these were the children who needed a home, and they wouldn't take them back no matter how often I complained," admitted one foster mother.

These comments were deeply unsettling to me, especially because they came off as exceptionally cruel and ableist. Linliang Qian, in her analysis of Chinese philanthropy in a Child Welfare Institute, describes a prevailing attitude of pity toward institutionalized children. Although she does cite ableism as dominating philanthropists' interpretation of institutionalized children as abnormal (2014, 258), she finds that the sociopolitical interpretations of children's abnormality as being without family and without usefulness also came into play. Visitors to the institution often remarked on the dirtiness of the place and the abnormality of the children, constructing a clear distinction between the clean, normal family environment and the unclean, abnormal institution (2014, 256, 261).

Appearances, both for children and adults, were the site of frequent commentary throughout my fieldwork. The sense that one's outer appearance bears mentioning sometimes connoted clear care and attentiveness ("You look skinny! You've lost weight!" "You look tired!"), yet at other times took on a definitive moral register, like the comments above that attempted to provide some order or even explanation for why these children were abandoned or abnormal. Foster parents, part and parcel of a competitive capitalist society, without subtlety voiced their concerns that children's appearances reflected their moral depravity, uselessness, or abnormality (J. Chen 2012; Kohrman 1999; Qian 2014).

Yet because foster parents' comments faded the more time I spent with families, they seemed to play a role in a narrative that foster parents were telling about their children's value and their own relationship to those children. Other people in their apartment complexes or their villages could readily perceive that their children were disabled, and they seemed to feel they owed them, they even owed *me*, an explanation of that disability. So what was really being communicated in those seemingly spiteful comments? What were they saying about the children, themselves, or their families?

One afternoon I spoke with a particularly jolly and warm white-haired couple who fostered a young girl with cerebral palsy alongside caring for their biological granddaughter. They spoke plainly of their rejection and discontent with their foster child in the beginning. "I remember how I used to go to the orphanage," the foster mother, Auntie Luo, said. "Because I'd fostered many kids and they'd all been adopted to America, none of them had been disabled, so I used to always tell the director to send me another beautiful one, like those on the wall." She gestured toward photos of a myriad of young toddlers that adorned the living room. "And I'd seen Ren Ren there. She was always dirty and pitiful and I used to ask the director, 'Who will ever adopt stinky Ren Ren?' I called her stinky Ren Ren [*chou Ren Ren*]!" She laughed, playfully brushing the twelve-year-old girl's shoulder, then added,

> But then one day the director called, and she said, "I want you to take Ren Ren." And I was, like, "Stinky Ren Ren? No!" And I didn't want to take her home, but she [the director] said she didn't have any healthy, beautiful children left, and so I took her home, all dirty and stinky, and I could barely stand to look at her. And gradually we realized that she wasn't developing normally, that she wasn't walking when all the other kids were, that her legs weren't steady, and I wanted to bring her back to the orphanage, because I thought, what am I going to do with this child that can't walk? But my husband said that we needed to give her a chance, we just needed to be patient and give her more time.

Auntie Luo's husband chimed in: "I knew she would walk. We just needed to be patient."

"Well, I wasn't," snapped Auntie Luo, "so I called the orphanage and said, 'Take her back,' and they told me she had cerebral palsy, and I didn't know what that was, but they said, 'It's a disease that affected her legs,' and so we began to take her to therapy, and when she was three years old, she eventually did walk."

It was not just foster parents, though, who struggled to accept orphaned children with disabilities as their own. In chapter 1, eight-year-old Dengrong roundly rejected the affection of her new foster mother and the urging of the orphanage monitors to articulate her feelings for her new foster parents. When Dengrong finally did cry out her father's name and bury her head in his chest amid sobs, there was the sense that she was defeated by the pressure to conform to her new family rather than truly willing and able to receive and give love. For children like Dengrong who remember their abandonment, psychological wounds run much deeper than the cerebral palsy or asthma that affects their bodies (Stryker 2010). Learning to love and trust again, let alone bonding to a new family, is anything but simple.

And yet, six months later when Huilan, the orphanage monitor, Older Sister Mo, the physical therapist, and I returned to Daling to visit Dengrong, there was a notable shift in both her physical state and her demeanor. Whereas a few months earlier we had found Dengrong so pale and weak that she could hardly move, on this morning she sat on a little chair outside on the front porch, basking in the sunshine, smiling pleasantly, and waving to neighbors who passed by. As we approached, Dengrong rose to her feet in the doorway and greeted us. The fever and cold sweats were absent, and the cough was much less significant as she gingerly puttered about the room with her tiny walker. Instead of refusing to speak or make eye contact, as before, Dengrong cheerfully referred to her foster mother as Mama; her foster mother, instead of calling Dengrong lazy, blinked back tears when Huilan complimented her on the excellent care she had been giving the little girl.

For "stinky" Ren Ren, a similar shift in acceptance was evident, especially on the part of the foster parents. Auntie Luo still criticized Ren Ren's shy nature, but she also advocated for "such a wonderful child" to find a permanent home in America. Ren Ren's foster father's affection for her was more obvious in the kind eyes and smile he held while speaking of their relationship. Yet Ren Ren's belonging within the little family became unmistakable in the way she cared for the couple's granddaughter and the way her foster family easily talked of how her presence had impacted their lives in both ordinary and extraordinary ways: they had become convinced that children with cerebral palsy could be clever even when their legs failed them, they avoided long car trips simply because Ren Ren was prone to motion sickness, and Auntie Luo and her husband hoped to count Ren Ren among the children that they had fostered over the years, the photos of which they gazed at adoringly.

FROM "UGLY CHILDREN" TO FOSTER SONS AND DAUGHTERS

But how did these shifts in relationship take place? How did foster parents go from "hardly being able to look" at foster children or being repulsed by their appearances to considering them like their own? How did foster children, often traumatized by their abandonment, learn to love and be loved? How did these needy persons in Chinese society come together to form meaningful relationships of care? What kind of practices and processes are integral to building kin relations among foster families, and how were these received by those who sought to monitor, understand, or evaluate these relationships in contemporary Chinese social life?

In this chapter, I explore foster mothers' motivations to foster (which come under scrutiny from state orphanage and INGO personnel), philosophies of caregiving, and affective bonding between foster parents and children through the establishment of belonging and obligation. I show how motivations that seem primarily economic and instrumental are interlaced with curiosity and adaptability and constitute a notable attempt on the part of poor older foster mothers to reposition their social vulnerability as an asset in parenting. Furthermore, I show how seemingly cruel teasing and community-brokered discipline actually reference culturally viable practices through which Chinese parents and children establish mutual obligation and belonging. Thus, in drawing on popular cultural codes in child-rearing, foster parents subtly establish orphaned and disabled children's belonging to these nonbiological families.

But this belonging does not just go one way. Additionally, I show how foster parents, in the raising of these children, are somewhat rehabilitated in the eyes of the state and society as they find purpose and respect in the commitment to raising a child. Although not all placements are so successful or transformative, this chapter, which emphasizes the traditional practices of child-rearing and discipline employed by the older foster mothers, demonstrates that daily caregiving, of a mutual nature, forges deep, affective bonds between foster parents and children.

While the chapter focuses heavily on foster mothers' motivations, practices of child training, and their effects, there are several other figures and arguments in the background. First, the children themselves (the focus of chapter 1) contribute in varied ways to the processes of fostering, illustrating that they are not passive recipients of cultural knowledge being socialized but active participants in the formation of these relationships of care.[2] I show that foster parents are often very forthright about their own needs for the children's companionship and care. Analogously, the children, despite the hierarchies between adults and children in Chinese culture, are dynamic social actors who do not take teasing, criticism, or the challenges of learning to love and respect new parents lightly. Thus, the foster relationship is not merely authoritative but also mutually dynamic and obligational.

This is a point that is better grasped in subsequent chapters, as this chapter tends to focus on the intentions and effects of foster mothers' parenting and motivations. Yet in highlighting mutual care in such relationships, this book supports critiques of care work from the field of disability studies that foreground the subjectivity and agency of disabled actors where they have often been mistreated as passive objects and recipients (see, for instance, Williams's 2001 critique of Tronto 1993).

Second, because abandoned children often first go to an orphanage before being placed into foster care, orphanage personnel are responsible for monitoring foster families' care for children and children's development. Additionally, various INGO actors who partner with the orphanage to provide finances, care, and oversight visit the foster children and their families every few months. During my eighteen months of fieldwork, I observed both orphanage and INGO staff members' efforts to facilitate the fostering process, as well as interactions between foster parents and their foster children without orphanage or INGO personnel present. By illustrating some of the preliminary differences between foster mothers and orphanage and INGO care workers' child-rearing strategies and motivations, this chapter also begins to explore some of the boundaries between foster families and biological families, as well as the state and family life (which will be the foci of chapters 4 and 6).

Still, the aim of this chapter is neither to examine the children's agency (or lack thereof) nor highlight the socializing efforts of the INGO personnel, but rather to unveil and understand the mutual, intersubjective processes that eventually make foster families kin to one another.[3] Making new families from the residue of broken ones is both arduous and meaningful, but if it is to be successful, the process is hardly one-sided. Indeed, in this chapter, I show how surprisingly mutual bonds of belonging emerge among foster parents and foster children through acts of "play," acts of teasing, traditional child-rearing practices, and acts of vulnerability and sacrifice that also make foster families belong increasingly to the category of family in the eyes of society and the state.

In so doing, both in this chapter and in chapter 4, I draw on literature on contemporary child-rearing in China that provides some cultural foundation for these practices of teasing, shaming, discipline, and care (Chao 1994; Fong 2004; Ho 1986; Tobin, Wu, and Davidson 1991; Wu 1996). In particular, Jing Xu's (2017) ethnography of moral development in a Chinese preschool identifies some of the ways that traditional modes of child-rearing are being complicated by a pervasive threat of immorality in Chinese society, the shift toward child-centeredness in family life, intergenerational parenting coalitions that fight for control of children, and a higher emphasis on moral education versus obedience from children. Still, Xu argues that the uniquely Chinese concept of *guanjiao*, an integration of approaches to discipline and care, provides a clear framework for socialization across Chinese society. Noting significant tension in negotiating *guanjiao* across multiple caregivers for single children, Xu (2017, 179–180) still finds that the tactics of shaming and ostracism, for instance, are common in Chinese preschool training. Even though she is Chinese, Xu remarks (2017, 23) that the public shaming of two- and three-year-olds by teachers appeared somewhat cruel, but highly effective. Her research finds that teachers and parents regularly used shaming, and exaggerated threats and techniques of ostracism, to discipline children; this may strike some Western readers as inappropriate or harmful to young children, but it serves distinct purposes in cultivating moral qualities for Chinese children.

Yet Xu's research with a typical preschool and middle-class families in Shanghai demonstrates that what may initially appear to be exceptional among foster families in terms of treatment, care, and disciplining of children actually references clear cultural codes and practices of child-rearing in contemporary China. Relatedly, Xu, as well as Teresa Kuan (in her 2015 ethnography that deals primarily with child-rearing of older children in contemporary China) both draw persistent attention to child-rearing as a site of dynamic cultural change in the People's Republic of China today and a site of much stress and conflict (*maodun*), particularly for mothers attempting to negotiate tension between autonomous yet filial children. Chapter 4 further explores how this tension plays out across generational and class differences as foster mothers and orphanage care workers struggle against one another's child-rearing sensibilities. But, for now, this chapter helps capture, describe, and analyze some aspects of the foster mothers' neediness with respect to their motivations to provide foster care for disabled and abandoned children.

Finally, this chapter extends yet another argument with which this book is concerned—that is, challenging the theoretical boundaries between need and care, emphasizing how need can be and is repositioned as a resource to care even as it is presumed or often interpreted as that which disenfranchises and dispossesses one of the very ability to provide care. Therefore this chapter plays (as does the entire book) on the double entendre of "needy alliances," emphasizing that both resiliency and creativity through need are repositioned as resources for care and for the building of relationships, and that the toxicity and inequality through which need is antagonized and undermined is that which prohibits and taints care, rendering it bereft and substandard.

"PLAYING" FOSTER FAMILIES

A common threat many Chinese parents make to their children is "Wo bu li ni" (I'll ignore you), meaning, "I'm not paying attention to you," "I refuse to acknowledge you (as a result of your behavior)," and even "I don't care." In response to disobedience or noncompliance, a parent will casually and nonchalantly offer this phrase, accompanied by the action of turning his or her back on the child briefly or pretending to walk away. When emotions are heightened, the phrase may be yelled at the child in question, the first or last in a series of piled-on threats that seek to reform the child's bad behavior.

What is starkly ironic in these very frequent exchanges between parents and children, however, is that these threats to ignore are hardly ever carried out: instead of ignoring the child, parents do just the opposite. Although the child's mother may pretend to walk away in order to get the child to follow, or turn her back for a brief moment, these threats of isolation are usually followed by more retorts, threats, or reprimands, and the child becomes the object of much social attention rather than being ignored.

Contrary to common ideals and portrayals of Chinese children as quiet and obedient and parents as commanding and authoritative, interactions between parents and children often took the form of "play" that anthropologist Jean Briggs has described among the Inuit. Drawing on her own extensive fieldwork with Inuit peoples, Briggs explains that questions adults ask of children often place children in personally threatening scenarios and then dramatize the consequences children choose in order to demonstrate the consequences of emotion and behavior in the larger context of Inuit social life (J. L. Briggs 1998, 2000). Further noting that children are often spoken to in exaggerated voices (that display fear, disgust, saccharine persuasion, tenderness, etc.), Briggs notes the incredibly difficult job for children to disentangle or parse relationships between content and emotion in Inuit language and culture (2000, 162).

Through multiple nuanced scenes of "teasing," a term Briggs rejects for its negative connotations and replaces with that of "play" (2000, 161), she shows how these interrogations can straddle the boundaries of saccharine affection and socialization:

> For the adult, the interaction is part idle pastime, part serious teaching device, and part test of how much understanding the child has developed; and more often than appears to *our* ears, it is a celebration of a child's existence and dearness. . . . Uninitiated children, who don't understand that adults don't mean exactly what they say, may be severely challenged by the questions, especially as the interrogations are often focused on transitions, even crises, that a child may be going through: weaning; adoption (very common in Inuit society); or perhaps the birth of a new sibling. (161)

What is rather uncanny is the parallels that the transitions Briggs describes have with the rhythms of foster care and how insightful her analysis of these multivalent dramatizations proves for the Chinese context, so foreign to that of the Inuit. Even the translations of the opening lines Briggs provides, which question whether a particular adult or the child in question is good or whether the child would like to go live in the home of a stranger or a relative, were almost perfectly echoed in my own research.

The culture that Briggs describes could hardly be more differentiated from the Chinese, however. Whereas the Inuit value their autonomy, avoid conflict, and are ambivalent about attachment, the lessons communicated through these pivotal Chinese parent-child exchanges have to do with the perils of social isolation, the important social roles children are to assume in deference to others, and the all-important sense of obligation a Chinese child and parent must develop toward one another to truly become family. Indeed, Chinese parents and foster parents alike, with grins on their faces, often questioned children as to whether they were good or bad (*guai bu guai*), whether they were willing to share or not (*gei bu gei*), or whether they wanted to go live in the house of a friend, relative, or stranger (*qu bu qu*). Children's differing responses dramatically shaped and transfigured the structure of these dialogues: especially with small children, the imperative to give a toy or a piece of fruit to another child or a parent was loosely enforced. Parents found the stinginess of young children to part with items hilarious and harmless just as often as they eventually corrected the disobedient behavior by reprimand or physical force (rarely spanking or slapping, but more often grabbing the aforementioned object out of the hands of the child in question).

Furthermore, the dialogues were often casually constructed, good-natured efforts by parents to carry out a curiosity or desire to illicit a reaction, enjoy the child's naïveté, and only secondarily test the child's abilities or teach a lesson. For instance, one afternoon when foster mother Auntie Ma and I returned with foster daughter Meili and her friend from a visit to the street food market, we bumped into another foster mother, Auntie Qin, and her nearly two-year-old grandson, Wei Wei, whom she had strapped to her back.[4] She told us that she had been out shopping with her older foster daughter and her young grandson, buying them new clothes, and she had gone home immediately to put one of the new shirts on her grandson, laughing about how adorable he was, how excited she was to dress him up, and showing us some of the other clothes she had in her bags.

We chatted on the street corner for a bit, and Auntie Qin took Wei Wei to pee behind a tree on the side of the road. When they decided they needed to head home, Auntie Ma tried to hand the little boy the bag with his new pants inside that she had been holding for Auntie Qin. When he would not take it, she replied, "Okay, I won't give it to you. But *waipo* [a term for grandmother, referring to herself] will wear your little pants then!" When she again got no response, she continued, "Well, then give me some of your *baozi* [the steamed bun that the boy was eating]."

"Yes, give some to *waipo*," his grandmother, Auntie Qin, encouraged. When Wei Wei silently refused, Auntie Ma removed his stuffed bear from another bag and asked, "Then why don't you give this to *waipo, hao bu hao* [okay]?"

Finally Wei Wei began to whimper, and walked over, snatching the stuffed bear out of Auntie Ma's hands and murmuring "Bu gei" (No, I will not give it). Both women chuckled.

"We'd better get going," Auntie Qin responded, and we all called out goodbye to them as they walked down the street to their apartment building.

In this lighthearted exchange, the older women seemed relatively unconcerned with Wei Wei's noncompliance in holding the bag he was given, sharing his steamed bun, or handing over his stuffed bear. Instead, the emphasis was on providing a playful, low-stakes environment for Wei Wei to practice making decisions regarding the demands of authority figures and also relative strangers. Wei Wei did not understand that Auntie Ma did not really want to (nor could she) wear his little pants, or that she probably had no use for his steamed bun or stuffed bear, so he played along, finally becoming disturbed at the thought of parting with the bear to the point of whimpering and audibly refusing. Both women seemed delighted and satisfied with his sour reaction. The point had seemed to implicate the young boy in an exchange that caused him to scrutinize his own choices and behaviors, and eventually to express himself through speech, however defiant.

Indeed, interactions between grandparents and young children like Auntie Qin and Wei Wei also serve to implicate the child in choices that demonstrate his or her social role vis à vis the family (J. L. Briggs 1998). For instance, while Wei Wei refuses his grandmother and Auntie Ma's requests, he is not shamed for his noncompliance; rather, his behavior is treasured as a feature of his naïveté and babyhood. As Briggs suggests, such interactions can contain multiple motivations, one being "a celebration of a child's existence and dearness" (2000, 161). Moreover, as Wei Wei grows and his grandmother and other adult figures can no longer tempt him into such games or dialogues, he will also find new social roles as a young boy and, finally, a young man. Despite their argumentative or teasing nature, then, these scripts are often imbedded with the importance of family harmony in Chinese society, wherein each individual plays his or her role and relates to others accordingly. Wei Wei, a baby, is not expected to speak up for himself or comply with each and every request that is made, and his interactions vis à vis the adults confirm that he is to be treasured for his babyhood while it lasts (J. L. Briggs 1998).

In other lighthearted exchanges, parents and foster parents asked children whom they wanted to sleep with at night—(foster) grandma or (foster) mama— and feigned hurt at being rejected, or rewarded children with affection when they were chosen. For foster families like Auntie Qin's, Auntie Li's, Auntie Luo's, and many others, the commingling of their own grandchildren or children with their foster children, as well as other biological and nonbiological kin side by side, created a climate wherein the same traditional, "playing," methods of childrearing and social conditioning played out among and between both biological and foster children. Thus, these comments about children that were ugly, noncompliant, or unsuitable, and these dialogues about where children would sleep and with whom they would live, which I initially received as teasing and perhaps even mean-spirited, started to make sense within mainstream cultural methods of Chinese parenting and belonging.

NORMALIZING FAMILY BONDS: FROM ISOLATION TO BELONGING

When many of the playful dialogues—offering children the choice of going to live with a relative, neighbor, or stranger, or staying at home with mom and dad—implicated foster children, the stakes seemed higher and perhaps more harmful. Owing to the futures the orphanage, these foster parents, and their foster children imagined in the United States or other foreign countries, my intrusion as a foreign face in the group often steered the conversation to news of America. In chapter 2, I described my discomfort with the foster mothers' pleas for me to save their pitiful children, whose future was not in China but in the United States, and the effect it had on the children, who fearfully sized me up.

Yet in addition to registering that these were exchanges that brought into play the power and inequality of intercountry adoption from China, I also discovered that these questions were variations on an attempt by foster parents to establish communication with their children and subtly transmit cultural ideas about authority, social roles, and social belonging. To be sure, these interactions were also a great source of knowledge given that the foster mothers prescribed roles to both the children and myself that we, in turn, resisted. The foster mothers interpreted my difference as one that constituted power, even imperialism, and the children were implicated in this complex relationship. This not only expressed the foster mothers' ambivalence to my power and participation in their community but also subtly underlined the power dynamics between Chinese parents and children. I learned that my social role as an adult was constituted by the hierarchical relations between Chinese parents and children and by my cultural association with adoptive parents who signified fear, uncertainty, and the disruption of foster relationships.

Xiaoyuan, whom we met in chapter 1, was a child a who, because her parents had reappeared at the orphanage years after her abandonment, would never be adopted abroad, and yet her foster mom's dialogue with her openly played out the option of where she would go to live after she was adopted. Despite their seemingly cruel nature, I want to suggest that paradoxically, these playful dialogues are just as important in establishing children's belonging and roles within a foster family (and parents' bonds to them) as initiating a particular transition associated with fostering and adoption.

As Xiaoyuan's foster mother asked her foster daughter, "Does Xiaoyuan want to go to America?" the dialogue was oddly scripted, with mom feigning surprise when Xiaoyuan refused, as if they had rehearsed this many times. It is true that Xiaoyuan's foster mother hopes against all hope that Xiaoyuan can one day be adopted, but she also takes great pleasure in the girl's reticence to go to America if her foster mother cannot come along, and Xiaoyuan's youthful responses to the questions ("Maybe . . . maybe I could text you," Xiaoyuan stammered). This dialogue between Xiaoyuan and her foster mother asserted bonds of obligation and belonging precisely because the fictional transition of adoption was approached with such dramatization.

Meanwhile, down the street, Xiaoyuan's neighbor, another foster child, Honghuan, was teased by her siblings and neighbors about going to America: "Do you want to go? Will you go? You're so lucky!" When her foster mother jokingly replied, "Yeah, I don't want you anyway!" Honghuan buried her head in her mother's chest. "Your new mother will look just like this auntie," her mom said, motioning to me. "Go take a picture with her." Honghuan eyed me suspiciously, and we all laughed.

In this short exchange, there was a threat of isolation ("Yeah, I don't want you anyway!"), but the foster mother continued to hold the child, and the community found Honghuan's suspicion of me understandable and endearing. Much like Wei Wei's refusal to share his items with Auntie Ma, Honghuan's "disobedience" was encouraged by laughter, establishing that despite Honghuan's uncertain future, her present home was very much secure with her foster mother and the gaggle of siblings and neighbors. Thus we see that although commonplace threats of isolation like "Yeah, I don't want you anyway!" smack of cruelty and exclusion, they actually serve to communicate distinct ideas about what it means to be a Chinese person given foster parents' unwillingness to ever truly leave a child alone.

In her famous study on the uterine family, Margery Wolf, an anthropologist of China, comments that it is not only isolation but also estrangement from family that constitutes the essence of social death in Chinese society. She writes, "Chinese children are taught by proverb, by example, and by experience that the family is the source of their security, and relatives are the only people who can be depended on. Ostracism from the family is one of the harshest sanctions that can be imposed on erring youth" (1972, 35). I am suggesting that, in coupling together threats of isolation ("Yeah I don't want you anyway!") with threats of being taken from one's family ("Don't you want to go to America?"), the emphasis is still on teaching children the relationship between obedience and social roles within the Chinese family. It is highly significant that despite the manifold references these threats may have for children who have been previously abandoned, foster parents continue to employ them.

In fact, I suggest that it is these threats that normalize the experience of family for these foster children. Despite the fear they drive into the children's hearts, the threats paradoxically serve to establish permanence, rather than the temporary nature, of foster family bonds. Only a child who belongs to a family—who plays the social role of a real child and is at once treasured, yet often disciplined—can truly be thrown out, ignored, or unwanted. The implication in these threats, though subtle and often seemingly subversive, is that the child in question is, in fact, very unlikely to be ignored, very much wanted, and very much treasured.

What is further important here, though, are the ways in which these exchanges solidify the bonds not only for the children but also for their foster mothers. As the mothers implicate the children in critique and play, they remind us that belonging, if it is to be realized, cannot be singular. In the following sections,[5] I expand upon how seemingly clear-cut financial motivations for fostering trend toward distinct sacrifices for the broader society and the state. Through the ostensibly trivial practices of child-rearing, coupled with the extraordinary arrangements among foster parents, foster children, society, and the state, the motherhood of these disenfranchised women takes on a broader valence. Belonging to the category of mother for these women then becomes a powerful moral category that makes their caring and the sacrifice evocative of "real families," a standing that the state cannot afford to ignore.

REMAKING MOTIVATIONS

Thus, these relationships between foster parents and foster children do not just confer a sense of social belonging for the children but rather establish such belonging in a subtle, mutual way, furthering the social standing and motherhood of the older women themselves. It is important to remember that many older foster parents with whom I did fieldwork in southwest Guangxi were both practically impoverished and socially marginalized. As I chatted with foster families in the villages, or even in the regional capital, the story was always the same: the foster parents' grown children had migrated to bustling cities to find work in factories, and depending on how far away they were, they returned on the weekends, monthly, or only once a year. In a society in which children are meant to care for their parents in old age (Potter and Potter 1990), many older people, despite fulfilling their sociocultural obligations to their children and society, found themselves physically and/or emotionally abandoned by children or other relatives who had left them behind to forge a future in the more prosperous cities.

Yet, when questioned directly about their motivations to foster, older foster parents candidly weighed differential and emergent reasons, crafting a narrative that reflected their awareness regarding both their social vulnerability and the substantial social benefits they gained from fostering. For instance, when Auntie Ma spoke about her decision to foster, her narrative reflected multiple motivations that developed and shifted over time. Like many other parents, through observation of neighbors' experiences, Auntie Ma gradually became interested in fostering:

Well, you know, my neighbors had fostered children, and I became curious. And I thought, to have a child, you know, I could do that, it's just me, and the government doesn't pay me much in retirement, so I also thought of the money. And so

I had one child, and she had to go back to the orphanage. But by that point I was used to having her around, and then I took in Meili, and she's been with me for six years. And you develop feelings, you know, you want more for them—like, me, what can I give her, really? Of course, I love her, but I want an American mother to adopt her to give her everything she deserves.

Auntie Ma's rationale for why she chose to foster begins with the motivation of curiosity. Next she mentions her [presumably physical and emotional] ability to do so, alongside the financial incentive of fostering a child. Additionally, she comments on the experience of "getting used to having a child around." Finally, she expresses the development of feelings for her foster daughter, Meili, and her desire to give her a better life.

Not unlike Wu Yuping, Han Xiaoyu, and Gao Qin, in their book on foster care in urban Beijing (2005), I also found that foster parents' motivations for fostering were multiple, overlapping, and emergent. But I want to suggest that for women like Auntie Ma, social vulnerability—a presumed disadvantage of their circumstances—was actually repositioned as a primary motivator in their acceptance and raising of abandoned disabled children. Indeed, following her assertion of curiosity, the intermingling in the phrasing of Auntie Ma's motivations is highly significant. When she states, "to have a child, you know, I could do that, it's just me, and the government doesn't pay me much in retirement, so I also thought of the money," her social vulnerability is certainly apparent but also subtly repositioned as a resource and an advantage in her ability to care for a child. She refers to her isolation and her solitary state as somewhat facilitating her ability to care, implying that if she had other obligations she would have to split her time and energy among them, but as a widowed older woman without biological grandchildren she is perfectly positioned to devote her attention to a foster child. Following on the heels of this reinterpretation of her vulnerability, Auntie Ma also frames her financial motivations quite candidly and matter-of-factly. Rather than shying away from her need, in both these circumstances Auntie Ma makes her vulnerability a primary pillar of motivation both in her willingness and competence to foster Meili.

FOSTER CARE AS SOCIAL REHABILITATION

Foster mothers cited many benefits through foster relationships that ranged from a boost in their own self-esteem to a raising of their status in the eyes of the community and even the state. Throughout my fieldwork, I observed that raising a child clearly gave these retirees a sense of purpose and heightened self-worth. Taking these children to the market or playground, or just out into the public courtyard, gave isolated older people an excuse to engage with their neighbors and their community. As foster parents developed pride and protective qualities regarding their children, they began to see themselves as valuable to community and society.

Hence foster parents often proudly cited the work they were doing for these "pitiful children" as *gongxian*, an act of civic sacrifice or duty. They felt that caring for a child, especially a child abandoned into the institutions of the state, recuperated their self-worth as active and important members of Chinese society. Most important, perhaps, the obligations created between children and foster parents reintegrated them into distinct social roles in family life, as they now became primary caregivers in family relationships. Although many of these children, especially because of their disabilities, could not or would not be able to offer the foster parents much care now or in old age, the mirroring of the intergenerational contract in these relations, wherein the children and elders offered emotional comfort and solace to one another in the face of abandonment by their biological parents and children, respectively, should not be overlooked (Croll 2010).

As poor older women took on the role of foster mothers, they became visible and notable in their sacrifice not only for their foster children but also for the Chinese state. In fact, their usage of the term *gongxian* to describe their motivations for fostering is highly significant in that it is the same term that the Chinese government once employed to solicit the service of its people for the Cultural Revolution and still uses to commend citizens for their sacrifices in the name of civic duty. Whether foster mothers were conscious of it or not, in suggesting that their kin work was a kind of *gongxian* they appropriated the language of the Chinese state, suggesting that their service had distinct ties to the maintenance of political life and order.

This type of repositioning is noteworthy given the state's own relative abandonment of poor older women, as well as middle-aged orphanage and INGO care workers' frequent criticism and prejudice against older foster mothers. Because the state orphanage provided the infrastructure and funding for foster care placements, it conducted quarterly visits to monitor the quality of the foster mothers' care. Due to suspicion of their motivations, as well as frequent criticism of their child-rearing and disciplinary methods, hygiene, and lack of education, the foster mothers often resented these visits and the surveillance in general. When I accompanied such middle-aged employees on their monthly visits, foster parents were often carefully compliant toward state orphanage workers, but when I returned on my own, they confided in me that they begrudged the disrespect and subordination these employees conveyed. As one foster mother complained, "To them we are nothing more than *baomus* [domestic servants]." In the presence of these monitors, their sacrifice, which had served to rehabilitate them, was subordinated to a needful, desperate kind of mothering.

Foster mothers also resented that they were left out of the loop in terms of being told to where and precisely when their foster children would be adopted. When children were adopted, the orphanage policies demanded that any visits between foster parents and adoptive families be conducted at the state orphanage or at a hotel. After adoptions, the orphanage also specified that any communication between adoptive families and foster families be conducted through the orphanage. Orphanage officials stated that the reasons for these policies were for the protection of the children and the adoptive families. They said they worried that foster families would try to solicit money from adoptive families, putting the state in an awkward position. But by concealing the foster families' homes and lives from view, they also frustrated some adoptive families who longed to have a relationship with their children's foster families.

Hence, one argument of this book is that the politics of moral family making are not limited to the confines of the home and the private sphere but necessarily disrupt the very conventions of other peoples' families (the INGO monitors), the wider society, and the state. Therefore, in this section, I have demonstrated some of the ways that through the bonds of foster care that develop between older foster mothers and abandoned, disabled children, foster parents experience certain economic, social, and political rehabilitation. In the final section and the following chapter, I elaborate how this rehabilitation is often perceived as a surprising affront to the very middle-aged INGO and orphanage workers who facilitate these foster care placements, thickening this intergenerational ambivalence and foreshadowing a remarkable reversal of intergenerational influence.

CHAPTER SUMMARY: DISPUTED MOTHERHOOD

Older foster mothers like Auntie Ma were often ridiculed by middle-aged orphanage workers who speculated that they were primarily and problematically motivated by their poverty to foster disabled children. As one INGO director once scoffed, "Who would take in these CP kids [children with cerebral palsy] if not for the money?" The same employees who spent many hours caring for disabled children in the orphanage and monitoring foster placements often muttered under their breaths that they themselves could not imagine caring for or taking in "such difficult children." In this way, middle-aged orphanage workers perpetuated the belief that only those in truly desperate circumstances, or commensurate circumstances of social abandonment, would take in such highly undesirable children. Whereas across the course of the foster care relationships, foster parents began to speak differently about children once called stinky, dirty, or worthless, middle-aged orphanage monitors often maintained a cautious, pitiable attitude toward to the children.

Furthermore, while foster mothers often felt that caring for a child was simple work, middle-aged orphanage workers imagined disabled children's care to be difficult. For example, one afternoon, in the village of Daling, Director Wang (of the Nanning Social Welfare Institute), Huilan, and I visited a prospective pair of prospective foster parents in their seventies. When Director Wang asked the couple whether they felt they could handle a disabled child from the orphanage, the old man responded, his eyes twinkling and with raucous laughter, "Suibian!

Suibian dai haizi!" (The phrase roughly means "No problem whatsoever" or "It's easy to raise a child!") The old man's laughter and words visibly alarmed Director Wang and Huilan, who shot back a whole host of admonishments about how children from the orphanage with diseases were fragile and required constant care, and that it would certainly not be as easy as this couple expected. The old man and woman, however, did not seem dissuaded. On many occasions I had heard foster mothers similarly scoff, "Why, it's easy to raise a child. To feed and clothe a child? How hard is it?"

Middle-aged orphanage monitors clearly bristled at this commentary, however, charging that older foster parents did not take seriously the time, energy, and expenses it takes to raise a child. The monitors were also angry that foster mothers often misunderstood stipends meant for the children as wages or other compensation. Foster mothers, however, remarked frequently and proudly on their own frugality, because they believed it was an important skill in being a parent and raising a child. They felt that by making the money they were given stretch further and further each month, they were managing their resources with the utmost care and responsibility. They were proud of their ability to skimp and save in ways that distinguished them from the middle-aged orphanage and INGO women who monitored their caregiving.

On the contrary, the orphanage and INGO monitors—particularly Teacher Liu (the director of Mercy Care) and Huilan—experienced stress in caring for their own biological families alongside their supervision of foster families. They were often critical of these older women's financial motivations, but they themselves complained of the economic constraints on their own family lives. As Teacher Liu once said to me, "It takes at least three people to raise a child; two just won't cut it!" She and Huilan relied on their parents and their in-laws to provide live-in care to their children while they worked long hours at their jobs. They often complained tearfully that raising children in modern China was arduous and draining, a stark contrast to the foster mothers' depictions of the relatively inexpensive, simple daily tasks requisite for child-rearing. In so doing, they positioned themselves as the real "state" mothers, making sacrifices for the state to care for their own families.

Yet even as middle-aged INGO and orphanage workers found foster mothers' vulnerability and poverty wanting,[6] older foster mothers exhibited pride and security in their ability to provide care to foster children as solo parents on limited budgets. This is significant because despite their "low status" in the Chinese imaginary and their attested vulnerability in aforementioned scholarship, older foster mothers did not view themselves as victims of their social circumstances, nor did they behave as confined or constricted by their limited finances. Foster mothers repositioned their social and economic vulnerability as a resource in their provision of good foster care and their work as good foster mothers.

Thus we see that this emergent intergenerational ambivalence about foster mothers' care for children, highly disputed by the middle-aged orphanage monitors, is actually a recognition on the part of the state that the biological boundaries of motherhood were being challenged and stretched to include these poor older women. Furthermore, it was primarily their neediness, not their care-giving, that foster care monitors found disruptive. Despite orphanage monitors' objection to the fitness of these foster mothers, the threat they presented (which will be taken up more significantly in chapter 4) connoted the efficacy of these social bonds and the power of their motherhood in the eyes of the state.

Therefore, despite the social rehabilitation afforded to poor older women in their assumption of the role of foster mothers (and especially sacrificial mothers for needy children of the state), these close bonds and formational kin relation-ships were not always celebrated but rather criticized by the orphanage monitors who also ostensibly wanted them to succeed. Such emerging tension between the need-based mothering put forth by older foster mothers, which proved to be para-doxically sacrificial and generative, contrasts with the state workers' need-based mothering that sought to reserve and preserve motherhood as a category of the privileged. Indeed, the specter of the adoptive family, which provides a further complication of these lines between class and motherhood, reminds us that even as these relationships play out on a small scale, they have significant ramifications for the politics of inequality that we see as embedded in family making in China and abroad.

Within this chapter the paradoxical use of threats and play to normalize foster relationships and reinforce belonging is also a notable political move by older foster mothers to embed their children within vital family relationships. The eth-nography in this chapter shows us how social vulnerability or need is reposi-tioned as a resource in mothering rather than a deficiency, thus challenging assumptions about who and what makes for a good mother in modern China. Whereas state and INGO monitors—with their suspicion of the foster mothers' financial motivations—seemed to demand a certain altruism (implying the means to sacrifice for others as a prerequisite to care), foster mothers found confidence in a more mutualistic notion of caregiving, where sacrifices and benefits shored up relationships and transformed need over time.

Foster mothering, by its very nature, relocates need to the center of kin relations and family making. Therefore, the political nature of family making crystallizes in these particular families, but in the process reveals something universal about kin-ship: need is certainly embedded in all family life, but it is presumed dispropor-tionate and in need of its own dissolution, its resolution. Yet, as we will see in chapter 4, need also knits together families, one to the other, complicating and commingling kinship, mothering, politics, and care altogether. The painstaking efforts to keep some families at the center, while others languish at the margins, are not so straightforward. The harder one pushes, the more one reveals the need at the center of such repulsions.

4 · ENVYING KINSHIP

"If you keep acting naughty, I'll send you back to the orphanage!" Teacher Liu, the director of Mercy Care, shouted to a room filled with foster mothers. "How many of you have said something like this to your child? Raise your hands."

Knowing smiles appeared on the withered faces of gray-haired women as they sheepishly raised their hands and broke into lively chatter. "Quiet, quiet please," Teacher Liu called out. "Now, how many of you have said things like, 'I'm so lucky to have you, I'm so happy you're my child'? Raise your hands again." This time only a few hands gingerly threaded the air, and the chatter reduced to a low murmur. Teacher Liu, flanked by two blond European women visiting from an INGO, began to stress the importance of positivity and encouragement in disciplining and raising foster children.

From my seat within the crowd, however, I overheard enduring protests from the foster parents. "So when a child misbehaves you're supposed to praise them?" one muttered. "That'll never work!"

"We all say those things," another whispered feverishly. "If we say the opposite, children will get the wrong idea, they'll never behave."

Meanwhile, in the corner of the room, a young foster child began to act up, and her foster mother began to yell and threaten to strike the child if she continued to misbehave. "Auntie," Teacher Liu addressed her, exasperatedly, "Can you please take the child outside? We're trying to run a lecture in here."

"GOOD FOSTER MOTHERS ARE HARDER AND HARDER TO FIND"

Every few months or so, I attended a training such as this one at one of the large state orphanages; they were often put on by foreign international nongovernmental organizations (INGOs), and often in partnership with foreign volunteers. And at nearly every orphanage I traveled to, and with nearly every INGO worker I talked to, I heard the complaint, "Good foster mothers are harder and harder to find." Whereas the overall number of children in orphanages had diminished since the 1990s, the proportion of children with disabilities in China's institutions had increased dramatically. INGO and orphanage workers cited the difficulties of enticing families to take in children with special medical needs, as well as the social stigma of disability. They complained that the older foster parents who were willing to take in such kids had "bad habits": they didn't discipline properly; they lacked education and basic parenting skills, especially in the areas of nutrition and hygiene; and they did not understand the special needs of children with disabilities adequately enough to provide appropriate daily therapy or training.

On the one hand, orphanage and INGO staff were convinced that older foster parents and abandoned disabled children created the perfect alliance. The former had time to spare, needed the money, and relished the reprieve from loneliness that the children provided; the latter benefited from foster parents' constant attention and affection, and were hardly valuable or attractive to anyone other than "needy old women." On the other hand, orphanage and INGO staff were often starkly critical of foster parents' methods of discipline, lack of education, and financially driven motives (see chapter 3). Thus, a puzzle emerged in my fieldwork: although older foster mothers were somewhat perfectly positioned to foster given their solitary lives and scant finances, they were also highly scrutinized by middle-aged orphanage and INGO monitors for these very reasons. Why were the features that at once motivated older women to foster so highly suspicious and problematic to their middle-aged counterparts?

It seemed reasonable enough that akin to analyses of Chinese state bureaucracy, state orphanage and INGO monitors may have merely been performing their duties by extending state surveillance into foster homes; after all, as was shown in chapter 2, foster care presents a highly contested site for the maintenance of family hierarchies that is reproduced by intercountry adoption (see Wang 2016). In addition, this critical relationship between state and INGO monitors and older foster mothers also certainly evoked insurmountable class differences: many older foster mothers were illiterate or poorly educated (having come of age during the Cultural Revolution), and nearly all were retired and without pension or much financial resources (see chapter 1).

Meanwhile, the government and INGO monitors were middle-aged women (though a few were as young as their twenties) who were college educated. While not rich, they were financially stable, technologically savvy, and spoke confident Mandarin, a signifier of cultural and economic prestige in linguistically plural and poor Guangxi. Many owned their own apartments, enjoyed a two-parent income, and were well supported by live-in parents or in-laws who helped provide childcare. Yet if older foster mothers were so radically subordinated to these middle-aged monitors in both class and bureaucratic status, why were their seemingly innocuous yet ignorant actions so unpalatable and emotionally disturbing to these state actors?

While doing my fieldwork, I initially and intentionally pushed the middle-aged orphanage and INGO monitors—who were in so many ways my age and class compatriots—away. I was in China to study foster families; what did these women have to do with that? Adamant to undo my own class privilege, at first I tried to avoid spending excess time with CWI, SWI, and INGO monitors and to keep them at somewhat of a distance. As Yunxiang Yan has argued so powerfully in his ethnography of Chinese family life, young people born in post-1980s China were becoming increasingly unfilial and uncivil, hardened to the needs of their elders and any societal responsibilities, "unbridled individuals" in search of a better life only for themselves (2003). I, too, found INGO and orphanage workers' dismissive attitudes toward elders, that smacked of self-centeredness, off-putting.

Yet as I spent more and more time traveling alongside foster care workers Huilan, Suling, and Teacher Liu, their frustrations and points of view grew on me. After all, they were spending days and weeks traveling to visit and accompany these fledgling foster families, and that meant leaving their own families behind. Teacher Liu talked openly and candidly about the challenge of living with both her husband and her mother-in-law in a two-bedroom apartment while she struggled to raise her only son. She was soft-spoken and demure, but she also had a steely determination. She had overcome a nasty divorce and made the transition to being the first Chinese employee of the adoption giant Holt International by virtue of the countless hours she spent studying English with foreigners and her own fortitude. Throughout my time doing fieldwork, I saw her navigate with sophistication and shrewdness a host of state blockades, tirelessly working for the good of the foster families.

And yet she was often quite critical of these women, questioning their commitments and their devotion to their children. When an American board member was moved to tears by her meeting with Auntie Ma, Meili's foster mom, Teacher Liu snidely questioned the board member, "What can possibly be so special about her?" Auntie Ma continually frustrated the orphanage and Mercy Care, as she talked incessantly, refused to comply with policies, was illiterate, and had no qualms about going behind the orphanage's back to get her way.

One afternoon, while waiting during our travels in the train station, Teacher Liu told the story of a birth family who came back secretly to check on their child at the orphanage. She told of how the orphanage demanded that the family pay money if they wanted to take the child back.[1] The shock must have shown on my face, and Teacher Liu replied, "Well, why shouldn't they [the orphanage] ask for money? They raised her all those years!"

But as we traveled from foster home to foster home, Teacher Liu also confided in me that she and her husband, despite their marital challenges, were ever hopeful to adopt a little girl. She was visibly exhausted, from staying up all night to nurse and care for her son, who was a poor sleeper, but here they were, longing for more children. They lamented that in China you could only have just one child and they had their eye on a beautiful little girl, one with minor cognitive disabilities, who had been abandoned into the state orphanage and was currently being fostered. While many of Teacher Liu's Chinese coworkers told me that their parents would never support adoption, Teacher Liu and her husband were remarkably warm to the idea. They did not speak of it in public, but when the foster families were out of earshot, they would often talk gingerly about the little girl, scrolling through photos on their phone. Every so often Teacher Liu's hard, tired face would break and swell and soften at the very thought of the child.

This chapter furthers the work of chapter 3 by analyzing motherhood as a site of ambivalence, stratification, and political maneuvering not just for foster mothers but for orphanage and INGO personnel. In positioning themselves as parenting experts, with elite, Western expertise, orphanage monitors asserted and maintained class hierarchies between themselves and foster parents. In conducting state business in Mandarin, they demonstrated their superior education and cultural status in contradistinction to local, older foster mothers who struggled to understand, speak, or write in Mandarin. Finally, in subtly undermining the normalization of children with disabilities through a discourse that emphasized poverty and pity, middle-aged orphanage monitors revealed their fear of becoming associated with the "needy families" and their "needy alliances." They themselves possessed a need to belong to an upwardly mobile, middle-class existence in which a "normal" biological family is prized and privileged.

Yet, given these tactics for maintaining and emphasizing class differences, it is highly significant that in private, Huilan, Teacher Liu, and other educated working women of their generation confided in me that they secretly resented the sacrifices of their middle-class livelihoods and, ironically, envied the older foster mothers they so arduously ridiculed and policed. Indeed, as I spent time with these middle-aged women I discovered that beneath the criticism lay a deep appreciation and envy for the work and family lives of the older foster mothers. As the family relationships of the foster families commingled with those of the middle-aged monitors themselves, they not only began to question their normative ideas of family but also revealed their own desires for unfulfilled intimacy in family life and their own social vulnerability. Far from simply uncivil, beneath their cold exterior the middle-aged state and INGO actors represented a remarkable and surprising intergenerational, emotional envy that fueled and interlaced their interactions with older foster mothers.

BUREAUCRACY AND CLASS HIERARCHIES

In the rural village of Daling one afternoon, one of the older foster mothers was becoming frustrated with her two-year-old with cerebral palsy, who kept sagging to her knees when the mother attempted to place her on a chair in the courtyard.

One of the ladies in the neighborhood came up and threatened, "If you keep misbehaving like that, you're going to go back to Nanning with them!" She gestured toward Huilan and Older Sister Mo from the orphanage and toward me. Huilan remarked to the older woman that she really should not be saying that, to which another foster mother chimed in, "We say those things all the time."

Huilan then turned to the foster mother of the misbehaving child, whom she was getting ready to interview. As they turned their chairs away from the child she told the foster mother to ignore her, not to draw more attention to the child or her misbehavior. One of the older ladies quipped to the little girl, who was still kneeling on the ground, "Yeah, if you're like that, we don't want you!"

Huilan turned, exasperated. "Not like that; just ignore her!" she reprimanded. And by then the little girl had started to smile again. "See?" Huilan asserted.

But then, a couple of minutes later, when the foster mother and Huilan still had their backs to the little girl and were firmly engrossed in their interview, the girl pushed the chair over the gutter, a large crack in the middle of the alleyway, and tumbled at least three or four feet into the sludge below. We all gasped, and I lifted her out. Thankfully, it was pretty clear that she was okay, and her foster father sweetly gathered her in his arms, carting her inside to help change her dirty clothes and handing her a cooked chicken leg. Meanwhile, however, after Huilan had gone inside with them, the older ladies in the courtyard began to mutter, "See, that way of discipline is ridiculous. You can't ignore a child. See what happens?"

Like Teacher Liu in this chapter's opening vignette, Huilan had sought to discourage the use of threats of abandonment (see chapter 3's analysis of "play") as a disciplinary technique given the psychological trauma children who had literally been abandoned onto the streets or into the orphanage had likely experienced. Indeed, in lieu of threats she had suggested that ignoring the child in question may be the best tactic, but that strategy was undermined by the fall of the child, which was witnessed by everyone present.

Child-rearing, especially discipline, became a site where class differences took on a moral valence as the inadequacies of older foster mothers, linked to their lack of education and low class status, threatened the quality of the parenting they had to offer and noncompliance with state policies. In chapter 3, an older couple's casual and nonchalant approach to the challenges of rearing a child with disabilities in Daling infuriated Director Wang of the Nanning Social Welfare Institute and foster care monitor Huilan. And in chapter 1, the visit to Dengrong's foster home that resulted in a dramatic display of emotion from the traumatized little girl centered around the lack of affection and support her foster mother, Auntie Huang, failed to express toward Dengrong. At the beginning of this chapter, Teacher Liu, alongside two Western INGO volunteers, critiques disciplinary tactics that shame and scold, preferring positive and encouraging interactions. Her willingness to align Mercy Care with Western psychological parenting practices elevates the INGO's status in the Chinese imaginary and in the foster mother's experience. Although Teacher Liu and her coworkers are younger than the foster mothers, their Western education lends them moral superiority.

Critical work in the field of childhood studies by Philippe Ariès (1960), Robin Bernstein (2011), Annette Lareau (2003), and Viviana Zelizer (1994), to name a few, has detailed the class politics of childhood in which only certain children are afforded the luxury of growing up without the pressures of economics, politics, and race. A childhood full of play and innocence, as a cultural ideal, is marked by privilege and inequality. Yet it is often misrecognized and misconstrued as universally applicable. Leslie Wang (2010b) notes how international conflicts regarding childcare and child-rearing in such a setting identify varied and stratified access to resources. In parallel, Sharon Hays's remarkable work, *The Cultural Contradictions of Motherhood* (1996), alongside the work of Shellee Colen (1995), and Faye Ginsburg and Rayna Rapps's concepts of stratified motherhood and reproduction (1995), identify how, within and across societies transnationally, class concepts alternatively uplift and undermine the work of certain kinds of mothers. Therefore, when educated, middle-aged state orphanage and INGO workers uplift the benevolent, emotional, individualized tactics of Western psychological motherhood, they are ardently allying themselves with, enforcing, and emphasizing a global politics of class and privilege that foster families are ill-positioned to attain. Through the everyday policing of modes of disciplining children, the orphanage and INGO workers undermine needy, poor, older women's ability to care effectively for foster children, reinforcing the boundaries of class between the two groups of women.

Furthermore, by firmly taking the upper hand in dispensing advice—on topics such as hygiene to child discipline—as the voice of the state, middle-aged monitors emphasize that certain markers of elite culture and citizenship become requirements for foster parenting. For instance, in late May 2012, Director Wang accompanied Huilan and I on a visit to Daling to celebrate Chinese Children's Day (traditionally celebrated on June 1). Early on the first afternoon, we gathered all of the foster mothers (and a few fathers) with some of their children in the living room of Older Sister Yang, the village foster care monitor. Director Wang and Huilan began their address with high praise for the foster mothers, stating that the rigor of their efforts was evident in the improvements of the children under their care. Huilan highlighted the work of a few mothers in the community, many of whom were new to fostering. "It's not that you all aren't doing a good job," she said, "it's just that these families are doing even more." Director Wang and Huilan practically talked over one another in their excitement, interspersing practical tips regarding parenting ("Bend from the knees when you lift these kids, as some of them are getting heavy") with seasonal announcements ("Now that it's getting warmer, the families whose children can't use the squatty potties in the home should buy a small toilet that disabled kids can start to use themselves").

When Director Wang and Huilan implored the group for feedback, however, the foster mothers fell rather silent. "We don't feel we can express ourselves in Mandarin," one foster mother muttered under her breath. A side conversation drifted into the frustrations families were having with disciplining their disabled children. One foster mother, Auntie Lu, complained loudly that her child would not sleep through the night, but she felt there was no way around it, since his mental disabilities presumably left him unable to string together sleep cycles. "He really can't do anything," she complained. "He doesn't understand anything."[2]

Overhearing, Director Wang and Huilan seized the opportunity as a teaching moment. "Don't say that," the middle-aged orphanage officials scolded the foster mother. "Never put your child down, especially in front of others. Children understand more than you know. You may be frustrated, but you can't talk that way." Auntie Lu looked at the cement below her feet sheepishly.

A few minutes later, Director Wang and Huilan implored Older Sister Yang to get up and give a small speech about the progress she saw in the community, but the village monitor also left her eyes downcast and muttered that she did not have anything profound to say. She merely thanked the mothers, Director Wang, and Huilan for their support, and then sat down abruptly. When Huilan began insisting that each child in the community has her own way of communicating, "like Xiao Pan communicates with her eyes," the mothers gradually spoke up, proudly, but still under their breaths, listing the accomplishments of their children.

The foster mothers commented repeatedly that they did not feel they could adequately express themselves in Mandarin, and fell silent or resorted to side conversations. Meanwhile, the orphanage workers continued to conduct the meeting in Mandarin, making few adjustments despite the foster parents' protests. When I followed the physical therapist, Older Sister Mo, on her house visits in Daling, I noted that most foster mothers there could barely sign their names, yet the orphanage insisted that each parent fill out monthly records of the child's therapy schedule. This bureaucratic priority emphasized both the authority of the orphanage and underlined the contractual nature of the relationship between the orphanage, or the state, and the foster families. But it also referenced a class-based disdain and prejudice against non-Mandarin communication. For instance, in an autism evaluation that took place at the Nanning Municipal Orphanage among a foreign psychological expert, orphanage staff, INGO staff, and a foster mother, the staff complained that the mother not only refused to speak Mandarin but, instead of answering the questions that were translated, "went on and on with story after story" in the presence of the "foreign expert."[3] In fact, orphanage and INGO staff complained incessantly that they could not get many of the mothers to speak Mandarin; interviews and conversations inevitably drifted into the local Cantonese vernacular or, worse, the seemingly infinite variants of the Zhuang minority dialect. An anthropology professor from Hong Kong who had also done research in Guangxi commented to me that many people seemed unable to avoid mixing Mandarin and *baihua*, the local dialect, as they spoke.

Yet for most orphanage and INGO staff this did not actually present a problem of comprehension. Director Wang, Huilan, Older Sister Mo, and Teacher Liu all spoke *baihua* fluently, and Suling, Xiao Wang, and others spoke variants of Zhuang. In most cases, staff members were not complaining about language differences because they could not understand the content of the conversation; instead they complained because speaking Mandarin denoted a certain status and education level, an everyday ability to live a modern Chinese life. In refusing to speak Mandarin these women were communicating not only a certain lack of ability or education but an unwillingness to conform to the language of the state orphanage's processes and protocols, and perhaps a certain defiance toward modern ways of life. These women's inability to speak Mandarin and their lack of communication skills were attributed to their lack of education, which thus often caused orphanage personnel to question their abilities to parent disabled children.

On a visit to a foster home one afternoon, after a foster mother had been complaining that her child had had nothing to eat because she had had a cold, Suling asked, "Has she been eating porridge?"

"Yes, but only porridge," the mother replied, "she hasn't eaten any rice." After we left, Suling went onto complain that foster parents often communicated imprecisely: here the mother was saying the little girl had had nothing to eat for days, when she had actually had porridge. These communication issues were often chocked up to the women's lack of education, or even their "backwardness," but such misunderstandings also seemed to reflect tangible differences in childhood experiences and thus philosophies of child-rearing. It was certainly true that many of these women lacked education, and that their education was interrupted by the Cultural Revolution.[4] Some of them were illiterate, many could hardly use cell phones or computers, and almost all of them complained that they could not help their foster kids with their homework. Yet their varying communication styles became a problem primarily in their interactions with middle-aged caregivers who sought to reform their speech and actions to fit modern, coherent forms.

Therefore, even as the practices of middle-class orphanage monitors highlight cultural and classist politics of mothering, it is also important to note how significantly such power plays flipped the generational script that had long made the senior generation the site of knowledge when it came to child-rearing and childcare in modern China. In his work studying practices among this younger generation, Yan characterizes them as unfilial given their individualist pursuits of pleasure at the expense of their parents in their early twenties (see Yan 2003) and into their experiences of childbearing, child-rearing, and parenting in their thirties and forties. In a later work, Yan characterizes an emerging "neofamilism" in modern China. In contradistinction to traditional familism, which Yan defines as the primacy of family interest over individual interests alongside the correlate values of obligation and self-sacrifice, neofamilism is marked by four distinct features: descending familism, or the directing of resources and energy toward younger generations; intimacy; materialism; and tension between individual and family interests (2018, 5, 11–23).

This last marker of neofamilism, a deeply rooted tension between individual autonomy and family happiness experienced by middle-aged Chinese, seems to be at the heart of the striking ambivalence and concealed envy that I describe in the second half of this chapter. Thus, it is important to consider that aggressive cultural and classist policing of the older generation may come from a place of deep insecurity or hurt, regarding familial change and transition in modern China. Indeed, in this second half of the chapter, I will explore how the lives of Huilan, Teacher Liu, and others in their generation express and palpably give voice to this familial tension, which is ironically played out in their relationships with not just their own families but with lower-class foster families.

INTERGENERATIONAL AMBIVALENCE AND ENVY

INGO and orphanage workers, Huilan and Teacher Liu included, often complained that they had lived a solitary childhood. This was surprising, especially because both Huilan and Teacher Liu grew up in the countryside and with siblings; in their thirties and forties, respectively, they were part of the post-1970s generation, that clearly distinguished itself from the post-1980s generation of only children. Yet, because their parents prioritized education, parents often split residence to support one or two children to get an urban education while others remained home in the countryside. Alternatively, many children from the Guangxi countryside began attending boarding schools when they were in middle school to minimize travel and take advantage of educational opportunities. Another Chinese foster care volunteer remarked, "I was, in a sense, raised by the school. I hardly lived with my parents from the time I was ten or so, because our home was so isolated in the countryside that I spent all my time in the dorms. My parents called to remind me of their sacrifice and implored me to study hard."

Huilan and Teacher Liu recalled childhoods spent bent over desks studying into the wee hours of the night, goaded by parents who piled their hopes for a bright future upon their slight shoulders. "Our parents weren't nurturing or understanding or kind," another informant commented. "They were hardened by their own experience during the revolution and determined to make something out of us. Their love was contingent on our success, and we knew it, so we studied hard. We treated it like a job." These middle-aged women were bitter that they had lost their childhood to schooling, and they blamed their parents for the loss.

Thus, the discontents and disconnects of the middle-generation INGO and orphanage staff were often supplanted onto older foster parents, who were at once criticized for being too indulgent and at other times too strict. The INGO and orphanage staff worried when foster parents could not help their foster children with homework, but they also resented that their own parents had never been there to help either. Their concerns about spoiling, meanwhile, mirrored the critiques they had of their own live-in grandparent caregivers regarding their only children. They charged that elderly foster parents were not rational thinkers when it came to discipline. They repeatedly alleged that it was important for parents to *jiang daoli* (reason with children), but older parents did not necessarily see kids as rational beings who could be reasoned with. Instead, to the older generation, repetition, force, and shaming were sometimes considered effective tools for teaching a lesson (see my analysis of "play" in chapter 3).

But there was certainly an ambivalence to these complaints: the middle generation simultaneously feared and admired the control the senior generation had over children. Several times when I went over to Auntie Li's house to provide English tutoring to foster child Pei Pei and her older sister Kaili (Auntie Li's biological daughter), Auntie Li asked if her niece, Yile, could sit in on the lesson as well. So the four of us sat in the Li family's cramped living room at the short table in miniature chairs as I struggled to get the three girls to complete their English homework. Auntie Li complained to me that Kaili was falling desperately behind in English, but she did not have the "big money," as she called it, to pay for the expensive training schools. Pei Pei, who was a good student, joyfully joined in the fun, but Yile was clearly the star student: she whipped through books that the other two girls could not begin to understand.

On one occasion Auntie Li and her younger sister-in-law, Mrs. Hu, walked me down the stairs and into the alleyway, and Mrs. Hu thrust a bottle of face lotion into my hands, lamenting that they had nothing to give me for all of my troubles. Then the two women began to hound me about their daughters. Mrs. Hu often asked me about the nature of my communication with Yile; on one occasion, when Auntie Li was not present, Mrs. Hu confided in me that she felt quite sorry for Pei Pei and her younger sister Yuping (also a foster child), but also for biological daughter Kaili, the oldest, whom she felt was often neglected because of the challenge of raising three children. She described Auntie Li's situation as "pitiable" because she had to take in so many children to make ends meet. Yet Mrs. Hu's own eyes welled up with tears when she lamented the many hours she and her husband spent working, which meant they barely knew their own child. She remarked that despite Auntie Li's desperate family situation, they were so close; the extra time Auntie Li had to spend with her children at home was something Mrs. Hu firmly envied.

She could not imagine raising "children like Auntie Li's," she said (both foster children had mild physical disabilities), and yet, she worried that her own daughter had become spoiled when over at Auntie Li's house, because at home she had no one with whom to share or communicate on a daily basis. She complained that Yile was getting rebellious and their communication was strained. Indeed, I had heard the young girl mock her mother's poor Mandarin, and Kaili and her cousin often whipped out their phones and giggled behind their mothers' backs. The tearful young mother asked me if I knew of any way to prevent this type of rebellion. Always wary of being put in these positions of authority, especially with no children of my own, I replied that I thought it was natural for young girls to be a bit rebellious, but nothing seemed to assuage Mrs. Hu.

While Auntie Li worried about some of the same concerns, commenting that in her day, rebellious children would have been beaten, she mostly troubled over Kaili's grades, Pei Pei's precarious foster care situation, and Yuping's possibly impending adoption. She noted that a young couple had come by to meet Yuping, but the orphanage had not told her anything about whether or when she would be adopted. When on one of the numerous occasions she complained to me that Pei Pei might be sent back to the orphanage, I implored her to speak with the orphanage officials about her concerns. She scoffed, repeating the remark I had heard so often from others: "To them, we're nothing more than *baomus* [domestic servants]."

What is so interesting about these interactions between Auntie Li and Mrs. Hu is that even though they are not institutional relationships like those between the older foster mothers and state and INGO workers, their intrafamilial dynamics reference similar intergenerational ambivalence, tension, and envy. While Mrs. Hu worries about her daughter's solitary childhood and her own lack of time to invest in it, she also pities her older sister-in-law's large household, in which she worries that children suffer from poverty and neglect. Meanwhile, Auntie Li concerns herself with the relationships of these children within and outside the family unit, and specifically their emotional security. Such a paradox suggests that while middle-aged parents often assume that seniors foster for financial gain, perhaps it is their own financial insecurity that is being projected onto others.

Furthermore, Mrs. Hu's attitudes toward children with disabilities mirror those of many of the middle-aged orphanage monitors' covert fear and distance. Although, in Daling, Director Wang and Huilan chide foster mothers for "putting down their children," especially in front of others, in chapter 3 an INGO director and employees admit to questioning whether foster mothers only take in children with disabilities for the money and that they, themselves, would be unlikely to raise or support these "difficult" and "pitiable" children. One could argue that Director Wang and Huilan are more concerned with appearances than with their own attitudes toward disabled children. Indeed, in chapter 5, we will further explore how attitudes of exceptionalism toward children with disabilities and their foster families, even when seemingly positive, often serve to maintain social distance and abnormality between disabled and able-bodied populations.

Mrs. Hu self-consciously shudders at the "pitiable" situation her older sister-in-law finds herself in because her family is so needy and desperate. Here her ambivalence is striking: she struggles to maintain her distance, yet she recognizes something attractive in the neediness that is so palpable—a neediness that is met in their brash intimacy and love for one another. Indeed, Mrs. Hu expresses a surprising envy for her "pitiable" elder sister-in-law Auntie Li when she contrasts her daughter's spoiled and disrespectful nature with the close camaraderie she experiences amid the Lis' poor, yet intimate, family unit. Even if such intimacy is idealized and contrived, it is both notable and ironic, especially given the harsh critique middle-aged parents often have of elderly foster parents. Mrs. Hu expresses simultaneous disgust and intrigue at the needy dependency she experiences in Auntie Li's household. How can it be that Auntie Li, who is so poor and pitiable, seems so free and satisfied in her makeshift, contractual, temporary family?

CHAPTER SUMMARY: AN EMOTIONAL STATE

In chapter 1, Huilan and Older Sister Mo seem satisfied by the emotional outburst they elicit from Dengrong, in which the previously despondent child clings to her new foster parents and calls out "Baba!" to her new foster father through tears. But that night, as Huilan and I washed the dust from our hands and feet, getting ready for bed in a small hotel room in Daling, I shuddered, pondering what had smacked of emotional manipulation in Dengrong's foster home earlier that day. While I was certainly troubled by Dengrong's foster mom calling her lazy, I was also very uncomfortable with the way in which Huilan and Older Sister Mo saw fit to coax desirable emotions from both Dengrong and her foster parents by referencing the alternative of returning to the orphanage for Dengrong or the contribution of Dengrong's foster father's wages as some sort of obligation for Dengrong to love him.

With her hair still wet and piled atop her head, and her body ensconced in a towel, Huilan seemed decidedly less authoritative, vulnerable even. She perched upon the bed next to mine. "Lin En," she asked, "how often does your husband tell you he loves you?"

"Everyday, I think." The words escaped my mouth instinctively, before I could find a way to soften them or contemplate why Huilan would suddenly ask such a question. "Why do you ask?"

"Well, that's just not something we say to each other—husbands and wives—in China. I'm not sure I remember my husband ever saying that. I mean I can tell he loves me—like, I guess, by what he does—but he doesn't say it," she murmured. "You know what, Lin En? These kids, they're like my children. I mean,

I was there when they were abandoned to the orphanage. When they lived there, I was there everyday; when they cried, when they laughed, I watched them grow. And when they go into foster homes, I can't believe how well they're doing. And I'm so happy . . ." Her voice trailed off. "But they also get to spend so much time together—these old men and women, they can be with their children all day. And I'm with them, while my husband, my in-laws, and my daughter are back at home."

I am sure I muttered some platitude about all the good that Huilan was doing. She had become one of my dearest friends during all the time we spent traveling together to and from Daling; she often commented on how lovely it was to have my company, because she would usually have to make all these trips alone. But in this moment, as in the ones inside Dengrong's foster home, or others when Huilan had cried bitter tears over her father's death or stared wistfully at the karst peaks as we rode on the bus, I was struck by the emotional complexity within which she lived and worked. For Huilan and Teacher Liu, the seeming boundaries that they sought to effect between themselves (as INGO and state orphanage workers) and Chinese foster families on account of class or institutions were actually woefully porous and permeable. As they ostensibly struggled with regulating relationships between foster mothers and foster children, with effecting proper affection and bonding, they struggled equally with the consequences of their own sacrifices and the lacks and challenges in their own familial relationships.

I realized that underneath some of the disparaging comments foster care monitors like Huilan made about foster mothers or their seemingly manipulative efforts to reform them lay a deep-seated envy and a personal longing for the emotional intimacy they so vicariously and eagerly sought to effect in foster families. Underneath the seeming austerity of policing contractual relationships that struggled to elevate lower-class women to upper-class parenting practices lay a murky, emotionally fraught ambivalence that left middle-class women struggling to build family relationships within a societal context in which social roles were constantly shifting under their feet.

Neofamilism is an intimate turn in Chinese family life; but whereas Yan's initial work demonstrated the "triumph of conjugality" over the patriarchal order (2003), dependence upon parental support among these young parents actually serves to depress conjugal intimacy. As Yan puts it, "the rise in intergenerational intimacy is paired with a decline in conjugal intimacy" (2018, 16). This is adamantly apparent in Huilan's wistful desires for her husband's affection; yet her own guilt and sadness at the fact that she must spend so much time away from her young child and aging parents in order to do her work with foster families also leaves her deeply ambivalent about whether personal sacrifice is worth her own familial discord. Indeed, what I think my fieldwork serves to illustrate is the profound tension young people like Huilan experience between pursuing their individual interests and supporting their family interests, and how the desire for familial intimacy is not necessarily synonymous with the experience of intimacy. Hence, Huilan and other middle-aged orphanage and INGO monitors are far from classist cultural elites, but rather find themselves emotionally embedded and envious of the very intergenerational intimacy fostered by their own efforts yet withheld from them personally.

What my relationship with Huilan and other state orphanage and INGO workers also taught me is that far from public and scholarly perception, the Chinese state was engaged in surprising, overtly emotional work as it navigated and arbitrated the politics of foster care. As Huilan's predicament illustrates, despite her own professionalism, private and public concerns for state orphanage and INGO monitors were not discontinuous but rather complicated the cultural notions of family and the character of the state in the practice of foster care. As we shall see in the following chapters, need is never neutral or acontextual; thus, this chapter demonstrates how state workers struggle to effect their needs for emotional and familial intimacy in tension with the lives of the foster families they manage.

In chapter 5 we expand our context to consider how the exceptionalism of foster families reinforces disability as an abnormal category within the Chinese imaginary. Furthermore, the abnormality of such children and their families is reinforced by the perception that such families exist merely to foster the formation of Western, "forever" families. This further compounds the politicization of need within a global context, in which some needs render families exceptional, temporary, and replaceable, whereas other need is subordinated and suppressed in order that family hierarchies be maintained.

5 · REPLACEABLE FAMILIES?

Director Wang, the woman in charge of foster care at the Nanning Municipal Orphanage, was proud of the people of Daling. After all, her own husband had grown up in the small village outside the county seat. He, like over 90 percent of people in Daling's county, spoke the Zhuang language that Director Wang, herself a speaker of a Cantonese-style *baihua* (vernacular), found so *buhao ting* (unpleasant to listen to). But she laughed knowingly as she said this, and the foster moms did not seem to fault her for her opinions—or at least their discontent did not show in the way they coddled and cuddled the children with physical and mental disabilities that now combed their village streets. Since October 2011, Director Wang and the Nanning state orphanage monitors had placed twenty-four kids with disabilities from the municipal orphanage into foster homes in a small village outside Daling. And things were going really, really well.

In contrast to the complaints about city folk, the familiar refrain uttered by the municipal orphanage workers and international nongovernmental organization (INGO) staff was that the people of Daling were different; they were "special" (*hen tebie*), "exceptional," or even "unusual." Orphanage workers frequently contrasted the people of Daling with others as *hen bu yiyang* (completely different, or "other") and commended them for being a *bangyang*, a shining example or model to other foster parents. "They really love these kids, when no one else would," explained Director Wang, smiling. "I don't know why they're different, but they just are. They love these kids just like their own [*gen tamende haizi yiyang*]." This assessment, and the success of the Daling project, traveled rapidly across the region. When I visited orphanages in the neighboring city of Qinzhou and Yongning County just six months later, I found that they had all heard of the Nanning Municipal Orphanage's project in Daling.

But Daling families and mothers were not the only ones who were referred to as possessing a special ability to love children with disabilities. Rather, in countless interactions with Chinese foster parents in the capital city of Nanning, where I conducted the bulk of my fieldwork, these parents self-consciously referred to their parenting of foster children as temporary, acknowledging and repositioning children's futures with families in America, the Netherlands, or

Spain. In chapter 1, Xiaoyuan's foster mother was beside herself, desperate for her daughter to be adopted to a "great family," as she called it, in America. As she and other foster mothers playfully teased their foster children about whether they would like to go to America, have an American mother, or be part of an American family, they acknowledged that their mothering and fostering would support the ultimate fate of their children being adopted into foreign families. When I asked foster families why they felt these children were better off with families in America, one foster mother replied, "Because they're kind, they want these children when no one else would.... I don't understand it, they're just special . . . I guess they really care."

WHAT IS SO SPECIAL ABOUT DALING?

Only in returning to my fieldwork years after the fact was I confronted by the striking symmetry between the exceptionalism attributed to both Daling foster families and future adoptive Western families. Whereas as an American, the racialized and economic stereotypes in these invocations of a special kindness and altruism among foreign adoptive mothers disturbed me, I gradually came to scrutinize a similar reductionism regarding the constructed "specialness" of the Daling foster mothers. I was uncomfortable with the way that specialness was often attributed by state orphanage workers to some pure, rural character that ignored both the subordinate social, economic, and political standing that may have compelled foster families to take in children in the first place and the hard work of caregiving that they were willing to do day in and day out for disabled children. In addition, that rhetoric of "special," "exceptional," and "unusual" served to further the distance between state orphanage workers and the foster families, just as the foster families afforded a special character to Western adoptive families that positioned them as familial outsiders.

In this chapter, I break again from the primary narratives of Dengrong, Meili, and Pei Pei to consider the exceptional cases of foster children who are rejected, marginalized, and unlikely to be adopted; the "special" foster families who care for them; and the "special" Western families—"forever" families—that orphanage officials and foster parents alike presume will adopt them. By beginning with the case of Jiaqi, a disabled teenage girl who is rejected from the special foster care pilot project in the village of Daling, I first demonstrate that such a dismissal is exceedingly rare. Whereas one might presume—given the rampant discrimination toward children with disabilities evidenced in the literature on China (Holroyd 2003; Qian 2014)—that such rejections are commonplace, Jiaqi's rejection shows just how strong a culture of familism is, not merely among biological families in China but also among foster families. Thus, although Jiaqi's inability to fulfill her social role to her family and her community references the familism that Chinese scholars have deemed central to Chinese social life for centuries (Fei 1992; Potter and Potter 1990; Qian 2014; Y. Yan 2003), it also shows that many disabled children can find belonging through foster families and local community in China. Subsequent study of Daling village's exceptionalism shows, however, that foster families' special abilities for care, and the exceptional progress of children with disabilities, often serve to further marginalize children with disabilities as "abnormal" (Qian 2014). Because recognizing the parents and the children as special also amounts to limiting their abilities or pitying their unfortunate status, I query what future such children have in this liminal state of foster care.

Finally, in analyzing the case of Pengfei, a young boy with multiple disabilities whom orphanage officials and his foster mother hoped would be given a diagnosis and also be adopted to America, I argue that Western desire for such disabled children, alongside the presumed replaceability of their foster families, renders them liminal within Chinese kinship and society. Even if such children are not eventually adopted through intercountry adoption (ICA), the perception *that they will be* (on both sides) reinforces the interrelated beliefs that disability is a condition that must be overcome through Western medical expertise, disabled persons are not welcome or able to function in Chinese society, and foster families do not have the resources to support such children with disabilities given that they are impermanent. Therefore, the demand for disabled children in ICA, however unintentionally, works in tandem with the practice of foster care to perpetuate the expansion of white, permanent, Western, adoptive, ableist, and heteronormative families at the expense of Chinese foster families.

JIAQI'S REJECTION

I will never forget Jiaqi: her chubby, pimpled face, the tattered sweater that hugged her round belly, and her gruff voice. Jiaqi had an awkward way of following our cohort of orphanage and INGO workers about when we came to Daling, a habit of staring and pointing, and sometimes she would drag her little sister so brusquely that the younger girl would all but have her face in the mud before Jiaqi noticed. Jiaqi could not be trusted to do childcare or any of the other tasks older children in villages like these were often expected to do, but then, neither could her foster mother, an aging woman whose hair had long gone white and whose husband was always off working in the fields.

Jiaqi's foster mom had taken in Jiaqi and two-year-old autistic Lili the previous October, but Lili, like many autistic children, refused to make eye contact and showed no signs of hearing or heeding her foster mother's speech, running up and down the dirt path through the town, and from door to door, leaving her old foster mother far behind. When we had come to visit the family months earlier, the foster mother had not been especially critical of Jiaqi, though she was a little mystified; she did not seem to understand that Jiaqi's mental capabilities were limited, even as she was growing into a young woman. The foster monitors noted that Jiaqi had grown plump in the home of this auntie, and the foster mother proudly commented on what a good eater her foster daughter was. Jaiqi's round-ness was a sign of being cared for by a mother who placed heaping bowls of steaming porridge in front of her morning, noon, and night.

Jiaqi was very happy in the village. She relished her freedom of going door-to-door, calling out "ayi" (auntie) and "jie" (older sister), simple kinship terms that expressed her delight in living life amongst a family and a village community. Jiaqi had been in the orphanage much longer than other children. The first time she had really left the institution's walls was to come here to the little town nes-tled within the craggy mountains. Hence, there were elements of her newfound freedom that she had come to abuse, creeping out of her home at night and standing outside the modest homes of the neighbors, calling from the street for her friends to come out and play. She had begun to hang around a group of boys her own age with Down syndrome who lived around the corner, and as these developments had been reported back to the orphanage by the village monitor, the orphanage had begun to worry.

And so, that morning over noodles at a hole-in-the-wall restaurant in the middle of the county seat, the women from the orphanage had told me that they were thinking of taking Jiaqi back that day. When I asked them why, they men-tioned the concerns for her safety and that she had become disruptive. I com-plained that it was a shame; for them, however, it was not the first time a foster placement had not worked out, that a child whom they knew had to "come home" (to the orphanage), as they put it.

The morning proceeded much like that of any other, but this time Huilan and I were accompanied by Older Sister Mo, the physical therapist, as we traversed the short streets of the little village, ducking in behind the shops to find life carrying on: the feeding and changing of diapers, and laughing and crying, within the concrete walls of the narrow homes often tucked behind their places of work. But when we began to weigh the little children in the crowded living room of Older Sister Yang, the village monitor, Jiaqi wandered inside and stepped on the scale. The foster mothers and fathers, crowding around with their little ones, whom they steadied and cradled in their firm arms, began to chastise her: "She's so fat, nobody wants her, she doesn't listen, she's not obedient, you should take this one back to the orphanage!"

Even Older Sister Mo commented on how fat little Jiaqi was as she perched on the scale, eerily silent in the face of all the accusations flying around the room. "She doesn't listen, does she?" Older Sister Mo responded. Then turning to Jiaqi, she said, "You need to do what your foster mother tells you."

Gradually it became apparent to me that the decision had been made at least a month earlier, and the orphanage monitors were merely waiting for the right moment to execute their plan. The white-haired foster mom came and stood in the doorway, dragging bewildered Lili by the hand and complaining to no one in particular, "She [Jiaqi] runs about the streets at night, and I've had it with her. She's disobedient. You need to take her back to the orphanage. Take her back and exchange her for another one!"

Huilan, the orphanage monitor, quietly took the foster mother aside, and said, "Yes Auntie, but we'll talk about it later." After a few minutes the old lady and Lili wandered back in. This time Huilan asked Jiaqi, "How would you like to go on a trip for the day and have fun with this pretty lady [Older Sister Mo]? Would you like that?" She prodded Jiaqi until she grunted "Hao, hao" (Okay, okay). Huilan took the foster mother aside and explained that she was going to take Jiaqi back to the orphanage because, if anything happened to her, it would be on her and Older Sister Mo's shoulders. She told the mother that they should go over to the house so Jiaqi could collect her things and say goodbye.

They began to walk Jiaqi, her foster mother, and little Lili down the street toward her home, and gradually a crowd of foster mothers and children and neighbors began to follow, exclaiming, "Let's go! Look, they're taking Jiaqi back to the orphanage!" The crowd filed into the home behind Jiaqi, her foster mom, and the women from the orphanage, peering into the little window to her room as Jiaqi packed her things. Not wanting to be part of the spectacle or the group of spectators, I took little Lili, whom the foster mom had left on her own, and we sat on the steps. Lili slumped to the step and was eerily still, nestling into my arms for the first time since I had met her, seemingly stunned by what little she could grasp of the situation.

I could hear the orphanage women's chorus of "Kuai yidian," urging Jiaqi to hurry up, gather her things, and get dressed to go. When Jiaqi emerged from her bare little room, the crowd stood watching. Huilan and Older Sister Mo asked her, "Well, do you have anything to say for yourself? Anything to say to your foster mother?" Gradually their questions turned to commands, "Say something to her; at least tell her goodbye." And when Jiaqi did not say anything, they commanded, "Say goodbye," to which Jiaqi grunted "Bye bye," hardly raising her head to look at her foster mother.

The crowd followed us onto the street, with Huilan and the neighbors now goading Jiaqi to say goodbye. The foster mom began wailing about how unthinkable and ungrateful it was that Jiaqi did not even want to say goodbye. How could the girl be so callous, after everything she had done for her? Huilan physically moved Jiaqi to face her mom again and say goodbye. As we walked off, Huilan kept telling Jiaqi that we were taking her to Daling, the county seat, to have fun, but meanwhile the neighbors murmured about her bad behavior and how she had to go back to Nanning.

Later, Older Sister Yang would murmur to Huilan about how the old woman's husband had recently gone into Daling proper to work in a factory and how, without him around, she could hardly keep track of Lili running about. And

Huilan mentioned that the foster mother did not understand, and she wanted another child, but how indeed they needed to look for a different family for Lili. When Jiaqi wandered up, Older Sister Yang smiled sweetly, asking her if she wanted to stay with her foster mom or go with this big sister, persisting repeatedly even when Jiaqi did not answer. As we led Jiaqi down the country path, by the river and out of the town, away from her old home, we saw the chubby chicken that Huilan had earlier said would be so tasty, and Older Sister Mo smirked at how it waddled. She told Jiaqi, "That's what you're going to be like when you get older, if you keep eating," and she and Huilan laughed.

We stopped in a rice noodle shop to grab lunch, and the women asked Jiaqi repeatedly whether her foster mother had fed her. She vehemently denied she had eaten, but when the bowl of noodles was placed in front of her she finally said that yes, she had already eaten lunch. Exasperated, the women told her to eat up anyway, and we all hurriedly scarfed down the soggy bowls of noodles, pressed for time to make the bus back into the big city. While we sat there, Huilan remarked that Jiaqi had made a lot of progress in terms of speaking and becoming more outgoing in the village, but she just was not right in the head, so when it came to sex and getting older, they just could not take the chance of having her out here, so far from the orphanage.

We got into a rickshaw with another foster mother and Older Sister Yang, and they all began to pepper Jiaqi with questions about whether she would come back to visit her foster mom, and when she finally said no, they all chuckled. When one of the women said something about Nanning, Jiaqi asked about Daling, and Huilan hurriedly replied, "We're going to Daling and then somewhere farther." The other foster mother told a story about how Jiaqi was out one night and went to one of the older boys' houses, and was yelling at the corner for him over and over, waking everybody up. Huilan mentioned that she thought a woman that Older Sister Yang had taken her to see would be a good new foster mother for Lili.

Shortly after we got onto the bus, Jiaqi, seated next to Older Sister Mo, began to throw up, and Older Sister Mo gasped, gathering up plastic bags, and scolding Jiaqi, "You don't understand, you have to hold the bag like this. Oh, it's so hard to teach her anything!" But when Older Sister Mo got off the bus to go to the bathroom, Huilan, who was feeling carsick herself, produced some tangerines from her bag and wordlessly slipped them to Jiaqi.

As the bus started moving and Jiaqi threw up again, Older Sister Mo chastised Huilan, "Why would you give her those?"

"She was crying," Huilan replied weakly.

"So let her cry!" Older Sister Mo snapped back.

A few weeks later I inquired about Jiaqi and how she was readjusting to the orphanage environment after what I considered to be a traumatic experience. "Oh, she's used to it here, this is where she grew up, she's doing fine," was the brusque response from Huilan. I never saw her again.

THE MORAL EXCEPTIONALISM OF DALING

I thought of Jiaqi often. I thought of how the gossiping around her unsightly appearance and her disobedient behavior served to unify the community against those who do not play by the rules, those who cheat, or those who are unable to fulfill their social roles, even though in this case the transgressor was just a child. Jiaqi's childlike behavior at the age of fourteen was misunderstood in a tight-knit community where each individual was evaluated by whether he or she fulfilled a proper social role. Jiaqi, unlike typical teenagers, was unable to care for her younger sister, Lili, and she was unable to interact with friends and neighbors appropriately. She was removed because her disruptive, unruly, and "abnormal" behavior posed a threat not just to her well-being but to the entire community and its social order.

In their work studying contemporary Chinese children with disabilities, both Eleanor Holroyd (2003) and Linliang Qian (2014) describe these disruptions that disability presents to the cultural logic of familism and the wider society. Much as I discuss in chapter 2, Holroyd confirms that among parents caring for disabled children in Hong Kong, disability was often experienced as a "disruption to the parent-child order" and a threat to the cyclical and reciprocal enactment of caregiving responsibilities that facilitates cultural personhood in a Chinese context (2003, 8, 18). This helps explain not only how Jiaqi failed to fulfill her own social obligations but how her malfeasance drew attention to a broader disruption of the natural social order. Yet, under their breaths, Huilan and others from the orphanage acknowledged that one of the major reasons they did not want to keep Jiaqi in the community any longer was because her foster mother could not provide the necessary care that Jiaqi needed.

Indeed, what I perceived as a deep injustice was that Jiaqi was seemingly scapegoated not just for her own misbehavior but also that of her aging foster mother. Such hierarchical relationships of community social roles complicate the personal trust that scholars such as Fei Xiaotong (1992) and Yunxiang Yan (2003) have emphasized in rural communities such as the village of Daling. As Sulamith Heins Potter and Jack Potter remark in their 1990 ethnography *China's Peasants*, children are not born with intrinsic value, but find value through the fulfillment of social relationships. Thus, they argue, "child care is a means to an end, a form of long-range self-interest" (1990, 229). Comparing the humanity that makes even *The Pirates of Penzance* sympathetic to the plight of the orphan in Western literature with the pity of the bandits for an old woman who will be left helpless in the world if they kill her only son in *The Book of Filial Piety*, Potter and Potter remind us that in China the moral emphasis is on caring for the old, whereas in the West it revolves around caring for the young (1990, 228–229). In their words, "[In China] to have children is to be protected from the pitiable situation, analogous to being orphaned, of being left without care in one's old age.

When villagers speak of having children so that old people may be taken care of, they are invoking a whole complex of cultural ideas embodying a definition of happiness resting on dependent security" (1990, 229). They stress that these cultural ideals in China exist at the level of assumptions that saturate, often subconsciously, everyday life for villagers. Although their ethnography was written over thirty years ago, and much has changed in the way of traditions of filial piety and family relations in China (see the introduction to this book and chapters 2–4), Jiaqi's rejection in Daling reveals the extent to which these assumptions regarding social hierarchies remain relatively intact or, at least, in tension (Y. Yan 2018).

Hence, while personal trust between villagers in Daling may preserve a certain moral culture that orphanage workers observe to be special or extraordinary, this moral culture necessarily makes its own exclusions based on individuals'— and especially children's—abilities or inabilities to fulfill their social roles. As Qian notes, a familist norm, which idealizes the family as the "axis of all other social relations," causes children who grow up anywhere other than with their family to be deemed not just "unfortunate" but "abnormal" (2014, 255, 256). Thus, among Qian's informants, a range of adults and children who sought to undertake philanthropic efforts and charity in state orphanages in China (with children with disabilities), this familist attitude of pitying such children or finding them useless given their "presumed unrelatedenss and isolation from responsibility" served to reinforce this stereotype of abnormality—ironically, further stigmatizing and ostracizing such children (2014, 261–262, 256).

A similar effect, however unknowingly, seemed to be operative among the orphanage monitors who removed Jiaqi, despite what I believe to be a sincere care and concern for her and her safety. Although Huilan and others from the orphanage acknowledged that one of the major reasons they did not want to keep Jiaqi in the community any longer was because her foster mother could not provide the necessary care that she needed, outwardly Jiaqi was blamed for her disobedience and her poor behavior; even her appearance became a subject of criticism. Thus, Jiaqi's ample weight, ironically a symbol of care and health among younger children, became the object of scrutiny among the community. While it is most accurately a signifier of her foster mother's neglect, no one dared to question the foster mother—an insider and an elder—regarding the lack of fulfillment of her social role. Instead, Jiaqi's weight became a symbol of her own undoing, her own lack of control, obedience, excess, and abnormality, for which she was ostracized from her foster family and the village community.

It is important to note that familism, arguably the vehicle for social rehabilitation for both foster mothers and foster children with disabilities in urban contexts, becomes their undoing in Daling. Yet, contrary to Qian's conclusions that a normal and repressive group of people excludes and reforms those with disabilities to consolidate their power (2014, 276), it is important to consider that in order to maintain familist cultural logic it may only be certain children with disabilities who are willfully and harshly excluded. After all, among the children in Daling, Jiaqi was the only one I ever saw returned to the orphanage in such dramatic fashion. In her case, her inability to be socially rehabilitated—like other children or even foster mothers—to make herself of service to the community may be more aptly attributed to her foster mother's failings than the severity of Jiaqi's disabilities or her inability to fulfill her social role. The familist commitments in Daling conspire to draw attention to her body—both her weight, as an emblem of her unruliness, and her disability, as the marker of her disobedience—rather than a mutually unsupportive family relationship or unfit parenting as the reason for her dismissal from the community. Here her abnormality is scapegoated so that the community can not only continue with its familist commitments but can continue fostering, preserving its special and extraordinary character.

THE SPECIAL, THE UNUSUAL, AND THE ABNORMAL

One of the reasons the foster care pilot project in Daling was so notable was that the goals for such a project, often proudly articulated by Director Wang, Huilan, and even local Daling officials, seemed quite distinct from goals that once supported the orphanage as a total institution or traditional foster care placements of typical kids bound for adoption. "Out here in the countryside in Daling," Huilan once said, surveying the expanse of green rice paddies nestled among Guangxi's famous karst formations that jut toward the sky, "our hope is that the children can learn some life skills. They can farm alongside their parents, they can sweep and help out around the house and become members of the community." With contrast to those children placed around the city and outskirts of Nanning, the futures of the twenty-four children who were placed in rural foster homes in Daling were often talked about with a rare, hopeful, permanence.

Here Huilan spoke explicitly about the abilities of the children (with no mention of their disabilities) to take on local household roles and to become integrated into the wider local community. The implication is that the life skills that disabled children would learn would grant them a place in these households and in the village that would solidify their family futures. Whereas many other disabled children who were placed in foster homes in Nanning heard frequently about the impermanence of these placements and the futures and families for which they were destined in foreign countries ("Would you like to live in America?" "Your future mommy is in America!"), the future that was imagined by the state orphanage personnel and local officials for these children included a productive, if not simple, lifestyle in the village of Daling.

By many standards, then, and not just the goals of the project, the Daling people themselves were construed as peculiar yet extraordinary: orphanage workers described repeatedly how they did not understand why Daling people were so exceptional and so much more willing to love these children as their own. Indeed, just a few months after the children had been placed in Daling, personnel from multiple INGOs; Director Zhou, the deputy director of the orphanage; and several others rode in on the bus with us to Daling to celebrate the new foster care placement and treat the mothers, children, and local Daling officials to a lunch to thank them for their participation. It was a wild afternoon of struggling to shove chopsticks full of duck and chicken into the kids' mouths, toasting with *bai jiu* (rice wine liquor) and beer, and affirmation from all sides of their commitment to the foster care project. Over and over the refrain rang out from Director Zhou and others that Daling people were special because they loved these kids just as if they were their own.

As she commended the village head on his willingness to support these children and their families, Director Zhou dipped her tiny goblet, as was customary, to clink below the gruff man's glass in a sign of respect. "These children couldn't walk or talk when they first came to Daling," the village head bragged. "But now, look around the room, listen to the chatter. Did you see them, sturdy and strong, on their way in? These things that they couldn't do, they've come to Daling, and now they can!"

A minute later Director Zhou leaned in and asked the village head about when these same young children would start attending the local kindergarten. He fumbled for his words and then hastily muttered that he just was not sure if these kids were smart enough for kindergarten, he would get back to the orphanage staff on that, he would have to ask around.

I thought back to a conversation that had happened just a few months earlier when we had visited eight-year-old Hongmei, the product of several urban foster care placements gone awry, in Daling. With minimal deformity to one of her eyes, Hongmei was small for her age, and had what the orphanage had described as numerous learning disabilities. Hongmei had performed poorly in urban schools, but she had also attended school only sporadically because her urban foster mother had been negligent. Given her experience in the city, orphanage officials felt she was a prime candidate for life in Daling.

Just a few months after being placed in Daling, Hongmei was thriving. She had come to her foster placement with what everyone called "bad habits" given that her previous foster mother had encouraged her to lie to orphanage monitors. When she first arrived in Daling she ate out of the garbage, lied to her foster parents, and exhibited a lack of social and cognitive skills. but after just a couple of months living with her new foster parents and sisters, her foster mother happily reported that she was able to "reason with her" and Hongmei showed interest and aptitude in learning simple spelling and math.

Yet the same day that Hongmei proudly wrote her name for us on a scrap of paper, introduced us to her new *nai nai* (paternal grandmother), and rattled off some new phrases in the local Zhuang language, I stood with Suling and a neighbor as they talked about her progress.

"I think she's ready for kindergarten," Suling, the Mercy Care worker, said excitedly.

"Oh, I don't know," said a neighbor—herself a foster mom to two older boys, one with cerebral palsy and the other developmentally delayed—with a shy smile.

"Why not?" Suling asked.

"Well, she's too old for kindergarten," the neighbor replied matter-of-factly.

"But she's developmentally delayed, so she needs to work at her own pace. She'd be fine in a kindergarten classroom," Suling urged.

"But these types of kids, they're different, like my Hengwei. If they were in the classroom, it really wouldn't be fair to all the other kids. They would bring all the other kids down," the foster mom replied. "I just don't think it's possible for them to go to school." Suling kept pressing, but the foster mother giggled nervously.

That evening a similar conversation escalated quickly over a meal of *kuaican* (fast food) in a local eatery. Huilan, Older Sister Mo, Suling, and I were exhausted after a full day of visiting with the foster families and had gone into Daling to spend the night. We ordered steaming plates of food and discussed the events of the day together. When we began to talk about Hongmei's much improved status, Suling spoke up. "Hongmei should go to kindergarten," she said.

"I don't know," Huilan hedged.

Older Sister Mo nodded indicating agreement with Suling, and added, "The foster mom should at least go to the school and ask. She hasn't even done that, and Hongmei really wants to learn. She needs to be around other kids, normal kids, not hanging around with those 'older Downs boys' down the street all the time."

"But you don't know the history of this project," Huilan complained. "I'm not sure we can ask the parents to push the school. Hongmei will stick out, she'll be uncomfortable there. She's so much older. Can you imagine the pressure? Do you remember what the pressure was like when we were kids? She can't take that kind of pressure!"

"You can't protect her from things like that," Suling shot back. "You can't protect her from life. This is the real world; don't you want her to live in it?"

"But I know what these kids can handle," Huilan retorted. "I've grown up with them in the orphanage. I can ask about kindergarten, but I'm not sure anything's going to change. I'm not sure about the upper limits of Hongmei's abilities, and neither are you. I don't want her to get hurt and to fail and for this community to suffer. I just want what's best for her, too."

Suling turned her eyes away.

In these interactions, the "special" character and care of Daling and its foster parents is complicated by their unwillingness, as well as the village head's unwillingness, to appreciate the right or ability of these disabled children to participate in state-sponsored education. The contrast between the jovial atmosphere of celebration, in which the children's developmental milestones are celebrated as a practical accomplishment owing to Daling's special character, and the village head's mutterings that the children were not smart enough for kindergarten suggests that the specialness of Daling and its people was not without its boundaries.

What is even more intriguing, perhaps, is the extent to which these boundaries were enforced by the very people caring for disabled children—namely, Hengwei's foster mother and the foster care monitor, Huilan. As Mercy Care monitor Suling interrogated these boundaries, Hengwei's foster mother cited a community ethic of harmony ("If they were in the classroom, it really wouldn't be fair to all the other kids. They would bring all the other kids down"), as does Huilan ("But you don't know the history of this project.... I don't want her to get hurt and to fail and for this community to suffer"), which reinforces that what is best for foster children with disabilities is what is best for the community.

On the one hand, Hengwei's foster mother and Huilan's apprehension regarding the integration of these children into local schools represents a genuine concern in rural China. In her review of state-sponsored and nongovernmental social services for orphans and disabled children, Anne Jane High (2013) remarks that even though disabled children are guaranteed a right to education, in practice they were often denied entry into local schools, discriminated against for their differences and disabilities (2013). Xiaoyuan Shang, Karen Fisher, and Jiawen Xie have also confirmed widespread discrimination and lack of institutional support for children with disabilities (Shang and Fisher 2014; Shang, Fisher, and Xie 2011). Indeed, Leslie Wang (2016) argues that by providing comprehensive governmental support to families with disabled children, China can curb the crises of abandonment that have made practices like foster care a necessity. Thus, the attitudes toward education for children with disabilities in Daling were not an anomaly.

Yet, much as Qian points out from her work with Chinese philanthropists (2014, 261), even attempts to "normalize" orphans with disabilities often served to reify social distinctions between those who were "normal" and "abnormal." I argue that a similarly coded exclusion is effected through the positive language of exceptionalism that is used by foster mothers in Daling, the village head who shows so much pride at their sacrifices and efforts, and the state orphanage staff who seek a better life for such children. Through this exceptionalism, the category and the boundaries of the "abnormal" are subtly reinforced with respect to these children with disabilities in their "special treatment." Thus, Qian argues, the two sides of familism that promote disability as abnormality in China—the one being outright rejection of disabled people on the basis of their uselessness, the other being a veiled form of rejection in pity—are both present in Daling (2014, 261–262). In the village head's embarrassing dismissal of the children's intelligence and ability to learn there is raw clarity regarding the children's lack of utility. In Huilan's insistence that Hongmei will crumble under the pressure of the expectations of the school and that the community may further suffer because of her failures there is pity and worry that softens the conclusion that Hongmei simply does not belong in school with typical kids. Even in Hengwei's foster mother's giggles and Huilan's apprehension about Hengwei bringing the whole classroom down, there is a subtle exclusion that finds not the community (which fails to include or educate) wanting but Hengwei himself lacking, deficient, or abnormal.

Much as Qian argues that, through the lens of familism, philanthropists attempt to normalize institutionalized children in China as those receiving love and care from the *shehui dajiating* (big family of the whole society), the pilot foster care project in Daling was an effort to normalize and further reintegrate these children into society (*huigui shehui*). But what undermines this normalizing are both the subtle ways in which the exceptional character of foster families and children in Daling promoted their exclusion from certain forms of society, like state education, as well as the fact that such children, unlikely to be formally adopted, remain in familial limbo. As Qian argues, "Despite the series of normalizing activities, as long as these children retain their institutionalized household registration and are not adopted into ordinary families, they will never be 'normal.' Here, the paradox in the operation of familist power surfaces: the only effective normalizing technique is adoption, which almost no philanthropists will try, because they think the children in the social welfare institute are not only socially but physically 'abnormal,' suffering from all kinds of diseases and impairments" (2014, 257). If foster mothers in Daling and across China are often legally prohibited—if not politically discouraged and economically disadvantaged—to adopt, does their emotional labor, however "exceptional," still serve to reinforce the abnormal character of disabled orphans? And if adoption of disabled children in China is unlikely, is the only method to normalize such children's permanent exclusion their exportation to Western countries? Finally, then, what of orphans with disabilities in China who are never adopted? Is familism and foster care in China to blame for their fates, or is there a similar exceptionalism operating through the practices of ICA that prefers certain children and uplifts certain families at the expense of others?

"ARE CHILDREN LIKE PENGFEI REALLY ADOPTABLE IN THE UNITED STATES?"

It was a rainy, dreary, winter day when, from the bustling street in the middle of one of the older neighborhoods in the center of Nanning, we entered the dank courtyard of the welfare housing building. I climbed the seven flights of steep stairs with the Mercy Care monitor to Pengfei's family's apartment. Once inside, there was the pungent smell of sour milk and mildew. Each time I would return there would be a different cluster of aunties or the couple's teenage children helping tend to the babies with cleft palates in the back room.

"Ayi, you're so generous, two babies and Pengfei; wow, you really are impressive!" the Mercy Care worker chuckled, smiling.

"Impressive! Ha!" the old woman scoffed. "As soon as one leaves, the orphanage thrusts another one into our arms, and how can we say no? They're so pitiful, these children." She rested one of the babies on her lap as she crouched in the sparse living room. Meanwhile, Pengfei, a blind, gangly boy of eight years, moved awkwardly about the room, clinging to the dingy walls, slapping his palms against them, and slapping his mother as he fumbled for her gaunt form in the doorway of the tiny kitchen.

As Pengfei's mother spoke, her voice shook and tears came from her eyes. She took Pengfei into her lap, cradling him as she fed him. She told us she had to restrain him to feed him so that he would not choke or hurt himself and to make sure he would eat. The family had cared for him since he was only a few years old, when he had started to speak and then suddenly stopped. She simply did not know what more they could do for him, how they could help him. She said someone at the orphanage had mentioned that he might be autistic. "What is autistic? Is he autistic?" she asked the Mercy Care worker. When he said he did not know, she turned to me, urgently begging for my evaluation. "What do *you* think? What does it look like to you?"

For months, Pengfei's foster mom protested that he needed to be reevaluated and rediagnosed. She complained, always tearfully, that he attended school at the orphanage, but the teachers ignored him because they did not know how to interact with him. Finally, at the monthly meeting at the orphanage, the Mercy Care workers, orphanage foster care monitors, and I discussed Pengfei's case. There was an American psychologist coming in a month, and it was decided Pengfei's mother would bring him to the school to be evaluated.

The meeting at the orphanage was a cacophony of English, *baihua*, Mandarin, medicalization, rehabilitation, and the wailing of a blind boy. Pengfei spent most of his time bolting to the door, swinging it open and closed and rejoicing in the muffled sound it made. The psychologist did the one thing no one wanted: she refused to deliver a diagnosis, instead encouraging Pengfei's foster mother, offering affirmation and creative ideas for how to stimulate the boy. Pengfei's foster mother annoyed the orphanage staff by answering each of the psychologist's questions with stories that meandered in and out of Mandarin and *baihua* and attested to the difficulties and joys of raising him. The orphanage staff annoyed me by scolding the foster mother for these long diatribes and neglecting to translate an ounce of the encouragement or affirmation the therapist offered. Pengfei's mom was anxious and perplexed as to why an American therapist could not or would not offer a decisive diagnosis, and frustrated that she was constantly being goaded to speak Mandarin when several of the orphanage staff spoke *baihua* just as well as her.

By the time the grueling evaluation was over, Director Wang, the exasperated orphanage workers, and Pengfei's foster mother all demanded to know one thing of me: "Are children like Pengfei really adoptable in the United States?"

CHAPTER SUMMARY: INTERNALIZING DEMAND, FAMILY HIERARCHIES

I cannot remember how I responded to such a question; at the time, over a year into my fieldwork in China, I had little idea which children were being adopted to the United States and whether Pengfei could be counted among them. But what was evident from our collective vantage point in China was how clearly both Pengfei's diagnosis of disability and his imagined future clung to knowledge and family decidedly positioned outside China, in the West. Although the intimate cultural politics of that meeting at the Nanning Municipal Orphanage far exceed the analysis offered here, I argue that the invocation of Western expertise and Western adoptive families in such an out-of-the-way place as Guangxi is not to be overlooked. By looking at the discourse regarding the special desire and care of American families for disabled children circulating among correspondingly "special foster families" like Pengfei's, we can see how, when it comes to disabled orphans, Chinese foster families are subordinated and marginalized with respect to future "forever" adoptive families in the West.

Although Pengfei's foster mother was heralded by an INGO worker as "impressive" (a term she notably dismissed), it is she who first tearfully pressed me, a Westerner wrongly presumed to have medical expertise, with the question as to whether he was autistic. A few months later, this question was put to a Western psychologist as both Pengfei's foster mother and the orphanage staff aggressively sought a diagnosis for Pengfei. Here the diagnosis, again presumably located at the site of Western knowledge, was treated as the source of not only a meaning but perhaps even a cure for the disability. The fact that Pengfei's foster mother had learned yet not comprehended the meaning of the term *autistic* further authorized the mysterious superiority of Western knowledge and the power of the diagnosis. In subsequent interactions with Pengfei's foster mother, I could see that she was clearly desirous and eager for this diagnosis because the orphanage had led her to believe that it would help Pengfei. The Western diagnosis was positioned as a key feature to Pengfei's medical rehabilitation, if not a cure.[1]

Therefore, the refusal of the Western psychologist to diagnose Pengfei dramatically and dangerously undermined the West as the ultimate site of medical knowledge, care, and rehabilitation—a threat that the orphanage staff, even more so than the Western expert, were eager to manage. As the Western psychologist not only refused to diagnose Pengfei with autism but listened intently to his foster mother's parenting anecdotes and affirmed her attempts to communicate with, teach, and discipline him, Pengfei's placement with his foster family was subtly substantiated. In other words, the implication of the interaction was that Pengfei was doing just fine in China with his foster family, that Western knowledge and diagnosis are not all knowing, and that rehabilitation or cure for a child such as Pengfei—who was blind, nonspeaking, and perhaps autistic—was a slow, not immediate, holistic medicalized process. Yet because Director Wang and Pengfei's foster mother both still believed a Western diagnosis was necessary for Pengfei to be rehabilitated, neither were satisfied by the psychologist's response. Furthermore, despite the finality and clarity of the interaction, both Director Wang and Pengfei's foster mother still inquired whether Pengfei might be adoptable in the United States, indicating that they still did not believe his socialization at home with his foster mother or schooling at the orphanage were adequate or sufficient; they did not believe that, without significant rehabilitation, Pengfei could continue to reside in China.

As demonstrated in the specific case of Pengfei, but also across hundreds of children with disabilities in my fieldwork, both the Chinese state orphanage and foster families, despite the efficacy of foster care placement, ultimately position these children's futures in the West as the ultimate site of benevolence and rehabilitation. Notwithstanding the validity of claims that children like Pengfei are wanted, readily adopted, and rehabilitated in America, this repositioning necessarily undermines the ability of foster mothers like Pengfei's to offer what is often touted as "special love and care." Despite their sacrifice, their extraordinary efforts are repositioned in the service of Western families who can provide these children with a permanent, stable, "forever" home, as well as the (albeit false) perception of "overcoming disability" through medicine and rehabilitation, all of which is preferable to foster care. Such discourse threatens to undermine, eclipse, or even erase the fostering of family by mothers like Pengfei's in China, and it also solidifies assumptions about discriminatory attitudes toward disability in China in conjunction with reifying hierarchies of kinship that take on a moral global register.

This is further significant because the perception that disability can and should be overcome through Western medicalization and rehabilitation is not a mere function of Chinese discrimination toward disability but a clear by-product of the increasing adoption of disabled children from China to Western countries. In many cases, adoptions of disabled children are expedited, and corrective and medical surgeries are frequently performed abroad and paid for by the adoptive family rather than the Chinese government. This not only serves to outsource intimacy and expense for the Chinese government, as Wang has alleged, but it also perpetuates the narrative that disabilities are somehow "overcome" in the West through therapeutic, surgical, or rehabilitative medicine. Yet, even if this is practically not the case, the fact that disability can seemingly be "cured" or rehabilitated through Western medicine highlights a global politics of ableism inherent in the current practice of ICA from China. Indeed, far from the West possessing a special ability to love and care for disabled children, it is that the West possesses a certain medical ability to cure and rehabilitate such children, who within China would seemingly remain problematically disabled. The West desires such children not just to care for them but to cure them, to subsume and incorporate such children into healthy families that provide a rich alternative to impoverished foster families.

In other words, even as scholars like Holroyd, Qian, and Wang have evidenced the way in which familist cultural logic undermines the personhood of disabled children in China, we have yet to consider how demand for such children with disabilities (internalized and reproduced by Chinese orphanage staff, foster mothers, and perhaps even the children themselves) complicates or exacerbates such concepts of disability and family within a global system of reproduction. What becomes clear in the example of Pengfei is that although a Chinese familist cultural logic may to some extent explain his abandonment, it is the magnification of Western desire, marshaled as medical expertise, that calls his foster family into question. And yet, the extent to which foster families are inherently unstable, predicated as they are on their presumed replaceability, is further complicated by the permanence afforded to certain foster families—namely, those in Daling.

What this draws our attention to is the way in which disability in China is not merely a consequence or a condition of cultural familism but a site where international desire subtly reinforces an exceptionalism with respect to children with disabilities and Chinese foster families that perpetuates social distance and discourses of abnormality. Indeed, what the statistics on disability in China show are that only a miniscule proportion of families in the Chinese population abandon disabled children (see chapter 2). Meanwhile, foster families are willing, if not eager, to take such children in. And yet, despite the increasing frequency, only another small proportion of these children is actually adopted to Western countries, making children like Honghuan and Meili the exception and not the rule. Thus, Jiaqi and Pengfei's cases are more commonplace than the literature, let alone the discourse on ICA, acknowledges. What we are left with is the shocking realization that in contradistinction to Director Wang and Pengfei's foster mother's hopes, neither Pengfei nor Jiaqi, nor so many children like them, will ever be adopted.

Therefore, the impermanence of their foster families—reinforced by the discourse of ICA and international demand, especially with respect to children with disabilities—serves to render them further liminal in Chinese society. The imposition of a future in which Western families are imagined as paramount and exceptional is not only alarmingly racist and sexist—as it conjures permanent family as white and heteronormative (Cheney 2014; Eng 2006)—but surprisingly ableist in that the work that such families do hinges on their rehabilitative and curative potential to not only rid China of disabled children but to reimagine such children within heteronormative, ableist, modern Western families (McRuer 2006). Thus, despite the scrappy resistance foster families seem to present to Chinese state actors and their conventional notions of family, we must ask whether such families are mere pawns in a system that not only furthers the chains of international adoptions but supports and reproduces hierarchies of modern family. How can foster families be disruptive if their very actors seek to undermine their existence?

6 · DISRUPTIVE FAMILIES

One morning a few months before I left Nanning, I climbed the five stories to Auntie Li's apartment to visit Pei Pei. On these occasions, I often ate with the family; roused the girls from sleepy stupors in order to take a walk in the nearby park; accompanied the family to the market; and chatted with Auntie Li, her older biological daughter Kaili, and her two foster children, Pei Pei and Yuping. This time, however, the youngest foster daughter, mischievous Yuping, was notably absent, and Auntie Li, Kaili, and Pei Pei all wore long, fatigued faces they struggled to hide behind polite smiles.

Conversation quickly turned to the broken hearts born by each of them at the departure of Yuping to a family several provinces away in China. "Oh, I should have spoiled her more while she was here, I should have appreciated her more," Auntie Li chided herself. "I shouldn't have complained so much about her naughtiness, I shouldn't have called her stupid," she said, laughing, but her laugh broke as tears streamed from her eyes and down her face. Auntie Li, Kaili, and Pei Pei huddled together on the wooden couch in the living room, literally clinging to one another with an affection that I had never seen displayed in the household.

"We've all been crying," Auntie Li explained, wiping tears away from her own eyes and gesturing toward and holding on to the other two girls. "I myself can hardly eat, can't sleep—I haven't slept since Yuping left." And then she told me how the ladies from the orphanage had come and told her that the only cure for a broken heart from one child was to foster another, so she had gingerly asked the orphanage for another child. But the subsequent child was almost one and a half and had never been fostered before. After coming to the family, she was completely out of sorts, crying inconsolably throughout the nights. Realizing that she could not handle it, Auntie Li had called the orphanage to take the child back.

The grief of losing a foster daughter and foster sister permeated the dirty walls of the tiny apartment, and I struggled to find words of comfort. When I snapped some photos of them, Auntie Li put out her frail arms to shelter the little family and huddle them together, and again, they tried so earnestly to flash smiles on their tear-stained faces. While Auntie Li told me how much comfort it was to still have her own daughter and Pei Pei by her side, I had been hesitant to make even that consolation. Given Pei Pei's advancing age, the orphanage had made it clear that they were not sure it was worth keeping her in foster care, and I had no information to provide to Auntie Li regarding Pei Pei's uncertain future. I knew if I mentioned Pei Pei's case, Auntie Li would pester me for information, and I would not be able to tell her definitively whether Pei Pei could stay.

"THE ONLY CURE FOR A BROKEN HEART IS TO TAKE ANOTHER"

When children left, foster parents often spoke of the loss as that of a broken heart and described the grief in poignant, physical terms. I had heard almost every foster mother repeat the same symptoms that Auntie Li had detailed: they could not sleep, nor eat—sometimes for weeks, months, or even longer. Yet when I traveled with orphanage monitors to courtyards and villages where parents had fostered for many years, they were the ones who encouraged these women, aging, alone, and frail to take yet another child. "I'm far too heartbroken from the last one," the women would complain.

"The only cure for a broken heart from one child is to take another!" an orphanage monitor would sing out with a bright smile. "I'll find a beautiful one, just for you!"

Such promises, alongside the palpable grief at the loss of a foster child, contrast sharply with the initial repulsion foster mothers like Auntie Ma felt at first sight of her foster daughter Meili's sickly appearance (see chapter 2). Even so, after learning that Meili would be adopted within a matter of months to America, Auntie Ma, like Auntie Li, expressed a desire to "spoil her a bit before she goes." Clearly the impending loss of a foster daughter with whom she shared daily life and had formed a kin relationship caused Auntie Ma to reflect on the changes in her and Meili's relationship over the nearly seven years they had spent together and how she desired to spend her last months with her. As those final months passed, the orphanage that had once expressed frustration with Auntie Ma for her demands and lack of discipline of her daughter began to encourage her to take another child after Meili left. But Auntie Ma provided excuses: she did not have any young children's clothes anymore, only clothes suitable for an older child, and she could not handle an older child at her age. She said that Meili, her third foster child, would be her last.

Then one Sunday in April we attended a picnic for all the Mercy Care foster families at a local park, where the Nanning Municipal Orphanage supplied games and food for the children and local sponsors attended with their families. An American board member from Mercy Care had brought a photo album that Meili's soon-to-be adoptive parents had sent along to introduce her to their home and their family, and she urged me to introduce her to Auntie Ma, and Meili so she could show them the album.

Auntie Ma, who had been sick with stomach problems, seemed almost transparent in her thinness and positively overwhelmed by the excitement of the moment. She clung to the American board member's hands nervously, her words tumbling over one another as she implored me to translate her assurances that Meili would be a dutiful daughter to this blond American mother whose face stared out from the glossy photo album: "I'm only an ordinary person, but I've tried to raise her to be a moral, good girl, to the best of my abilities. She may not be beautiful, but she's kind, and she's smart, and she has beautiful hands that speak to a prosperous future," Auntie Ma stammered, grasping at Meili's hands awkwardly.

Her words moved the board member, who tearfully replied that Meili's adoptive mother had been waiting for seventeen years to adopt a child and would certainly love Meili no matter what—she did not need to be perfect or obedient. Meili sat meekly and stoically nearby. She eventually ran off to play with another foster child, seemingly disinterested and embarrassed by her foster mother's rush of emotions. But before we left, I caught Meili and her friend with their noses buried in the photo album, marveling at the horses and the beautiful rooms featured in the photographs. When I came by Auntie Ma's apartment a few days later, she confirmed that Meili had been poring over the book each day.

Just a few days later, Auntie Ma telephoned in the evening to ask me to meet her at her home. Along with the photo album, the adoptive parents had sent along a necklace for Meili, and Auntie Ma said she had something she wanted me to deliver to the adoptive family by way of the American board member who was returning later that week to the United States. In the meantime, I telephoned Mercy Care's director to find that, as I suspected, I would not be able to deliver anything directly to the board member, because all exchanges like this had to first pass through the authority of the municipal orphanage.

That evening, when I got off the bus, Auntie Ma was eagerly waiting for me at the stop. Taking my arm, she suggested, "Let's not climb the stairs all the way up to my apartment; let's just duck into one of these shops, and I can show you what I've brought." We settled on a tiny photo development store and perched on the iron chairs. Then I delivered the disappointing news to Auntie Ma that I would not be able to take the letter that Meili had helped her write to the adoptive mother to the American board member. Auntie Ma tried to persuade me that the orphanage would never know, but I mentioned the orphanage's kindness to me in sponsoring my research project, and how I simply could not do anything to compromise that relationship.

Crestfallen, she began to flip through faded photos she had brought along of Meili as a child, commenting this time on how small and cute she was when she first came to her. Then, struggling to read the letter line by line to me and explaining the choices of her words, she implored me to memorize them so I could tell the American board member what to relay to the adoptive mother. When

I assured her that I could pass the letter on to the orphanage and they would get it to the adoptive mother, she smirked, remarking that the orphanage did not care about her and they would not deliver the letter. She continued to read the heartfelt words that relayed the story of Meili's abandonment and detailed her obedient qualities and her substantial talents to her new mother.

After we finished reading, Auntie Ma took both my hands in hers and let out a tearful sigh. "You know, I'm not a perfect person, but I've always prayed for a family for Meili," she said. "Perhaps even more than my own daughter, I've loved her with all my heart. And now, I think I can rest easy. I know now that I've done one thing right with my life, to raise a daughter who will have such a bright future to go live in America."

These emotional outbursts—the tears, the impassioned pleas, the physical ramifications of heartbreak—were such unusual displays from usually stoic, matter-of-fact, even brisk women like Auntie Li and Auntie Ma. I wondered how such hearty women could suddenly shrivel in the face of heartache when they had seemingly gone on before unscathed. Indeed, international nongovernmental organization (INGO) and orphanage staff had certainly cajoled them to cure their broken hearts before; were these sudden bursts of emotion signs of weakness and failure? What would become of these women, Auntie Li, Auntie Ma, and also Auntie Huang, and their tiny, fledgling foster families? Were they and their foster children, Meili, Pei Pei, and the fragile Dengrong, to disappear as if they never existed? Was their brokenness representative of their resignation to the fates of their families to fade into the background as quietly and emphatically as they had once come to exist and thrive? Or was there something fertile, resistive, albeit unselfconscious in the everyday protests they made against taking another foster child or refusing to let this one go?

In this chapter, I demonstrate the effect of excessive emotion, generated by relationships of foster care, on both foster mothers and Chinese state orphanage and INGO workers. I argue that despite the seeming brokenness of these foster mothers and their families when facing the impending departure of a foster child, or enduring a recent departure, the emotional excess produced in these confrontations and exchanges represents an unselfconscious resistance (Modell 1992; Wozniak 2002) to Chinese state orphanage and INGO workers. As the chapter goes on to demonstrate, even though Chinese state orphanage and Mercy Care workers take pains to maintain the boundaries of the contractual relationships between foster mothers and their foster children, they are nevertheless affected by these emotions, suggesting that the boundaries of not just foster families but all families are much more porous than they may seem. This also shows us that even the seemingly impenetrable Chinese state is vulnerable to emotion, precisely because the bonds of fosterage are not merely temporary but transformative, powerfully exceeding the confines of the foster family's existence. By using the phrases "emotional excess" or "excessive emotion" I do not mean to indicate that these emotions are truly exceptional or inappropriate. Indeed, the expressions of emotion displayed in this chapter at losing a child are actually rather commonplace and justified. However, I use the qualifier of "excess" because of the way in which they overflow to complicate and implicate the boundaries of the contract and the impermanence suggested by the foster care relationship. The adjective also identifies the way in which these emotions become disruptive both to the foster mothers who experience them and to the state and INGO monitors that receive them. The emotions are not judged excessive: rather the point is that foster relationships produce an excess of emotion that cannot and will not be contained. Finally, within the broader argument this book makes about need and kinship, I show how the neediness of Chinese foster families serves to disrupt the production of international adoptive families and further undermine the normativity of Chinese biological families.

EVERYDAY RESISTANCE

The first few times orphanage and Mercy Care staff returned to monitor Dengrong, the young girl with cerebral palsy who had been placed in the village of Daling in October 2011, they were visibly and audibly dismayed with the substandard care they felt her foster parents were providing. With a hyperactive, autistic foster sibling, they noted that the quiet, obliging Dengrong was being slighted by the foster mother's attention and affections. On numerous occasions, Huilan, Older Sister Mo, and Suling had all taken turns chastising the mother for her lack of leadership.

"You're the adult," Huilan had charged. "*You* have to lead, *not her*. So if she has a cold and a fever, you can't give her lychee fruit simply because that's what she wants to eat. Everyone knows that those kinds of foods raise the internal temperature and make a fever worse. She may not eat much porridge, but you have to tell her that she can't have any of those fruits or candies until she gets better." Huilan swiped at the burning forehead of the young child, bundled up and slouching feebly in a chair.

Auntie Huang complained that Dengrong was lazy and refused to practice walking with her walker, as she urged her to do. "Well, make her do it," was the callous response from Huilan, Older Sister Mo, and Suling. When we were out of the mother's earshot, Suling made allegations of favoritism, and complained that the mother did not take the admonitions seriously enough.

"She needs encouragement, though," Huilan replied. "I know what it's like with these mothers. If you shame them, they retreat into themselves. They need to feel that they can do it, care for these difficult children."

In truth, I had never seen a child so ill as the second time we visited, and it had been on that occasion that Huilan refused to see Dengrong, urging the foster mother to take the little girl to the county seat immediately for an injection, telling her we would come back the following day. The next day Huilan dropped off a host of donated prescription medicines and inhalers from the West, instructing the woman on how to administer them. Auntie Huang not only seemed to mis-understand the seriousness of Dengrong's condition but was also burdened by the fear and embarrassment that Dengrong was one of the sickest kids in the village. Because everyone knew the story of how a child had died in Daling six years earlier, and all the children had been removed as a consequence by the municipal orphanage, foster mothers were extremely nervous caring for children with extreme medical conditions. Finally, the cultural belief that children who die before their parents are unfilial and may return as wandering ghosts was not altogether dismissed in the countryside, especially where death and disease were more constant companions than in the larger, more modern, cities.

On the third visit, however, we found Dengrong standing at the doorway, greeting us, smiling, the fever and cold sweats absent, and the cough much less significant as she gingerly puttered about the room with her tiny walker. Huilan smiled widely and complimented Auntie Huang on the care she had been giving Dengrong. Had she been using the medicines or the inhalers? What had she been feeding her? Gradually Auntie Huang admitted that she had not used the Western medicines much—she did not know how, and she had not seen that they had had any effect. But on one occasion when she had been at the county seat she stopped by the office of a local healer, who suggested that she boil a tea with some local grasses and roots, and she admitted, rather timidly, that she felt this local remedy might be responsible for Dengrong's recovery. Huilan seemed unfazed and happily accepted the local solution. She insisted on reimbursing the foster mother for her medical expenses, and when the mother replied that the old man did not give receipts like many local healers, and it was a pittance, Huilan pressed her that the scrawling of his signature with an amount on paper would suffice. She reminded the woman that medical expenses were to be covered by the orphanage, and this, like injections, certainly qualified.

This example shows how in the absence of INGO or orphanage monitors, foster mothers seek out local solutions to their children's impairments and medi-cal complications. Far from demonstrating noncompliance, which both the orphanage and the INGO felt they had observed in the first two months of Den-grong's care, within just three months Auntie Huang had proactively sought the advice of a local expert when she felt Western medicines were not inducing the change she sought to see in the care and health of her foster daughter. Her hesitancy to express her methods and remedies to the INGO and orphanage officials is likely linked to the class and social hierarchies between middle-aged, middle-class monitors and poor, older, foster mothers that I describe in chap-ters 3 and 4. But it also suggests there may have been local or reasonable explana-tions to the difficulty of Dengrong's transition and her poor health in the first two months that remained uncommunicated because of differences in approach and because of inequality between INGO and orphanage monitors and the foster mothers themselves. Again, perhaps it was not so much that Auntie Huang did not understand Dengrong's precarious condition so much as that the condition needed time to be ameliorated and interpreted within her own local community, way of life, and constellation of beliefs.

Thus, although foster parents frequently commented that foster children belonged in the United States or other developed countries, and that they themselves were old, uneducated, even "backward," and unable to care for them, this did not mean that they did understand their children's disabilities and medical needs in a sophisticated way or that they lacked the resources and the wherewithal to become advocates for these children (see chapter 2). In their study of foster care in Beijing, Wu Yuping, Han Xiaoyu, and Gao Qin (2005, 97) describe the development of local methods of rehabilitation and care among foster families (*tu banfa*) and note that, while they are different from the care given in the confines of an institution, they are nevertheless ample adaptations to children's needs. In chapter 3, I discussed how the disciplining and "playing" techniques that foster parents employ with both disabled and nondisabled children effectively communicate Chinese ideas of belonging and social personhood rather than merely disadvantaging or confusing disabled children. Thus, my research confirms that despite orphanage monitors' complaints regarding foster parents' lack of education and spotty compliance to therapy and disciplinary methods (see chapters 3 and 4), there were often other ways that foster parents adapted to the needs of their children.

A month later, when Director Wang and Huilan had called a village meeting in Older Sister Yang's living room to update the community on the status of the foster care project, Huilan had singled out Auntie Huang as one of the parents who was doing exemplary work. "We all know how sick Dengrong was when she came to Daling," Huilan said, grinning proudly, "and this foster mother has gone above and beyond, healing such a sick child." Auntie Huang, usually brash and gruff, shyly blinked away tears.

Auntie Huang's advocacy expresses both the deep understanding of foster children and changes in subjectivity that the process of fostering produces alongside the practical concerns of trying to provide care for disabled and sick children in more rural settings. Not unlike Auntie Ma, who constantly stressed her status as an ordinary woman without sophistication, foster parents like Auntie Huang purported to know little of disabled children's special needs and often humbly and dutifully accepted parenting advice from professional women like Huilan and Older Sister Mo, who were twenty to thirty years their juniors. Although women like Auntie Huang appeared and even acted compliant, it is important to note that they also subtly spoke up in defense of their behaviors and adaptations, which ultimately benefited the children and testified to a radical shift in relationship between the two.

To its credit, the Nanning orphanage was, and continues to be, willing to place children with disabilities outside the orphanage walls and even negotiate care and medicine at the local level. Nonetheless, setbacks due to state infrastructure, technology, and distance continue to establish practical limits to these rural foster care models. For instance, Director Wang's praise of the foster mothers in Daling was heartfelt, but she also acknowledged the limits of Huilan's one-woman supervision.

Yet we might also read Huilan's insistence that the orphanage cover the medical expenses for Dengrong's local healing as a way for the state to assert control and boundaries over foster care relationships. If Auntie Huang began to cover these expenses out of pocket, the foster family would begin to tread dangerously close to the boundary of a legitimate, biological family, which would not be subsidized for these expenses. Yet these efforts by orphanage and INGO workers to codify the terms of these relationships chafe against the excess of emotion and feeling that are present in them, and the efforts highlight an emerging challenge and overlap between temporary foster families and the biological or adoptive families that are sought after by the state. Indeed, as Huilan insisted on the reimbursement of Auntie Huang for her efforts, she subtly reinscribed the temporary nature of the relationship between Auntie Huang and her foster daughter Dengrong. Dengrong, regardless of the care she finds in the household of Auntie Huang, remains a ward of the Chinese state, her final destination oriented toward a family that is not Auntie Huang's.

THE VULNERABILITY OF THE STATE

For foster mother Auntie Li and her tight-knit makeshift family, the challenge that foster families presented to the state was even more overt, contested, and significant. On an evening a few months prior to Yuping's adoption, when cool breezes blew through the streets of Nanning, Auntie Li, foster daughters Pei Pei and Yuping, foster care monitor Suling, and I clamored down the stairs and walked the few blocks to the park at the end of the street. The air was festive as children rode blinking bumper cars in the town square, women danced, and men played chess in the concrete pavilion.

Yuping, the younger foster daughter, began to hassle her mother for tickets to ride the carts. "Oh, I forgot them at home," Auntie Li muttered. "Stupid me! Oh well, Yuping, you and Pei Pei will just have to play on the equipment." Yuping began to pout, but eight-year-old Pei Pei grabbed Yuping's hand and led her over to the monkey bars, where Pei Pei proceeded to dazzle us with her gravity-defying stunts.

"You try, Suling!" Pei Pei gestured, and gangly Suling slipped off her high heels and with great gregarious giggles scaled the rungs to the monkey bars. "Ahh!" she exclaimed, slipping off the bars; turning to Pei Pei, she told her how strong she was in comparison.

"Now you, Older Sister Lin En," Pei Pei beckoned in her quirky speech. "Oh, all right," I conceded, scaling a few rungs before I, too, dropped off.

Auntie Li clasped her hands together in delight. "Pei Pei's the best!" she squealed. As Pei Pei sidled off to lift Yuping on top of the lower bar, helping her somersault around it, Auntie Li's eyes brimmed with tears. "It isn't fair, what's going to happen to Pei Pei," she whined. "She's part of our family now, she's doing so well here, but the orphanage says it's a waste of money to keep her with us, they want to take her back when she's twelve, when she starts going to middle school."

In previous conversations with Auntie Li and Pei Pei, the effects of a faulty cleft palate repair for Pei Pei were evident and numerous—including, but not limited to, her original abandonment, the discrimination against her in school and society, and her struggles to communicate with others. Although Auntie Li's household—comprising her biological daughter, two foster children, and adult son—was one of the poorest I visited, with five individuals crammed into a two-bedroom apartment, the family noticeably banded together around Pei Pei, so effortlessly translating her speech when others failed to understand her that they were perplexed by others' assertions that Pei Pei had a disability. Indeed, as I observed on the monkey bars that evening, Auntie Li, a poor, retiree, took great pride in Pei Pei's abilities, found joy in the reintegration her foster children provided her in wider society, and considered Pei Pei an irreplaceable part of their family.

But, as illuminated in Auntie Li's tearful comments about the orphanage's plans for Pei Pei, there was more to this story. Though her situation was somewhat unique, because Pei Pei's biological mother was actually alive but incarcerated (see chapter 1) she was not eligible for adoption. Because Pei Pei did not have the capacity to be adopted within China or abroad, then, the orphanage failed to see the benefit of expending time and resources to keep her in a foster family. In fact, as Auntie Li complained, the orphanage began to doubt its investment during the time that I knew Pei Pei, her foster mother, and her foster family. The orphanage reasoned that it would be more cost-effective to send Pei Pei to the local orphanage school rather than continue her foster placement and pay the school fees for a placement out of district. On the one hand, Pei Pei's case reveals how the state can be complicit in the abandonment of children by excluding certain individuals from vital familial and societal relationships. By keeping children of the incarcerated like Pei Pei in administrative limbo by binding them to biological families that fail or are unwilling to care for them, the state prevents certain children from being fostered or permanently adopted.

Yet Pei Pei's case also demonstrates the way in which bonds of foster care tend toward an emotional excess that troubles the very power and boundaries of the Chinese state. Auntie Li never gave up her quest to retain guardianship of Pei Pei, constantly pleading with the various orphanage monitors and officials to allow her to continue raising Pei Pei into adulthood, so formative was the bond between them. Clinging to INGO and state orphanage workers' arms when they paid her visits, exclaiming in a loud whining tenor the urgency of her requests, visiting the orphanage, and hounding these officials for information or promise of her foster daughter's fate, she disrupted the character of these relationships in which she was meant to conform to the state's demands on her service. Auntie Li, scrappy, effusive, and poor, was a bane to the workers' existence because her tactics were so demanding and disruptive.

What is further intriguing about Auntie Li's resistance is the ways in which it not only foregrounded her emotion but also reinterpreted her need. As Auntie Li indicated to Suling and me ("It isn't fair, what's going to happen to Pei Pei. She's part of our family now, she's doing so well here . . ."), the objection came from a conviction that Pei Pei belonged with her foster family because she was thriving in that environment; therefore, the state would be going against not just Pei Pei's best interests but the very family it had helped to form if it tore them apart. In her complaints, Auntie Li subtly repositioned Pei Pei and her foster family as not being in need of the state, but in need of one another, thus emphasizing the resources of these families to provide care for one another. Even as her emotions decried the injustice of the situation and her tactics seemed to position her as begging the powerful state for reprieve, her requests also uplifted the import of the foster family as a contributor to social welfare. This invocation of the validity of the foster family to stand on its own in a service to the state is even more significant given the way in which previous chapters have highlighted the replaceability and invisibility of Chinese foster families who exist in order to support the formation of Western adoptive families.

Several months after returning to the United States, I received an email update from Suling, who confirmed that Auntie Li's lobbying had paid off—Pei Pei would be allowed to stay in her foster home until adulthood. Therefore, in contrast to the seeming limits of foster care relations and the marginal character of foster families, Auntie Li's triumph shows that even in the face of seemingly insurmountable obstacles of bureaucracy and institutions, poor uneducated foster mothers are motivated by the experience of caring for children and the love they have for them to seek what they feel is best for them.

Despite Auntie Li's diminished social stature, she won a great battle against the state due to her persistence. In allowing Pei Pei to stay in Auntie Li's foster household until adulthood instead of confirming any legal obligation to her biological mother, the state radically recognized that foster families can provide legal personhood, as well as emotional benefits, that parallel—and, perhaps, exceed—those of biological families. The Chinese state, despite its policies that affirm the temporary nature of foster families, the foster care contract, and a cure for "broken hearts" in the routinization of contractual fostering, was extraordinarily and surprisingly vulnerable to the emotion that it helped nurture. Indeed, although foster parents were clearly in a subordinate position with respect to the authority of the state orphanage and INGO employees, their relationships with their foster children often compelled them to resist the power and purview of the state. Although these relationships were temporary, the emotion they produced had lasting and disruptive effects in compelling the Chinese state to respond and conform to foster mothers' demands.

EMOTIONAL INDICTMENT

In this section, I depict how emotion, at once encouraged by the Mercy Care and state orphanage staff, angers and undermines those staff members' own sensibilities and the state's ability to process intercountry adoptions (ICAs). Even as the outset of this chapter shows that Meili's impending ICA triggered feelings of nostalgia and warmth for her once reticently welcomed foster daughter, Auntie Ma's inability to control her sadness at Meili's departure reveals the disruptive and often unselfconscious power of foster care's emotional excess.

The orphanage generally did not permit foster mothers to meet adoptive mothers, especially at the orphanage or at their private homes—for fear, it said, that foster families would beg the adoptive families for money; instead, it preferred to have foster families meet adoptive families briefly at the adoptive families' lavish hotel. Such concerns demonstrate the orphanage's desire to control the neediness exhibited by the foster families to the adoptive families. Having made countless visits to homes ranging from modest to squalor, I certainly believe that the neediness of the foster families made evident to the adoptive families would have certainly troubled any notion of a reciprocal exchange. And yet, in this case, at the request of Meili's adoptive mother, the orphanage had made the exception to let this exchange proceed at the orphanage.

So when the time came for Meili to go to America, Auntie Ma accompanied her to the orphanage to say goodbye, and though her words expressed her gratefulness and deference to the new American mother, her gaunt frame, her red eyes, and her sobs expressed her loss palpably. At one point she clung to Meili, wailing loudly, and the orphanage officials frowned disapprovingly, and quickly prying her from her daughter's arms. "Stop crying," the orphanage monitors whispered feverishly and petulantly, but it was no use: Auntie Ma had already made the scene they had been wanting to avoid.

Judith Modell reflects on how the child as gift attempts to "rearrange the hierarchical dimension" evident in the socioeconomic inequalities of adoption by "altering the bases for the transfer of a child, from a comparative measure of fitness to an individualized gesture of solidarity" (1999, 38). And yet, as Marcel Mauss has pointed out, "objects are never completely separated from the men [*sic*] who exchange them" (1990, 31). Hence, as much as the orphanage intended to control any exhibition of neediness in this exchange between mothers, Auntie Ma's excessive sadness tainted the gift of Meili to her adoptive mother, the transaction smacking of a lack of reciprocity given the paucity of kinship inflicted upon Auntie Ma in the very exchange. Even as the orphanage tried to placate Auntie Ma with another child as a gift following this exchange, Auntie Ma's excessive emotion communicated that this was clearly a loss on her behalf, not an "individualized gesture of solidarity."

Thus, when Auntie Ma confided in me regarding her intent to spoil Meili, cried out dramatically as she said goodbye, and refused to take in another child following Meili's departure, she signaled that her care and affection for Meili were singular and genuine and that Meili's place as her foster daughter could not be replaced by another. Indeed, Pei Pei's mother Auntie Li demonstrated similar emotions following the adoption of her younger foster daughter, Yuping. When I visited her in her home with her other children, the usually stoic Auntie Li wept petulantly regarding Yuping's departure; she was overcome with emotion, anger, and sadness. Although she reluctantly took in another child at the request of the orphanage, she eventually ended up returning the child to the orphanage shortly thereafter, much to the orphanage's chagrin, and falling into a deep depression. Whereas this brokenness at the departure of a child was understandable, its excessive, extended, transformative effects on the state orphanage and INGO monitors was somewhat surprising.

For instance, when Auntie Ma expressed raw, uncontrollable emotion at Meili's departure, such excess flew in the face of the orphanage monitors, who insisted that the exchange must proceed without undue disruption or emotion. Auntie Ma's emotion at releasing Meili to her adoptive mother infringed upon the state orphanage monitors as an emotional indictment regarding their inability to understand the depth of relation and care effected through the foster care relationship. Suddenly it was they, the arbiters of the contract, who were ostracized from its very effects, and they were dumbfounded, uneasy, and afraid. It was the very foster families that state orphanage workers helped to create, and with whom they so earnestly sought to effect emotional bonds, who suddenly rose up to disrupt their own emotional and political sensibilities, rendering the state monitors threatened and perturbed.

Additionally, Auntie Li and Auntie Ma's noncompliance about taking another child threatened to disrupt the state processes of foster care and ICA, and the orphanage monitors were placed in a subservient relationship to them, practically begging them to take in another child. Indeed, as I show in the next section, as foster mothers lobbied for higher wages or assert their control over the fosterage relationship via child-rearing practices frowned upon by orphanage monitors, they subtly confronted the political and social hierarchies that render foster care a sublimated form of kinship.

A FINAL ACT OF RESISTANCE BY NEEDY FAMILIES

Several months before I left China, foster parents in Daling organized to demand higher wages from the Nanning Municipal Orphanage. Throughout my fieldwork, foster parents' discontent over money, complaints, and requests for higher wages were ubiquitous (see for instance, chapter 3). In Guangxi, where moderate incomes measured around 1,000 yuan per month (roughly US$165), the stipends of 700 yuan per child for healthy children and 800 yuan per child for children with disabilities paid by the orphanage (and in part by Mercy Care) were salaries comparable to the median incomes of other professionals, and commensurate to or greater than many state pensions.

Even as the orphanage discussed these requests for higher wages at its quarterly meetings, it complained that with its own budgetary limitations (the state provided the orphanage 1,000 yuan per child per month), it could hardly afford to pay the foster mothers more. The orphanage also explained that if it were to continue and expand foster care programs, it would have to let longtime internal staff go, and sometimes these moves, especially if staff were relatives of government cadres or had political connections, could be controversial.

But the main disconnect between the foster mothers' requests for higher wages and the orphanage's refusal to comply reflected a difference in understanding as to the purposes of the wages themselves. Orphanage personnel viewed the wages as reimbursement—a stipend to cover children's expenses and meager supplemental income for foster parents, as they were required to meet a minimum income level in order to legally foster. Over the course of my fieldwork, however, I discovered that few parents who fostered either met the minimum income level or had other income (from pension) of their own. For many foster parents without family or government assistance, this stipend was a primary source of income. As I noted in chapter 3, foster parents also believed their frugality as far as the children were concerned (perhaps owing to their experiences of scarcity during the Maoist era) demonstrated their effectiveness and competence as parents. As this ethnography has illustrated, older foster parents were *needy* in every sense of the word—disenfranchised from political, social, and economic life in modern China—and their relationships with their foster children provided so much more than economic compensation.

Therefore, it was highly significant that in March 2012, when foster mothers in Daling organized to demand higher wages from the Nanning Municipal Orphanage, they did so not just with money in mind but also their labor. While at first glance such conflict may appear to confirm their self-interested or financially driven motives, foster mothers in rural Daling were not merely lobbying for more money but also for the privilege of taking in additional children. So motivated and compelled were they by the needs of these children that each of them agreed to take on an additional third child, but they also demanded that compensation be raised. Because of a significant shortage of foster mothers, the orphanage, which was in a superior position as monitor of these relationships, suddenly found itself subordinate to the foster mothers' demands.

But the state orphanage and INGO staff also found themselves in the uncomfortable position of being confronted with these older women's—and their makeshift families'—neediness. Cautious to make sure the women could provide for higher numbers of children, the officials were reticent to grant them additional children. Yet by withholding children they were placed in the position of acknowledging the raw extent of these women's neediness. And had the need been merely financial or transactional, the state would presumably have had no problem in turning these women away or looking beyond them. There was something morally resolute and deeply convicted about the neediness of these families that referenced not poverty but provision. Out of their need, these foster families saw fit to give to more children: thus, their need did not just amount to demands but an unexpected excess that transcended the contract they made with their foster children and the state through foster care.[1]

CHAPTER SUMMARY: DISPARATE TRAJECTORIES

These foster mothers, in their visible and excessive displays of emotion and their ordinary and extraordinary acts, began to transcend familial and state boundaries of social life, demonstrating long-lasting effects of seemingly temporary relationships and challenging the authority of the state to regulate and control such relationships. As I noted in chapter 4, the local valence of these confrontations makes even middle-class, middle-aged orphanage monitors and INGO employees such as Huilan, Suling, and Teacher Liu question their own normative notions of family. Indeed, the transformative, emotional effects of foster care relationships powerfully exceed the very boundaries state and INGO workers presumed to place upon them.

Just a few months after I left Guangxi, Huilan emailed to inform me that Director Wang had left her position as foster care director at the Nanning Municipal Orphanage, and Huilan had accepted the promotion. Struggling to reconcile the increased responsibility of overseeing the entire Nanning department, in addition to the Daling project, Huilan confided in me that her own insecurities as a parent made her often feel hypocritical, ineffective, or listless. Noting that age was not a prerequisite to caring, she praised some of the older foster parents she had known over the years, but, like many others, she wondered who might take their place. In a world in which these children were being abandoned by people in her generation, and their foster parents (older women) were growing older and more feeble, who would emerge to adopt them, foster them, or value them as persons?

An article regarding changes to the foster care policies in 2014 expressed similar concerns. These new regulations undermined the Daling foster parents' demands, actually decreasing the maximum number of children from three to two per foster family, and elevating the requirement that parents have nine years of formal education and average financial status in the region. Although the standards were developed to protect children from abuse, they also practically threatened to undermine many poorer families' abilities to offer care (*China Daily* 2014). The need for foster families remained self-evident given the increasing number of children with disabilities in state institutions,[2] but the supports and incentives for foster families, like all families caring for disabled children, remained scant. Even as the government had raised the requirements to foster, it had kept the stipends stable: would that attract more middle-aged, middle-class caregivers, or would the number of foster families simply dwindle under the new stipulations? As Huilan had once whispered to me under her breath in Daling, "I love these children, but even I couldn't imagine caring for them myself."

In that same email Huilan divulged that Dengrong had been sent back to the orphanage because her health remained too fragile. But I learned from Huilan that this occurrence was not due to negligence of care but a result of genuine health complications. Living over three and a half hours by bus outside the capital city of Nanning, and with her guardianship and medical insurance still managed in the orphanage, it became too impractical for the fragile Dengrong to reside out in the village, where there were few modern facilities or treatments. Huilan told me that Dengrong's foster parents traveled several times from Daling to Nanning to visit her in the orphanage, where she continued to recover.

Over Skype one evening, Meili, who had been adopted to America just three months after I left China, was eager to try out new words in English. Several months later, she insisted on only speaking in English with me, blurting out short phrases in a sing-songy cadence. Auntie Ma was busy trying to learn how to type on a computer in order to communicate with her, she reported. Her adoptive mother had discovered that Meili was quite nearsighted, and she now wore glasses that framed her round face. Her adoptive mother emailed me often to thank me for helping with Meili's transition—it had been virtually seamless. It was hard for her and her husband to remember a time without Meili. Yet, back in Nanning, Auntie Ma, who refused to foster another child, grew thinner and more frail.

Pei Pei would remain in the foster home of the triumphant Auntie Li seemingly into adulthood, but what then? Would her fate remain tied to her incarcerated birth mother or her *hukou* (household registration) transferred to the orphanage, forever marking her as abandoned and without a family, or would foster care— especially given its slightly more permanent nature in her case—provide her the social capital with which to find a role and a place in Chinese society?

The varied trajectories of these three foster children, as well as those of their foster mothers and some of the orphanage and INGO workers who played such key roles in their family making processes, speak to some of the ways in which—

despite its seemingly marginal character—foster care intertwines and expands families across contemporary Chinese society and the world. In this chapter, I have tried to show the surprising ways in which foster relationships both disrupt and complicate notions of which families are viable, valuable, and powerful. I have endeavored to show that despite their temporary qualities, such relationships are imbued with real emotions that disrupt the processes of state control and international adoption. In so doing, it is my intention to avoid romanticizing this emotion or resistance (Abu-Lughod 1990) by also contextualizing the precarious nature of this family making, the sincere and painful losses that come with losing children, and the tremendous neediness that hangs in the balance. Indeed, in both this chapter and the conclusion that follows, I hope the reader will assess that foster mothers' need is not being merely instrumentalized for generative, theoretical purposes. Rather, within a context of inequality, I demonstrate that such need still poses a rich challenge to ideals of modern family and those who have power and influence. Hence, in this chapter, I have also aimed to show that such disruptive actions by foster mothers, foster families, and Chinese state orphanage and INGO monitors are not marginal or idiosyncratic; they deeply complicate the notion of which families are in need and which families we need.

CONCLUSION
Families We Need

There is a chilling thought in every anthropologist's mind that he or she has returned from the field failing to answer the very questions they went there with. My case is no different. That basic human and deeply anthropological question of why these foster mothers would be willing to foster child after child after child, enduring sincere heartache and bureaucratic abuse, and seemingly gaining little for it, still hovers over this book. But as I have reflected, I have found not the foster mothers themselves but the question itself to be wanting. It is both fundamentally unanswerable in simple terms and audaciously distancing, predicated as it is on the belief that my desire for family, my own need, is and has always been so profoundly different from these foster families and their state and international nongovernmental organization (INGO) counterparts whom I came to know and cherish. Research questions provide necessary distance in anthropological fieldwork, framing the project as one that takes place patently *between* social worlds.

But we also cannot undertake anthropology as anything other than the people we are, people who are very much from certain places and in relationships with certain people. And so, what I have come to analyze in this conclusion is not just who these foster families were, what they did, and why it mattered to them and to China, but why it matters to you and to me—why the intermingling of families in China suggests something greater about families across the globe and why my research question need prompt a rich starting point from which to ask deeper, more nuanced questions about families we all need.

FOSTER CARE: A NEEDY KINSHIP

As has been shown throughout the book, this experience of being confronted with the contractual, often emotional excess of these relationships, was jarring and riveting for the middle-aged Chinese state orphanage and INGO workers. Despite the class-based criticism they leveled at older women for their "backward" hygiene, their lack of education, and their scant discipline of foster children, they found the emotions conveyed by foster families real, excessive, and striking. Indeed, in spite of the underside of these generational frictions, my intent has also been to rehabilitate these seemingly "uncivilized" and "immoral" subjects (Yan 2003, 2011a, 2011b) by ethnographically conveying the social pressures they experience and the ways in which their own ability to perform parenthood and personhood had become intimately intertwined with the needy foster families they served.

What happened in the envy that emanated from these INGO and orphanage monitors who found themselves emotional outsiders to the very foster relationships they had helped to develop was that both foster families and nuclear, biological families—those championed by the state's interpretation of tradition— became real and viable family forms. Far from merely existing in contracts brought forth by the state, foster mothers' seeming noncompliance with the contract— lobbying for more children and better wages; refusing to foster because the pain of losing a child was so great; or demanding to keep the children they had been raising, despite legal constraints—confronted, critiqued, and even exceeded practices and emotions conferred in biological families and kinship. Thus, state and INGO employees were bitter with and envious of foster families because they saw a simple, intimate, and enjoyable experience of family among them that they themselves found wanting. This signaled a powerful critical ambivalence with respect to modern neofamilism (Yan 2018)—a surprising challenge regarding the makeup of the modern family emerging from the margins in contemporary China.

Although when children with disabilities are adopted, they are adopted by and large outside of China today, during my eighteen months in the field I met more and more Chinese families who were willing to consider children with Hepatitis B and Down syndrome for adoption. An increasing awareness beyond not just the foster mothers but of others in society suggested that ideas about disability and disease might be shifting. Indeed, even as notions of disability in China undermine notions of personhood and can often lead to child abandonment (see chapters 1 and 2), this fact is arguably exacerbated by the demand for disabled children that comes primarily from the West in intercountry adoption (ICA) and the Chinese government's eagerness to send such children abroad (see chapter 5). Therefore, more research is needed to explore the way local understandings of disability interact with international processes, something the field of disability studies must take seriously.[1]

Meanwhile, the broader integration of disabled children into societal life—as shown in my ethnographic findings in foster care both in the city and the countryside, as well as in the increasing acceptance for children with disabilities within their foster families—is important to note. Because it is legal for parents with one child to adopt a second with a disability, or from an orphanage, more and more families with the financial capabilities and the social connections, like Teacher Liu, are considering such an option. It has only been five years since the government's official expansion to a two-child policy, and it was only in 2021 that it announced a three-child policy. Although initial reports suggest that few couples are motivated to expand their families, it remains to be seen whether the three-child policy will encourage parents to keep children with disabilities and whether in response to increasing populations of children and adults with disabilities the Chinese government will expand its meager support for such families.

Still, one might query how significant local patterns are in light of China's regional diversity, massive demographics, and popularly referenced strong central state. The everyday acts of resistance to which this book speaks have not sparked a widespread revolution whereby older and disabled citizens in China have come to enjoy profound rights or even a more robust citizenship. Indeed, even as Orna Naftali detects an increasing culture and recognition of children's rights in China, her work takes place among middle-class teachers and parents in Shanghai. Thus, she also acknowledges that some children, like those of migrants (and, I would argue, children with disabilities and orphaned children), remain problematically outside the Chinese state's notion of child rights (Naftali 2014, 135). Because such children are viewed as property of the patriarchal family under adoption law, which also makes no stipulations for guardianship, these children remain outside the category of modern citizens to whom certain rights are afforded (Shang, Morris, and Fisher 2011). For those who are older and poor, especially, the Chinese government's tacit commitment to their filial superiority has meant little practical change. They still find themselves isolated and marginalized, even within their own families, as the best of fates leaves them indentured to their own grandchildren's childcare.

But my ethnography also shows that the status quo for middle-class, nuclear, modern families in China is increasingly untenable. As Huilan and Teacher Liu express, their own social networks are often bereft of the very affection and emotions they seek to effect in the foster families they monitor. Thus, my ethnography shows that even as the Chinese state nationally denies certain benefits and futures to disenfranchised populations, such as children with disabilities and poor older people, state workers are emotionally vulnerable to foster families and their needs. Incrementally, then, it is the power of these bonds of foster care to disrupt the familial lives of middle-class and middle-aged state orphanage and INGO workers against the rigidity of state policies that mark the wide circles of social change afoot in an out-of-the-way place like Guangxi. In this way, I have shown that these seemingly marginal families are not so marginal after all in that their emotional bonds of kinship infiltrate the normative modes of the state in their everyday interactions with state orphanage and INGO workers. When it comes to kinship in China, "nature for once has not already had the last word" (Levi-

Strauss 1969, 31), just as the state has not been the final arbiter of personhood and citizenship. From the seemingly trivial rearing of disabled children by poor older parents comes a notion of modern personhood that troubles the boundaries so archetypal of modernity in China. From the everyday acts of rearing the next generation come the families that foster change.

BEYOND CHINA

This book has argued that contemporary state-sponsored foster care in China does not present an idiosyncratic, temporary form of kinship but instead a formidable challenge to family life in China, state power, and public and anthropological assumptions about the limits of foster kinship. In this section, I review the theoretical contributions of each chapter of the book to the field of kinship studies and present an overarching argument for why need presents a promising concept for a reinterpretation of modern familial relationships.

Chapter 1, "Abandonment, Affinity, and Social Vulnerability," has demonstrated the parallel abandonment and social vulnerability of disabled and orphaned foster children and poor older foster mothers, illuminating how they are not only stigmatized by disability and presumed futility but chiefly disadvantaged by lacking the requisite family and obligations to function as social persons in contemporary Chinese society. At the outset, the neediness of these foster families seems to justify both their subordination and replaceability. Chapter 2, "Fostering (Whose) Family?," has identified the growing proportion of orphaned children with disabilities in state institutions and state-sponsored foster care, as well as the symbiotic relationship between state-sponsored foster care and ICA. Therefore, beginning with chapter 2 the book asks how foster families fit into the constellation of Chinese kinship given the presumed destination of their children for Western adoptive families and their replaceability.

Chapter 3, "Needy Alliances," has shown the parallel social rehabilitation for foster children and foster parents that occurs alongside efforts by orphanage INGO personnel to patrol the emotional bonds of these relations. Chapter 4, "Envying Kinship," has explored the underlying vulnerability behind the contempt that middle-aged INGO personnel often present to elderly foster mothers, illuminating their unfulfilled desires for intimacy in their own modern family lives. Thus, families that once seemed pitiable for their desolate social vulnerability became enviable in their emotional resonance, disrupting local notions about what it may really mean to be family.

Chapter 5, "Replaceable Families?," has considered how narratives of exceptionalism with respect to disabled children and their foster families served to marginalize them with respect to international adoptive families, both undermining their significance and their pertinence with respect to Chinese kinship. Finally, chapter 6, "Disruptive Families," has illustrated the unselfconscious resistance foster families present to the Chinese state in their emotion, which exceeds the temporary character of their relations. Thus, these chapters argue that foster care transcends its temporary, contractual nature in the firm challenge it presents not only to the state but to other normative constructs of kinship in modern China and a contemporary anthropology of the family.

One of the challenges my ethnography presents to studies of contemporary kinship is that it makes foster care legible as a viable form of kinship in that it can no longer be construed as fictive, temporary, or replaceable. The very emotional excess generated by foster care is what troubles state and INGO workers who struggle to maintain its contractual boundaries. But as Auntie Li and Auntie Ma especially remind us, children in foster care and the families they produce are neither temporary nor replaceable. Thus, foster care does not just upend its own fiction (J. Goody 2004) that renders it seemingly temporary or replaceable but confronts a rigid preference in adoption processes (Yngvesson 2004) and a hierarchy in ideological kinship for the permanent or "complete" family (Strathern 1988). Indeed, we cannot conceive of the adoptee as fundamentally temporally oriented toward the adoptive family precisely because the foster family, in the emotional bonds it effects, exists and persists beyond its temporal contract in the adoptee, the foster parent, and even the adoptive parents.

As my ethnography clearly shows, the bonds of foster care and the emotions they confer—far from quickly dissolving at the close of the contract—intervene and threaten to disrupt the work of the state and even the processes of ICA. Yet despite the prominent role foster families play in both effecting and disrupting ICAs, they are noticeably obfuscated from international sight, national public news, and scholarly discourse. The absence of such families maintains the myth that they are truly replaceable, performing a mere contractual service to effect the chains of ICA and build permanent "forever" families.

But whereas foreign adoptees can ultimately be remade into elite citizens of developed and resourced nations, foster parents—harbingers of a backwardness that defy modernity—remain remarkably absent from the ICA narrative as well as contemporary anthropological studies of kinship. In so doing they both allow for and reproduce hierarchies that favor and privilege the modern, nuclear Western family while failing to acknowledge that such families are not only mythic but interlaced with the temporalities of foster families. Thus, although they are conceptually simplistic, foster families remind us that family does not exist on a hierarchy from temporary to permanent but demonstrate a multitude of overlapping, needy relationships that are not linear or permanent but lingering and simultaneous.

This leads to a second reason why foster families are so deeply needed in our landscape of contemporary understandings of kinship and that is their ability to complicate another myth of modern family: singularity. In her argument regarding open adoptions in the United States, Judith Modell (1994) argues that such relationships complicate the nuclear family ideal of two parents and a child by making way for a third parent, or a third mother (in addition to the two mothers already present in the adoptive triangle—namely, the biological mother and the adoptive mother). My ethnography shows just how disputed the motherhood of these foster parents was by the state orphanage and INGO monitors, who sought to manage these relationships (see chapters 3 and 4), marking motherhood as so many others have done as not an unassumingly private but intensely political, stratified, and contested site of social practice (see, for instance, Colen 1995; Ginsburg and Rapp 1995; Layne 1999; and Taylor, Layne, and Wozniak 2004).

If these women's motherhood was so radically disputed by the very women who employed them, it makes sense that the multiplicity of mothers evident in the process of foster care to adoption threatens the validity of singular, freestanding, (adoptive) family forms.[2] Despite the pivotal role of the foster mother in the triad of birth, foster, and adoptive mothers, she is once again notably expunged from tales and studies of adoption. This serves to reinforce not merely the temporary nature but the singular, bifurcated entities of birth and adoptive families, which fundamentally eschew the place and plurality of the foster family as a viable family player. Indeed, even as the field of kinship studies has tried to make way for alternative, viable, and perhaps especially multiple forms of family (Carsten 1996; Franklin and McKinnon 2002; Howell 2006; Schneider 1980; Weismantel 1989; Weston 1991), my study of foster care and its ties to ICA showcases the way in which certain mothers and certain families are crowded and cleaved from the pure nuclear family in a way that invites important reflection and revision.

Finally, the need inherent to the formation of foster families, which so visibly disturbs and disrupts state orphanage and INGO foster care monitors' own notions of family, presents a formidable challenge to the concept of kinship by choice that has often permeated modern practices and studies of family. Anthropologists of kinship have long foregrounded the notion that all kinship is created, thus undermining a false opposition and hierarchy between "natural," biological kinship and choice-based, "manmade" forms (Schneider 1980, 1984). Although what Kath Weston and Judith Modell were arguing for in the 1990s with a notion of choice-based families very much sought to fundamentally undermine this opposition, the popular interpretation of choice undermines both its universality and desirability as mere derivative for those who cannot or do not have viable biocentric kinship options (Laurie and Stark 2012). Thus, contemporary studies still struggle against reinforcing created kinship as secondary, derivative, "deviant," or mimetic of a prior, superior biological form (Butler 2004; Weston 2005).[3] Therefore, any reconfiguration of kinship and its alternative forms is still searching for an underlying unifying concept that can move beyond the expendable notion of choice and its prior biological reference.

Indeed, what I mean to suggest is both that families need and use other families to make themselves powerful, visible, and enviable, *and* that, beneath it all, we are all emphatically needy, human, and vulnerable. Thus, the common, disruptive need for relationship undergirds all of human kinship. The very politics of modern family making are neither devoid of power nor propped up by pure, calculated, and liberal choice. It is just that acknowledging foster families means laying them bare in the dramatic politics of global family making for all to see. Foster families remain sublimated within the chains of ICA, national narratives, and the "new studies of kinship" (Carsten 2000; Franklin and McKinnon 2002), because their visibility threatens to naturalize and equalize need and vulnerability, highlighting that the global struggle for kinship has unevenly eclipsed some families in the service of others. Indeed, it becomes painfully clear in my ethnography that foster families do not merely need the Chinese state, the children broken biological families provide them, or the rescue of a Western adoptive family; instead, Western adoptive families, state orphanage and INGO workers and, of course, disabled children palpably and emphatically also need foster families to be family themselves. Can it be that if the replaceability of foster care constitutes the ultimate fiction, then the chosen, Western modern nuclear family represents its mythic counterpart?

THE PARADOX OF NEED

It is hardly surprising that even as studies of foster care in the United States reference a similar transformation in foster mothers and a profound utility to the role foster care plays in forming permanent families (Wozniak 2002), foster families' replaceability in contradistinction to emphases on reunification or adoption makes them both unintelligible and subordinate among other forms of family. Thus, the binary oppositions of permanent versus temporary, singular versus multiple, and biological versus chosen across national contexts serve to bury the fact that all families, in spite of their forms and power, are driven and operate within a common economy of need. Meanwhile, it is traditional, biocentric forms of kinship that preserve the ultimate fiction. Seemingly set apart from processes distinctive to modern family making like ICA, they appear devoid of need—let alone any need for foster families.

And yet, within the economy of the family, needs are constantly being met and displaced, qualified and catalyzed, in the dynamism of transformation, transition, and certain disruption. Huilan's or Teacher Liu's families perhaps help us to see the need most plainly because they are seemingly divorced from our context, but their longing for intimacy, affection, connection, and mutual belonging were so profound that they threatened to stay hidden and only manifest in the contempt they felt for the needs of foster families. Accordingly, we might ask ourselves, what contempt manifests in America for the single-parent household, the extended immigrant compound, or U.S. foster families whom we render poor, self-serving villains in order to conceal the rampant need across our country and our own relationships? Thus, if our own need for family does not make itself paramount, we need only look to the way in which we displace it onto contempt for "lesser families" to expose the hierarchical politics of family making that disguise our common humanity.

Suddenly, my research question belies not a mere quest for knowledge but so clearly my own prejudice, ignorance, and unwillingness to admit and cast myself as needy also. Indeed, if an anthropological study of kinship has only been able to effect patterns and purposes of isolated groups and nationalities, it has little distinction. But to see family making for the communal, mutually implicated political practice that it is and find our critical concepts impoverished precisely because they assert themselves over and against our need for one another seems a ripe use of ethnography and a powerful promise for our understanding of kinship. I am convinced that the answer to my question then lies not so much in foster families' need for family but in mine and my own willingness to dismiss it. The paradox of needy families, needy kinship, and families we need is that need laid bare brings not so much poverty but unexpected excess—an excess that transcends boundaries and contracts and temporalities and forms. The paradox of need is that it is at once the great equalizer and indicter in the human web of kinship and simultaneously the most seductive exploiter and divider that the human family has ever known.

EPILOGUE

I am finally coming to terms with one of the reasons I struggled for so long to write this book: because the stories of these foster families and their foster children with disabilities have bled together with my own story in ways that are trying, uncomfortable, and also excessive. As mentioned briefly in the prologue to this book, it was these women, their extraordinary love for their extraordinary children—their extraordinary families—that inspired my husband and I to become parents ourselves.

After returning from China and wandering through the loss of culture shock and a miscarriage, I gave birth to a seemingly healthy baby girl in February 2014. But just a few short months after her birth, we noticed that Lucia was extremely irritable and inconsolable, and her difficulties went far beyond her feeding challenges. Indeed, an MRI and subsequent seizures revealed severe brain damage, which just a few months shy of her first birthday showed itself to be progressive rather than static. What testing revealed thirteen months in is that my husband and I were both recessive carriers for a very rare genetic disease, a degenerative disease of the brain; many children die in early childhood, and the interventions— surgeries, feeding tubes, muscle relaxants, and ventilators—are significant for daily life.

But after what we witnessed among foster families in China, living life with Lucia could hardly take on a tragic quality. Indeed, despite the many challenges Lucia's life presents, I am filled with awe, wonder, and joy when I look at my child, and I know I draw such inspirations from the ways in which women like Auntie Huang, Auntie Li, and Auntie Ma celebrated the lives of their children, however temporary these relationships were. Without assuming to know the mind of God, I can't imagine how such journeys aren't just merely intertwined but meaningful; that our families so deeply resound seems so ultimately fitting and yet presents a notable, painful loss for me—perhaps the loss of China.

That I have not gone back and that I may never go back to China now— precisely because of the medical challenges that traveling away from or taking along a disabled child would present on such a journey—rings as a cruel, cosmic joke on some of my darkest nights of the soul. There are, of course, the questions unanswered, the paths unfollowed in research that will lay bare and fallow because of this. But much more so, there is the sense that although our lives now are definitively connected through our labor of love and love's transformations through raising disabled children, things are not as intertwined as they may seem. I bear the understanding that the debts of the fieldworker, and perhaps especially mine, can never be repaid, and that is a hard but important truth. I begin to recognize just how astounding it was that these women not only welcomed these children temporarily but also why anything otherwise would have been so much easier.

I hinted in the prologue that Mercy Care's work had become even more precarious under new legislation that placed increased restrictions on foreign nongovernmental organizations operating in China. In 2017, despite numerous efforts to register legally according to the new legislation, and when they were prevented from doing so, Mercy Care staff became subject to heightened surveillance due to their foreign connections. Under tremendous pressure from the authorities in May 2021, Mercy Care made the difficult decision to sever its relationships with orphanages in China, close its support for Chinese foster care programs, let its Chinese staff go, and cease all operations there. Later that summer, after a year of trying interrogations related not just to the operations of Mercy Care charity but also her Christian faith, Teacher Liu decided to flee China with her family and seek asylum in the United States. The future of foster care programs in these areas where Mercy Care has withdrawn its support, and the future for its former Chinese staff (still under government scrutiny), remains uncertain and dangerous.

The COVID-19 pandemic had also brought a screeching halt to the international adoption market, forced foster children back into the orphanages, and undermined support networks for families with disabled children both in China and the United States. Many have pointed to the way in which COVID-19 has not so much instigated as exposed a global care crisis of startling proportions. My hope is that even though ethnography is small, particular, and time-sensitive, this book sheds a light on why modern family making is so essential and yet so inequitable, inviting us all to rethink and reimagine our participation in local, national, and global politics. I hope this book reminds us that what local actors do—and here I am thinking particularly of Auntie Ma, Auntie Huang, Auntie Li, Dengrong, Huilan, Meili, Pei Pei, Suling, and Teacher Liu—matters even in the face of startling national and international factors. These families remind me that I am not alone in either my need or my substantial fortitude, and if we could all not just imagine but experience a net of connection, care, and support, perhaps this book would never have been written. I can only hope that the future renders the book's struggles outdated, even if its protagonists will never become obsolete.

In my corner of the world, I have become an advocate for persons with disabilities, seeking to create the care infrastructure that can support needy families like my own. I am always struck by the efficacy of making my family's neediness apparent in advocacy, but also by the costs to that vulnerability. It makes me realize that even when needy families are constantly demanded to put their lives on display in order to receive basic rights and supports, they are also rendered invisible, as their marginality is constantly held against them in countries like China and the United States, which only want families to be strong, modern, and infallible. A world away from foster families, I suppose this is the small way that I continue to try and fight and struggle for better lives for families with disabled children.

In meditating on the loss and separation I feel regarding China and these families, and the changes afoot that I am helpless to impact, I glimpse the costs of love that biological families all too subconsciously assume—and which I myself had somewhat eschewed. I find that the things I wished for most upon embarking upon this journey—these types of connection with my informants and with my family—are all at once possible, and flawed, and yet they drive a hard, hard bargain. I find that we fieldworkers are not miracle workers, omniscient observers, or even equal partners with our informants; rather, at best, we emerge from the field as limping, scarred debtors. That we live to tell these stories is our liability; that we wrestle fitfully with them may speak to our integrity. But that we cannot, we will not, we do not, in any way repay them is my deepest and most painful truth. I recognize that my own transformation, my life's meaning, rests squarely upon their defiant, transcendent love, and I achingly wonder now how I ever existed without it.

ACKNOWLEDGMENTS

This book is based on fieldwork I conducted in Nanning, Guangxi, China, from 2010 to 2012 for my doctoral dissertation in anthropology at Princeton University. The dissertation was submitted and defended in November 2014, and my PhD was conferred in 2015. As with any large-scale research and writing project, there were many voices and hands that went into it. And, as is especially the case with ethnography, this book simply would not have been possible without the partnership and collaboration of remarkable interlocutors.

I begin by thanking the foster mothers and foster children who welcomed me into their intimate family lives during the time I spent in China. I am grateful for all the insight they provided me on Chinese culture, disability, family, and kinship, of course, but also the deeper lessons they taught me about love, acceptance, perseverance, and advocacy.

To the state orphanage officials and international nongovernmental organization personnel, especially the staff and board members of Mercy Care, I am deeply in debt. Their willingness to take me under their wings, share their own struggles with life and child-rearing, and introduce me to the work of foster care in China made this project possible. By translating the complexities of Chinese governance and culture for me, they offered an invaluable contribution to the breadth and the nuances of this project.

Alongside the foster families who made it possible, this book is dedicated to my dissertation adviser, Isabelle Clark-Decès, who died tragically while doing what she loved—teaching and doing fieldwork in India—in 2017. Isabelle's commitment to me never wavered, nor did she ever back down from giving sound critique and ardent advice. Her academic collaboration and her effusive support were some of the most cherished gifts of my doctoral experience. Her willingness to regard me not merely as a student but as a whole person has made me aware of my own strengths and shortcomings and more confident of who I am as a scholar, a teacher, and a person. I will always treasure the time my husband and I spent with her and her late husband, Jim Clark, in conversation in their home, and their unparalleled generosity. I remember meeting Isabelle for coffee shortly before she left for India in 2017. I had just received a three-year appointment to teach at Princeton Theological Seminary, and she told me with tears in her eyes that she was proud of me. What a thrill it was to be loved by her! Isabelle was deeply invested in my life and success, and I miss her terribly. I think of her often when I am teaching or meeting with students.

At Princeton University, I thank the Department of Anthropology, the Department of East Asian Studies, the Program in Gender and Sexuality Studies, and the Princeton Institute for International and Regional Studies for their support of the research that made this project possible. I am also grateful to Amy Borovoy, who provided not only generous feedback at the dissertation stage but also demonstrated sustained interest in this project and its success. Rena Lederman and Everett Zhang contributed rich insights at the dissertation stage as well. Carol Greenhouse was always there to talk as I was revising this manuscript into a book, and Carol Zanca is not just an academic mentor but a confidant and friend.

I never would have finished writing my dissertation without the camaraderie and support of my PhD cohort at Princeton. From supporting one another through our graduate exams, to learning alongside one another in the classroom, to phone calls in the field, and then to an amazing year of writing up our dissertations, shoulder to shoulder, I'll always be so grateful for the unique and unparalleled support they gave me. Thank you, Eva Harman, Pablo Landa, Daniel Polk, Saul Schwartz, and Marissa Smith; you are true friends and colleagues. Having Megan Steffen and Serena Stein as colleagues has also been pivotal to this work. And getting to know Susan Ellison as I was writing, and her constant love, mentorship, advice, and friendship, has really gotten me to the finish line.

This book would also not have been possible without the early support of the Princeton Writing Program, where I taught from 2014 to 2017 under Amanda Wilkins's direction and where generous feedback and support of this project from true colleagues was never in short supply. To my friend and writing partner found there, Alex Davis, there's no way to thank you for the substantive feedback on this work, your belief in me, and your wisdom. I can't tell you how much I appreciate your friendship and support. My colleague and friend Anne Moffit's intellectual and emotional support has also been essential and constant.

I thank Fuji Lozada, my thesis adviser at Davidson College for his unwavering support, and for never giving up on his dream of rerouting me to China. I'll always cherish the moment I called to tell him I was finally going! My college roommates and dear friends, Christina Cupani Jarvi, Beth Daniel Lindsay, and Erin Spalinski, have all stuck by me and this project, encouraging me to finish, which has made all the difference.

I'm grateful to my colleagues at the Center of Theological Inquiry and Princeton Theological Seminary for their support of my unconventional career and this project. I'm especially grateful to Victor Aloyo, Eric Barreto, Kenda Dean, Deborah and Lindsey Jodrey, Josh Mauldin, Gordon Mikoski, Hanna Reichel, Abigail Visco Rusert, and William Storrar for their support. I am also thankful to colleagues with whom I studied and became acquainted at the seminary and shortly thereafter— namely, Katherine Anderson and Andrew Brown, Mike Angeloni and Taylor Brown, Kim Copeland, Rob and Lindsey Hankins, Jessie and Jason Lowry, Natalie and Ransom Portis, Ben and Emily Robinson, Brent and Erin Raska, and Zack Shaeffer and Kristina DeMain—for their lifelong friendship. Christie Chow and Joseph Tse-Hei Lee have provided much insight and encouragement as well.

I am thankful to colleagues at the Chinese University of Hong Kong, and especially Joseph Bosco; Cati Coe at Rutgers University–Camden; Guangxi Education College; the late Kay Ann Johnson and Barbara Yngvesson at Hampshire College; Kate Kaup at Furman University; Maochun Liang of the Social Welfare Institute in Guangzhou; the University of Hong Kong; Shunjie Xu and Guangxi Minorities University for their investment in this project.

I am thankful to my Chinese friends, especially Amy, Huan Huan, Helen, and Wendy, who provided invaluable moral and practical support throughout this project. I am also thankful to friends whom I met in China and along the way, including Pam Bowman, the late David Bridgman, Rachel and Jason Deutscher, Caitlin Dwyer and Henry Young, Chris and David Holland, Peter Lim, Brenda Lisenby, Don Snow, and Claire and John Wadsworth. Discovering China alongside all of them was thrilling, and I am thankful for their love and patience with Evan and me.

I am deeply grateful to Barry Federovitch and Sylvia Roberts for providing nursing care for my daughter, Lucia, that has enabled me to finish this book and provided tremendous support to my family.

I thank my family: my parents, my sisters, my parents-in-law, my sister-in-law, my nieces, my aunt, and my husband. I owe a deep debt of gratitude to my mother, not only for all the wisdom and support she has always provided but for her encouragement to enroll in beginning Mandarin in that first semester of doctoral study, when this project was but a twinkle in my eye. She had great vision then and continues to advise me in the most cogent ways both personally and professionally. I thank my father for his undying support and love. I thank my sisters for their companionship and belief in me. I thank my Auntie Lynn for her love and support. I thank my in-laws for their support and for daring to make their first trip out of the country, all the way to China. I also cherish the time we spent with my dad and sisters traveling in Guangxi, and our visits from aforementioned seminary friends. I remember my paternal grandparents, as well as my maternal grandmother and also my maternal grandfather, whom I lost while I was in China but whose life continued to inspire me while I completed and wrote the dissertation and later this book.

Finally, I thank my husband, Evan Schneider, who is my best reader, my best friend, and my true love. I thank him for inspiring this project in so many ways, for his deepest companionship in China, for all the joy he brings to my life and continues to bring, and for giving me our daughter, Lucia Jayne.

We were both so inspired by the foster families' love for their children that we returned from China with a desire to have our own child. This book would not have been possible without those families, my husband, and our daughter, Lucia.

NOTES

PROLOGUE

1. I demonstrate in the introduction that "one-child policy" is a misnomer given the regional variations and implementations of China's birth planning policies from 1979 to the present.

INTRODUCTION

1. I find the nuances in Fei's (1992) theories of Chinese rural and urban life and social relationships rather unappreciated by contemporary anthropologists of China, and yet quite essential to an understanding of an out-of-the-way, rural, yet rapidly transforming place like Guangxi.

2. In this book, I use the terms *children with disabilities* and *disabled children* alternatively to reference both the experience of disability as embodied impairment *and* a social experience of discrimination and marginality; see, for instance, Shakespeare 2006. These *are not* local terms that establish how children with disabilities are viewed in Guangxi but rather theoretical terms that recognize the relationship of my arguments to disability studies theory and justice work. The local and contentious nature of disability in China and its relationship to global politics and family theory is explored further in chapters 1, 2, and 5. In chapters 1 and 2, I go into much more detail regarding the politics of abandonment, foster care, and ICA from China.

3. It is very difficult to gauge an average stay for a child in a foster home because, due to local circumstances, international paperwork, health challenges, and the like, timelines varied considerably. Still, young children with minor disabilities were usually adopted within six months to two years from the time they started to be fostered. For the main three children this books follows, one can easily glean the variance and the ambiguously temporary nature of foster care: one child was fostered for about seven years, another for less than a year and then returned to the orphanage, and another was fostered indefinitely.

4. The expression *"forever" family* is an English-language one used by American and European adoption agencies, and especially by adoptive families. Although Chinese foster families themselves did not use this term, they, alongside state orphanage officials, frequently imagined and positioned their foster children's futures in Western countries and with Western families.

5. The term *elderly* has largely been abandoned by scholars and practitioners of older adulthood for its pejorative connotations. In this book I use *older adults* and *seniors* to refer to Chinese women who are over fifty, because this is the retirement age for women in the People's Republic of China.

6. Daling is a pseudonym used to protect the identities of the foster families and children who live there.

7. Mercy Care is a pseudonym for an American INGO with which I worked closely and which sponsored foster care placements in Guangxi and several other provinces in China from 2004 to 2021.

8. Because CWIs and SWIs still provide institutional care to children and were commonly referred to by locals as *fuliyuan* (orphanage), throughout the book I also use the term *orphanage* to refer to a CWI or SWI.

9. Johnson is trained as a political scientist rather than an anthropologist, but her detailed work relies on hundreds of local interviews alongside a local team of researchers over decades.

10. Meanwhile, the rates of birth defects are skyrocketing, due to pregnant women's exposure to coal smoke and pesticides (Lyn 2011). The number of birth defects has grown 40 percent since 2001, with one million affected children being born each year (Hu 2007). According to population research (Shang 2008a), birth defects have come to replace gender as the most significant category for institutionalized children.

11. Major adoption agencies, such as the Chinese Children Adoption International (CCAI) and Holt International, who now process adoptions of children with disabilities exclusively from China stipulate that all children who go through ICA be fostered prior to their adoptions. Again, although foster care is widely appreciated to be a critical part of readying children for ICA, it remains in the background of such agencies and their work in China.

12. Jing Xu (2017, 61) writes, "I prefer the terms *imagined Chinese* and *imagined Western* instead of *Chinese* and *Western* because this dichotomy has no fixed meaning or boundaries in itself. It only resides in popular imaginations that are subject to changing contextual factors and fluctuating individual experiences." Yet in both their writing on Chinese-Western adoptions, Kay Ann Johnson (2016) and Leslie Wang (2016) establish that whereas the West is often idealized by both Chinese and Westerners, China is vilified by the mass media for its expulsion of infant girls. I agree with Xu that there are no fixed meanings for these terms, but I want to use them both for their imagination and idealism, and therefore I do not qualify them in and of themselves but seek to do so in my analysis.

13. Modell borrows this language of "unselfconscious resistance" from Jean Comaroff (1985, 261), who suggests that resistance may construct counterhegemonies of which individuals are unaware. Modell, in fact, argues that "the *experience* of adoptive kinship involves a *reinterpretation* of American kinship" (1991, 12). It is this reinterpretation that foster families offer of Chinese kinship, and not necessarily the outcome, efficacy, or even force of it, in which I am interested.

CHAPTER 1   ABANDONMENT, AFFINITY, AND SOCIAL VULNERABILITY

1. Johnson's work powerfully illustrates that even at the height of intercountry adoptions in 2005, ICAs from China never exceeded 30 percent—meaning that children, and particularly girls, were being adopted domestically through orphanages and private channels in China all along. As indicated in this book's introduction and as elaborated on by Johnson, the Chinese government's active suppression of domestic adoption was to blame for the explosion in ICA in the early 2000s. Today ICAs have dramatically decreased due to a host of factors and healthy infants are almost exclusively adopted within the PRC; yet one-eighth of those adoptions, as of 2020, were still attributed to foreigners (*Economist* 2020).

Hence, domestic adoption is somewhat an exception to the argument that children abandoned into the orphanage are marked and marred by cultural stigma. Yet, as we see throughout this book, because public attitudes toward such children remain ambivalent, secrecy is often preferred in domestic adoption. Domestic adoption is not widely acknowledged or accepted, indicating that there is still a reticence on the part of locals to appreciate domestic adoption as a viable mode of modern family making. This book will develop similar arguments about foster care and foster families.

2. Portions of this section appeared in Raffety 2017.

3. For a critique of the conflation of the legal category of abandonment with voluntary relinquishment in China, see Johnson 2016, x, 12–13, 23. Indeed, *abandonment*, like all terms, is an imperfect one, which is why I often pair it with the term *social* to advance the argument that it is the social consequences of abandonment that make it so damaging, especially to orphans with disabilities and older persons in China today.

4. For the protection of the informants, all names are pseudonyms.

5. Whereas residential patterns have shifted in many parts of China, my fieldwork demonstrates that brides still traditionally move in with their in-laws following marriage in Guangxi. This leaves families without sons particularly vulnerable and helps explain the extremely skewed gender ratios in regions like Guangxi.

6. For more on the way in which experiences during the Cultural Revolution produced frag-mentation of the self and internal censorship which caused many individuals to keep silent about their suffering, see Kleinman et al. 2011.

7. Given the myriad of cultural definitions of what it means to be an orphan in contemporary China, statistics regarding the number of orphans are often variable. For instance, the statis-tics vary considerably whether one counts only children in state institutional care, or children in kin fosterage, or whether one includes street children and children of the incarcerated. For relevant statistics and for more on these definitions and their importance, see the introduc-tion to this book. Regarding the relevance of considering the cases of orphans, street children, and children of the incarcerated together in order to further characterize and understand the consequences of abandonment, as well as social disability and personhood in Chinese society today, see the summary at the end of this chapter.

8. In his work on American kinship, David Schneider deconstructs the premise that kinship is primarily oriented around biology, arguing that "blood" and biocentrism are symbolic yet flimsy in actually establishing kinship ties; see Schneider 1980, 1984. Perhaps similarly, readers will see throughout the book that although biological families in China warrant a much-sought-after ideal—as many authors have shown elsewhere, and I hope this book helps further—they are but one form among many in contemporary China.

9. While the Chinese government suggests that around ten thousand children are trafficked every year, some experts estimate that number may be as high as seventy thousand (McDon-ald 2012). In Guangxi, the poverty of neighboring Guizhou and Yunnan Provinces, as well as the porous border with Vietnam, presented a particularly precarious situation for trafficking, and during my time there numerous busts of elaborate child trafficking circles were reported by the local police (Z. Yan 2011). Charles Custer and Leia Li's documentary *Living with Dead Hearts* (2013) follows families whose children have been abducted and children who find themselves growing up in strange homes.

Johnson complicates the way in which government policies that have restricted domestic adoptions have made it more difficult for would-be adopted children and their parents to secure *hukou* registration, effectively regulating and trafficking children and funds into state orphanages and abroad; see Johnson 2016, especially chap. 5.

10. For more on how these "playful" interactions between foster mother and foster daughter, while often appearing cruel or disinterested, actually serve to cement the affection and emo-tion of bonds of kinship between the two parties, see chapter 3.

11. Another important political force behind child abandonment in China, especially in the modern era, is the careful structuring of the birth planning and domestic adoption laws that make it very difficult to legally relinquish a child for adoption. In fact, although it is rarely prosecuted as such, several Chinese statutes explicitly list abandonment as a crime, including the Adoption Law, the Law Protecting the Rights and Interests of Women and Children, the Marriage Law, the Protection of the Disabled Law, and the Protection of Minors Law; see High 2013, 133–134. The Adoption Law of the People's Republic of China (first published in 1990), chapter 1, article 3, states explicitly and up front in the general provisions that "adoption shall not contravene laws and regulations on family planning." Chapter 2, article 18, further clarifies, "Persons having placed out a child for adoption may not bear any more children, in violation of the regulations on family planning, on the ground of having placed out their child for adoption." Yet as the conditions for placing a child up for adoption, the law ambiguously

states in chapter 2, article 5 (3), that parents must present "unusual difficulties" that leave them unable to rear children. These conditions are variously interpreted by local officials, who—especially in autonomous regions like Guangxi—have jurisdiction to develop their own implementation policies for these types of laws and overall, make it very difficult to legally relinquish a child. For more on this, see Johnson 2016.

12. What some have called threats, following Jean Briggs (1998, 2000), I label "play," the intersubjective development of relationships (see also Howell 2006) between parents and children that thrives on retorts and questions and often contains layers of complex cultural meaning. Regarding these cultural interactions between parents and children, and the surprising way in which these comments contribute to cultural and familial formation for foster children, see chapter 3.

13. For more on these interventions, see chapters 3 and 4, where I develop the argument that middle-aged state orphanage and INGO monitors were actually threatened by the emerging affection evident in foster families, and lacking in their own family lives, and began to envy these makeshift foster families.

14. For more on *canji* (from *can*, a verb, meaning "to injure or spoil, to destroy or oppress" and *ji*, a noun, meaning "sickness, disease, or pain"), see Kohrman 1999, 892nn10–11.

15. Disability scholars, especially those who support the social model of disability, have often made a general distinction between impairment, a functional limitation of the body, and disability, an experience of discrimination due to society's unwillingness or inability to accommodate those limitations; see, for instance, Shakespeare 2006. Yet, as this chapter shows and as many scholars have pointed out, such distinctions are artificial and often culturally meaningless; see, for instance, Crow 1999 and Siebers 2008. Rather than reinforce the social model of disability, I try to specify in this chapter how perceptions of disability in China are critically tied to personhood, thus broadening the category of who is socially vulnerable beyond disability.

16. The 1950 Marriage Law stressed reciprocal obligations of parents and children for the welfare of the family. The 1980 Marriage Law, which replaced it, clarifies children's obligations to provide for their parents and gives parents the right to prosecute their children if they fail to do so. In collaboration with the 1980 law, the Family Support Agreement, a voluntary contract between parents and children, has been widely implemented throughout rural areas since 1985. A government white paper titled "Development of China's Aging Affairs" (2006) encourages parents and children to sign the Family Support Agreement. In August 2012 China's National Bureau of Senior Affairs released the New 24 Filial Exemplars, which aim to protect the rights and interest of seniors by further conscripting their children into obligatory care. Hence, far from obsolete, the institution of filial piety is being notably reinvigorated by China's government, even as it is being reinterpreted by families and scholars of social life.

17. The concept of social vulnerability is informed by an analogous concept of social psychosis as developed in Biehl 2004 and related to "social suffering" in Bourdieu et al. 1999; Kleinman, Das, and Lock 1997; and Mauss 1979b.

18. Qian 2014 and Wang 2016, both regarding children with disabilities, are two notable exceptions.

CHAPTER 2   FOSTERING (WHOSE) FAMILY?

1. Qian 2014 and Wang 2016, who both focus on disabled children in Chinese welfare institutions and whose work features prominently throughout the book, are two notable exceptions.

2. This argument will be revisited with respect to further ethnographic material in chapter 5.

3. Portions of this chapter first appeared in Raffety 2019.

4. Major adoption agencies such as CCAI and Holt International, which now process adoptions of children with disabilities exclusively from China, stipulate that all children who go through ICA are fostered prior to their adoptions. Although foster care is widely appreciated to be a critical part of readying children for ICA, it remains in the background of such agencies and their work in China.

5. For more on trafficking, see chapter 1.

CHAPTER 3   NEEDY ALLIANCES

1. In chapter 1, I argue that while many children are abandoned because of mental and physical impairments, abandonment in contemporary China makes people socially vulnerable because it deprives them of important social roles and family networks that constitute social personhood. For instance, I show that while Meili was abandoned as a result of a divorce (and not a disability), her story nevertheless references the social abandonment that poor older women and disabled children alike have experienced that makes them eager for the affective, emotional, and social bonds that foster care can provide.

2. In her foundational work on intergenerational caregiving, Esther C. Goh (2011, 16–17) argues for a bidirectional model of caregiving in order to supplement previous models of studying Chinese family relationships that focus unilaterally on parental transmission of values and behaviors to children rather than children's active participation in caregiving. While Goh's argument is instructive, I think that—given the lack of focus in scholarship on Chinese children's personhood and agency—her paradigm of bidirectionality emerges primarily from theoretical debate rather than her ethnographic or quantitative data. In fact, bidirectionality can be misleading in that it does not specify when or how relations between parents and children proceed in *reciprocal, interactive* ways, and thus obscures the authority many Chinese caregivers ultimately retain with respect to their children. In this book and elsewhere (Raffety 2015), I have attempted to remain open to the emergent cultural, interactive, and reciprocal relations between children and adults, acknowledging children's important participation in child-rearing and fostering, in light of a paradigm in which authority in child-rearing still very much rests with the senior generation in China today.

3. In using these words *mutual* and *intersubjective*, I reference Marshall Sahlins's (2013, 28) theorization of Rupert Stasch's interpretation of kinship as based on living lives and deaths together rather than biology. While I think Sahlins's theory does good work in breaking down some of the persistent barriers between biological and fictive or created kinship (see Schneider 1980), I am interested in illustrating more specifically how belonging is created in Chinese foster families by way of particular practices such as play and repositioning social vulnerability.

4. Although the two mothers in question are foster mothers, Auntie Qin is Wei Wei's biological paternal grandmother, and thus this interaction notably straddles the boundaries of play within foster families and biological families.

5. Material from these last three sections has previously appeared in Raffety 2017.

6. According to middle-aged orphanage monitors, such needy alliances were understandable given both foster parents and foster children's social abandonment, but they were also disadvantageous because poor older women were of "low quality," meaning they lacked the requisite education and culture to rear Chinese children poised for adoption to prominent Western nations; see Wang 2010b, 2016. State orphanage and INGO monitors' prejudice against poor older women were reflective of government-sponsored discourse that emphasized the making of modern individuals into "high-quality" citizens through education, enterprise, and development. This emphasis on high-quality (*suzhi*) employed by the Chinese government in population campaigns to express the goal of modernity not only to decrease population size but

also to improve population quality has been widely studied; see Anagnost 1997, 2004; Bakken 2000; Friedman 2006; Greenhalgh 2010; Jacka 2009; Murphy 2004; Sigley 2009; and Wang 2016. Given the perception of retirees as physically and socially marginal, orphanage and INGO workers were skeptical about whether such persons could be remade into "high-quality" citizens and thus subjected them to much scrutiny, surveillance, and critique.

CHAPTER 4   ENVYING KINSHIP

1. For an explanation of *chuxian*, see chapter 1.
2. This phrasing is reminiscent of the complaints of the *ayis* (aunts) that Leslie Wang has observed in an orphanage for disabled children in central China (2010b). American staff were miffed at the Chinese staff's attention to only the children's present and physical needs, as they preferred to see each Chinese child as an individual with unique preferences and future goals. Whereas American and Chinese caregivers attributed these differences to culture, Wang attributes them to class, arguing that certain views of childhood are commensurate with variances in class. While class necessarily comes into view here, my argument also points to the way in which important and deep-seated class and state relations masked intergenerational envy.
3. This example is explored further in chapter 5.
4. Teresa Kuan (2015, 77) discusses attitudes among individuals who referred to themselves as members of the *laosanjie* generation, junior high and high school graduating classes from 1967 through 1969, when urban youths sacrificed education to go down to the countryside "in the spirit of modernization." Many feel that their sacrifice impacted their future, preventing them from benefiting from postrevolution market reforms.

CHAPTER 5   REPLACEABLE FAMILIES?

1. Wesley Ellis (2019) uses disability theology to critique the centrality of diagnosis in caregiving.

CHAPTER 6   DISRUPTIVE FAMILIES

1. In the introduction, I note the 2014 policy change with regard to implementing a two-child maximum, a nine-year formal education minimum, and average financial standing for couples who foster (*China Daily* 2014). At the time of this confrontation, three children were often granted to urban couples who fostered, and before I left the field in 2012, that policy remained. In 2009 and 2010, however, the Ministry of Civil Affairs did clarify minimum standards of living for foster care and orphanage placements—not raising the wages, as Daling foster mothers had advocated for, but attempting to curb abuse toward children.
2. In their scoping review of Chinese foster care as of 2020, Yanfeng Xu and colleagues (2020, 2) argue that finding qualified and motivated foster parents, especially in urban areas, has become a challenge. Most children are being placed with foster families in rural areas, and many children, perhaps owing to their disabilities and the overall decrease in ICA, are not being adopted.

CONCLUSION

1. In my article, "Special Needs Adoption, Demand, and the Global Politics of Disability" (2019), I explore just how international processes of adoption have fostered persistent and

subtle ableism under the guise of benevolence in developed countries as they have simultaneously perpetuated abandonment of disabled children in countries like China. Because disability studies is such an interdisciplinary field, there are few cultural anthropologists at work seeking to provide comprehensive understandings of disability on the ground and even fewer concerned with making sense of these local understandings in tension with international processes and politics of inequality. Thus, I hope my own fieldwork can be repurposed to add and strengthen this interdisciplinary conversation with respect to the contemporary politics of adoption and disability.

2. It is particularly notable that in the case of China, whereas foster parents are prevalent, disclosed, and relatively easy to locate through ICA processes, it is Chinese birth mothers, notoriously difficult to find, who are eagerly and frequently sought out as adoptees return to China on homecoming or roots trips (Yngvesson 2004). Remarkably, in the case of China, the temporal relationships of mothers also prove a flimsy qualifier for motherhood: whereas birth mothers are present in children's lives for short periods of time before children are often abandoned in China, as my ethnography shows, foster mothers often raise children for lengthy stints.

3. In my own fieldwork, I certainly discovered parallelism and interplay between forms and practices of foster kinship and biocentric kinship in China; for instance, older foster parents employed playful teasing strategies that reinforced the belonging of foster children precisely on the basis of their ability to be rejected from what already smacked of biocentric kinship (see chapter 3).

Chen, Feinian. 2005. "Residential Patterns of Parents and Their Married Children in Contemporary China: A Life Course Approach." *Population Research and Policy Review* 24 (2): 125–148.

Chen, Feinian, Guangya Lu, and Christine A. Mair. 2011. "Intergenerational Ties in Context: Grandparents Caring for Grandchildren in China." *Social Forces* 90 (2): 571–594.

Chen, Janet. 2012. *Guilty of Indigence: The Poor in Urban China, 1900–1953.* Princeton, NJ: Princeton University Press.

Cheney, Kristen. 2014. "'Giving Children a Better Life'? Reconsidering Social Reproduction, Humanitarianism and Development in Intercountry Adoption." *European Journal of Development Research* 26 (2): 247–263.

China Daily. 2014. "China's Faltering Steps on Family Foster Care." December 1, 2014. http://usa.chinadaily.com.cn/china/2014-12/01/content_19001696.htm.

Cohen, Myron L. 1993. "Cultural and Political Inventions in Modern China: The Case of the Chinese 'Peasant.'" *Daedalus* 122 (2): 151–170.

Colen, Shellee. 1995. "'Like a Mother to Them': Stratified Reproduction and West Indian Childcare Workers and Employers in New York." In *Conceiving the New World Order: The Global Politics of Reproduction*, edited by Faye Ginsburg and Rayna Rapp, 78–102. Berkeley: University of California Press.

Collier, Jane, Michelle Rosaldo, and Sylvia Yanagisako. 1982. "Is There a Family? New Anthropological Views." In *Rethinking the Family: Some Feminist Questions*, edited by Barrie Thorne and Marilyn Yalom, 31–48. New York: Longman Books.

Comaroff, Jean. 1985. *Body of Power, Spirit of Resistance: The Culture and History of a South African People.* Chicago: University of Chicago Press.

Crary, David. 2010. "Adopting China's Special-Needs Kids." *NBC News*, March 28. https://www.nbcnews.com/health/health-news/adopting-china-s-special-needs-kids-flna1c9449418.

———. 2019. "Foreign Adoptions Fall to US Fall by 14 percent Continuing Trend." *AP News*, March 14, 2019. https://apnews.com/article/4d9bacba78da438aa02aa6549cbac3a6.

Croll, Elisabeth J. 2010. "The Intergenerational Contract in the Changing Asian Family." *Oxford Development Studies* 34 (4): 473–491.

Crow, Liz. 1999. "Including All of Our Lives: Renewing the Social Model of Disability." In *Encounters with Strangers: Feminism and Disability*, edited by Jenny Morris, 1–21. London: Women's Press.

Custer, Charles, and Leia Li, dirs. 2012. *Living with Dead Hearts.* Songhua, https://vimeo.com/70711924.

Davis, Deborah, and Stevan Harrell, eds. 1993. *Chinese Families in the Post-Mao Era.* Berkeley: University of California Press.

Demick, Barbara. 2009. "China Blames Pollution for Surge in Birth Defects." *Los Angeles Times*, February 2, 2009. https://www.latimes.com/archives/la-xpm-2009-feb-02-fg-china-birth-defects2-story.html.

Dorow, Sara K. 2006. *Transnational Adoption: A Cultural Economy of Race, Gender, and Kinship.* New York: New York University Press.

Economist. 2020. "For People in China, Adopting Chinese Children Is Getting Easier." June 4, 2020. https://www.economist.com/china/2020/06/04/for-people-in-china-adopting-chinese-children-is-getting-easier.

Ellis, Wesley W. 2019. "Diagnosing Adolescence: From Curing Adolescents to Caring Young People." *Journal of Disability and Religion* 22 (4): 390–407.

Eng, David L. 2006. "Political Economics of Passion: Transnational Adoption and Global Woman: Roundtable on Global Woman." *Studies in Gender and Sexuality* 7 (1): 49–59.

Evans, Karin. 2008. *The Lost Daughters of China: Adopted Girls, Their Journey to America, and the Search for a Missing Past*. New York: TarcherPerigee.

Fei Xiaotong. 1992. *From the Soil: The Foundations of Chinese Society*. Translated by Gary G. Hamilton and Wang Zheng. Berkeley: University of California Press.

Fisher, Karen R., and Xiaoyuan Shang. 2014. "Protecting the Right to Life of Children with Disabilities in China." *Journal of Social Service Research* 40 (4): 560–572.

Fong, Vanessa. 2004. "Filial Nationalism among Teenagers with Global Identities." *American Ethnologist* 31 (4): 631–648.

Franklin, Sarah. 2013. *Biological Relatives, IVF, Stem Cells, and the Future of Kinship*. Durham, NC: Duke University Press.

Franklin, Sarah, and Susan McKinnon, eds. 2002. *Relative Values: Reconfiguring Kinship Studies*. Durham, NC: Duke University Press.

Friedman, Sara. 2006. *Intimate Politics: Marriage, the Market, and State Power in Southeastern China*. Cambridge, MA: Harvard University Asia Center.

Ginsburg, Faye, and Rayna Rapp, eds. 1995. *Conceiving the New World Order: The Global Politics of Reproduction*. Berkeley: University of California Press.

Global Times. 2015. "Homes for the Abandoned." August 2, 2015. Accessed November 17, 2021. https://www.globaltimes.cn/content/935066.shtml.

Goffman, Erving. 1963. *Stigma: Notes on the Management of Spoiled Identity*. Englewood Cliffs, NJ: Prentice-Hall.

Goh, Esther C. L. 2009. "Grandparents as Childcare Providers: An In-Depth Analysis of the Case of Xiamen, China." *Journal of Aging Studies* 23 (1): 60–68.

———. 2011. *China's One-Child Policy and Multiple Caregiving: Raising Little Suns in Xiamen*. New York: Routledge.

Goody, Esther N. 1982. *Parenthood and Social Reproduction*. Cambridge: Cambridge University Press.

Goody, Jack. 2004. *Comparative Studies in Kinship*. London: Routledge.

Greenhalgh, Susan. 2010. "Governing Chinese Life: From Sovereignty to Biopolitical Governance." In *Governance of Life in Chinese Moral Experience: The Quest for an Adequate Life*, edited by Everett Yuehong Zhang, Arthur Kleinman, and Weiming Tu, 146–162. New York: Routledge.

Greenhalgh, Susan, and Edwin A. Winckler. 2005. *Governing China's Population: From Leninist to Neoliberal Biopolitics*. Stanford, CA: Stanford University Press.

Guan Xiaofeng. 2006. "Nationwide Plan for Better Care of Orphans." *China Daily*, December 29, 2006. http://www.chinadaily.com.cn/china/2006-12/29/content_770291.htm.

Guo Jinhua and Arthur Kleinman. 2011. "Stigma: HIV/AIDS, Mental Illness, and China's Nonpersons." In Arthur Kleinman, Yunxiang Yan, Jing Jun, Sing Lee, Everett Zhang, Pan Tianshu, Wu Fei, and Guo Jinhua, *Deep China: The Moral Life of the Person; What Anthropology and Psychiatry Tell Us about China Today*, 237–262. Berkeley: University of California Press.

Hays, Sharon. 1996. *The Cultural Contradictions of Motherhood*. New Haven, CT: Yale University Press.

High, Anne Jane. 2013. "China's Orphan Welfare System: Laws, Policies, and Filled Gaps." *University of Pennsylvania East Asia Law Review* 8 (2): 126–176.

Ho, David Y. F. 1986. "Chinese Patterns of Socialization: A Critical Review." In *The Psychology of Chinese People*, edited by Michael Harris Bond, 1–37. New York: Oxford University Press.

Holroyd, Eleanor E. 2003. "Chinese Cultural Influences on Parental Caregiving: Obligations toward Children with Disabilities." *Qualitative Health Research* 13 (1): 4–19.

Howell, Signe. 2003. "Kinning: The Creation of Life Trajectories in Transnational Adoptive Families." *Journal of the Royal Anthropological Institute* 9 (3): 465–484.

————. 2006. *The Kinning of Foreigners*. Oxford: Berghahn Books.

Hu, Bi Ying, and Judit Szente. 2009. "The Care and Education of Orphan Children with Disabilities in China: Progress and Remaining Challenges." *Childhood Education* 86 (2): 78–86.

Hu Yinan. 2007. "Baby Born with Birth Defects Every 30 Seconds." *China Daily*, October 30, 2007. http://www.chinadaily.com.cn/cndy/2007-10/30/content_6214736.htm.

Human Rights Watch Asia. 1996. *Death by Default: A Policy of Fatal Neglect in China's State Orphanages*. New York: Human Rights Watch.

Jacka, Tamara. 2009. "Cultivating Citizens: Suzhi Discourse (Quality) in the PRC." *Positions: East Asia Culture Critique* 17 (3): 523–535.

Jimmerson, Julie. 1990. "Female Infanticide in China: An Examination of Cultural and Legal Norms." *UCLA Pacific Basin Law Journal* 8 (1): 47–79.

Johnson, Kay Ann. 2004. *Wanting a Daughter, Needing a Son: Abandonment, Adoption, and Orphanage Care in China*. St. Paul, MN: Yeong and Yeong.

————. 2016. *China's Hidden Children: Abandonment, Adoption, and the Human Costs of the One-Child Policy*. Chicago: University of Chicago Press.

Joyce, Kathryn. 2013. *The Child Catchers: Rescue, Trafficking, and the New Gospel of Adoption*. New York: PublicAffairs.

Kasnitz, Devva, and Russell Peter Shuttleworth. 1999. "Engaging Anthropology in Disability Studies." *Position Papers in Disability Policy Studies* 1(1): 1–37.

Kaup, Katherine Palmer. 2000. *Creating the Zhuang: Ethnic Politics in China*. Boulder, CO: Lynne Rienner.

Keyser, Catherine. 2009. "The Role of the State and NGOs in Caring for At-Risk Children: The Case of Orphan Care." In *State and Society Responses to Welfare Needs in China: Serving the People*, edited by Jonathan Schwartz and Shawn Hsieh, 45–65. New York: Routledge.

Kipnis, Andrew. 1997. *Producing Guanxi: Sentiment, Self, and Subculture in a North China Village*. Durham, NC: Duke University Press.

————. 2011. *Governing Educational Desire: Culture, Politics, and Schooling in China*. Chicago: University of Chicago Press.

Kleinman, Arthur, Veena Das, and Margaret Lock, eds. 1997. *Social Suffering*. Berkeley: University of California Press.

Kleinman, Arthur, Yunxiang Yan, Jing Jun, Sing Lee, Everett Zhang, Pan Tianshu, Wu Fei, and Guo Jinhua. 2011. "Introduction." In Arthur Kleinman, Yunxiang Yan, Jing Jun, Sing Lee, Everett Zhang, Pan Tianshu, Wu Fei, and Guo Jinhua, *Deep China: The Moral Life of the Person; What Anthropology and Psychiatry Tell Us about China Today*, 1–35. Berkeley: University of California Press.

Kohrman, Matthew. 1999. "Grooming 'que zi': Marriage Exclusion and Identity Formation among Disabled Men in Contemporary China." *American Ethnologist* 26 (4): 890–909.

————. 2005. *Bodies of Difference: Experiences of Disability and Institutional Advocacy in the Making of Modern China*. Berkeley: University of California Press.

Kwok, Siu Ming, Dora Tam, and Roy Hanes. 2018. "An Exploratory Study into Social Welfare Policies and Social Service Delivery Models for People with Disabilities in China." *Global Social Welfare: Research, Policy, and Practice* 5 (3): 155–165.

Kuan, Teresa. 2015. *Love's Uncertainty: The Politics and Ethics of Child Rearing in Contemporary China*. Berkeley: University of California Press.

Lafraniere, Sharon. 2011. "Chinese Officials Seized and Sold Babies, Parents Say." *New York Times*, August 4, 2011. https://www.nytimes.com/2011/08/05/world/asia/05kidnapping.html.

Lareau, Annette. 2003. *Unequal Childhoods: Class, Race, and Family Life*. Berkeley: University of California Press.

Laurie, Timothy, and Hannah Stark. 2012. "Reconsidering Kinship: Beyond the Nuclear Family with Deleuze and Guattari." *Cultural Studies Review* 18 (1): 19–39.

Layne, Linda S., ed. 1999. *Transformative Motherhood: On Giving and Getting in a Consumer Culture*. New York: New York University Press.

Lederman, Rena. 2013. "Ethics: Practices, Principles, and Comparative Perspectives." In *The Handbook of Sociocultural Anthropology*, edited by James G. Carrier and Deborah B. Gewertz, 588–611. London: Bloomsbury Academic.

Leinaweaver, Jessaca B. 2013. *Adoptive Migration: Raising Latinos in Spain*. Durham, NC: Duke University Press.

Levin, Dan. 2014. "Many in China Can Now Have Second Child, but Say No." *New York Times*, February 25, 2014. https://www.nytimes.com/2014/02/26/world/asia/many-couples-in-china-will-pass-on-a-new-chance-for-a-second-child.html.

Levi-Strauss, Claude. 1969. *The Elementary Structures of Kinship*. Boston: Beacon Press.

Liu Huawen. 2004. "The Child's Right to Birth Registration—International and Chinese Perspectives." Research Note, Norwegian Centre for Human Rights, Oslo.

Lyn, Tan Ee. 2011. "Birth Defects Linked to Coal Smoke, Pesticides: China Study." *Reuters*, July 18, 2011. https://www.reuters.com/article/us-china-pollution-birthdefects/birth-defects-linked-to-coal-smoke-pesticides-china-study-idINTRE76H50J20110718.

Maine, H. S. 1861. *Ancient Law*. London: J. Murray.

Malinowski, Bronislaw. 1930. "Parenthood—The Basis of Social Structure." In *The New Generation: The Intimate Problems of Modern Parents and Children*, edited by V. F. Calverton and Samuel D. Schmalhausen. New York: Macaulay.

Marre, Diana, and Laura Briggs, eds. 2012. *Somebody's Children: The Politics of Transnational and Transracial Adoption*. Durham, NC: Duke University Press.

Mauss, Marcel. 1979a. "The Notion of Body Techniques." In *Sociology and Psychology: Essays*, translated by Ben Brewster, 95–119. London: Routledge and Kegan Paul.

———. 1979b. "The Physical Effect on the Individual of the Idea of Death Suggested by the Collectivity." In *Sociology and Psychology: Essays*, translated by Ben Brewster, 35–56. London: Routledge and Kegan Paul.

———. 1990. *The Gift: The Form and Reason for Exchange in Archaic Societies*. New York: W.W. Norton & Company, Inc.

McDonald, Mark. 2012. "Buy, Sell, Adopt: Child Trafficking in China." *New York Times*, December 26, 2012. https://rendezvous.blogs.nytimes.com/2012/12/26/buy-sell-adopt-child-trafficking-in-china/.

McDonell, Stephen. 2021. "China Allows Three Children in Major Policy Shift." *BBC News*, May 31, 2021. https://www.bbc.com/news/world-asia-china-57303592.

McRuer, Robert. 2006. *Crip Theory: Cultural Signs of Queerness and Disability*. New York: New York University Press.

Meier, Patricia J., and Xiaole Zhang. 2008. "Sold into Adoption: The Hunan Babytrafficking Scandal Exposes Vulnerabilities in Chinese Adoptions to the United States." *Cumberland Law Review* 39 (1): 87–103.

Ming, Yang. 2021. "China to Raise Retirement Age to Offset Funding Shortfall." *Voice of America*, March 17, 2021. https://www.voanews.com/a/east-asia-pacific_voa-news-china_china-raise-retirement-age-offset-funding-shortfall/6203387.html.

Modell, Judith S. 1994. *Kinship among Strangers: Adoption and Interpretation of Kinship in American Culture*. Berkeley: University of California Press.

———. 1999. "Freely Given: Open Adoption and the Rhetoric of the Gift." In *Transformative Motherhood: On Giving and Getting in a Consumer Culture*, edited by Linda L. Layne, 29–64. New York: New York University Press.

Murphy, Rachel. 2004. "Turning Peasants into Modern Chinese Citizens: 'Population Quality' Discourse, Demographic Transition, and Primary Education." *China Quarterly*, no. 177, 1–20.

Myers, Allan, dir. 2005. *China's Lost Girls*. Washington, D.C.: National Geographic Video.

Naftali, Orna. 2014. *Children, Rights, and Modernity in China*. Basingstoke, UK: Palgrave Macmillan.

Office of Children's Issues. 2013. *FY 2012 Annual Report on Intercountry Adoption*. Washington, D.C.: U.S. Department of State, Bureau of Consular Affairs.

Ong, Aihwa. 1999. *Flexible Citizenship: The Cultural Logics of Transnationality*. Durham, NC: Duke University Press.

———. 2006. *Neoliberalism as Exception: Mutations in Citizenship and Sovereignty*. Durham, NC: Duke University Press.

Oxfeld, Ellen. 2010. *Drink Water, but Remember the Source: Moral Discourse in a Chinese Village*. Berkeley: University of California Press.

Parsons, Talcott. 1955. *Family: Socialization, and Interaction Process*. Glencoe, IL: Free Press.

Potter, Sulamith Heins, and Jack M. Potter. 1990. *China's Peasants: The Anthropology of a Revolution*. New York: Cambridge University Press.

Qian, Linliang. 2014. "Consuming 'the Unfortunate': The Violence of Philanthropy in a Contemporary Chinese State-Run Orphanage." *Dialectical Anthropology* 38 (3): 247–279.

Raffety, Erin. 2015. "Minimizing Social Distance: Participatory Research with Children." *Childhood: A Journal of Global Child Research* 22 (3): 409–422.

———. 2017. "Fostering Change: Elderly Foster Mothers' Intergenerational Influence in Contemporary China." In *Transnational Aging and Reconfigurations of Kin Work*, edited by Parin Dossa and Cati Coe, 92–111. New Brunswick, NJ: Rutgers University Press.

———. 2019. "China Special Needs Adoption, Demand, and the Global Politics of Disability." *Disability Studies Quarterly* 39 (2). https://dsq-sds.org/article/view/6662/5249.

Ragone, Helen. 1994. *Surrogate Motherhood: Conception in the Heart*. Boulder, CO: Westview.

Ripley, Will. 2015. "'They Don't Deserve this Kind of Life:' Meet China's Abandoned Children." *CNN*, August 12, 2015. https://www.cnn.com/2015/08/11/asia/china-orphanage-children /index.html.

Sahlins, Marshall. 2013. *What Kinship Is—And Is Not*. Chicago: University of Chicago Press.

Sangren, P. Steven. 1995. "'Power' against Ideology: A Critique of Foucaultian Usage." *Cultural Anthropology* 10 (1): 3–40.

Scheper-Hughes, Nancy. 1993. *Death without Weeping: The Violence of Life in Everyday Brazil*. Berkeley: University of California Press.

Schneider, David. 1980. *American Kinship: A Cultural Account*. Chicago: University of Chicago Press.

———. 1984. *A Critique of the Study of Kinship*. Ann Arbor: University of Michigan Press.

Shakespeare, Tom. 2006. "The Social Model of Disability." In *The Disability Studies Reader*, edited by Lennard J. Davis, 2nd ed., 197–204. New York: Routledge.

Shang Xiaoyuan. 2002. "Looking for a Better Way to Care for Children: Cooperation between the State and Civil Society in China." *Social Science Review* 76 (2): 203–228.

———. 2008a. "The Role of Extended Families in Childcare and Protection: The Case of Rural China." *International Journal of Social Welfare* 17: 204–215.

———. 2008b. *Zhongguo ruoshi ertong qunti baozhu zhidu* [System of Social Support for Vulnerable Children in China]. Beijing: China Social Sciences Academic Press.

———. 2010. *Zhongguo er tong fu li qian yan wen ti* [Discovery report: Emerging issues and findings for child welfare and protection in China]. Beijing: China Social Sciences Academic Press.

———. 2011. *Zhongguo ertong fuli qianyan wenti* [The front lines of Chinese children's welfare]. Beijing: Social Sciences Academic Press.

Shang Xiaoyuan and Cheng Jianpeng. 2006. "Zhongguo gu'er zhuangkuang fenxi" [Analysis of the situation of China's orphans]. *Youth Studies*, no. 10, 8–12.

Shang, Xiaoyuan, and Karen R. Fisher. 2014. *Caring for Orphaned Children in China*. Lanham, MD: Lexington Books.

———. 2016. *Disability Policy in China: Child and Family Experiences*. London: Routledge.

———. 2017. *Young People Leaving State Care in China*. Bristol, UK: Policy Press.

Shang, Xiaoyuan, Karen R. Fisher, and Jiawen Xie. 2011. "Discrimination against Children with Disability in China." *International Journal of Social Welfare* 20 (3): 298–308.

Shang, Xiaoyuan, Morris Saldov, and Karen R. Fisher. 2011. "Informal Kinship Care of Orphans in Rural China." *Social Policy and Society* 10 (1): 103–116.

Shang, Xiaoyuan, and Xiaoming Wu. 2011. "The Care Regime in China: Elder and Child Care." *Journal of Comparative Social Welfare* 27 (2): 123–131.

Shang Xiaoyuan, Wu Xiaoming, and Li Haiyan. 2005. *Shehui zhengce, Shehui xinbie yu Zhongguo de ertong yiqi wenti* [Social policy, social gender and the problem of infant abandonment in China]. *Youth Studies* 4 (1): 1.

Shen, Qing, Helen McCabe, and Zhaoyang Chi. 2008. "Disability Education in the People's Republic of China: Tradition, Reform and Outlook." In *Disability and the politics of education: An International Reader*, edited by Susan L. Gabel and Scot Danforth, 177–200. New York: Peter Lang.

Siebers, Tobin. 2008. *Disability Theory*. Ann Arbor: University of Michigan Press.

Sigley, Gary. 2009. "*Suzhi*, The Body, and The Fortunes of Technoscientific Reasoning in Contemporary China." *Positions: East Asia Culture Critique* (17) 3: 537–566.

Smyke, Anna T., Charles H. Zeanah, Nathan A. Fox, Charles A. Nelson, and Donald Guthrie. 2010. "Placement in Foster Care Enhances Attachment among Young Children in Institutions." *Child Development*, no. 81, 212–223.

Sohu News. 2015. *Daibiao tijiao yi'an fandui she qi ying dao cheng zhi bianxiang guli yiqi* [Representative submitted a motion to oppose baby hatch on basis that it encourages child abandonment], May 11, 2015. http://news.sohu.com/20150311/n409607601.shtml.

Solinger, D. 1999. *Contesting Citizenship in Urban China: Peasant Migrants, the State, and the Logic of the Market*. Berkeley: University of California Press.

Strathern, Marilyn. 1988. *The Gender of the Gift*. Berkeley: University of California Press.

———. 1992. *After Nature: English Kinship in the Late Twentieth Century*. Cambridge: Cambridge University Press.

Stryker, Rachael. 2010. *The Road to Evergreen: Adoption, Attachment Therapy, and the Promise of Family*. Ithaca, NY: Cornell University Press, 2010.

Sun, Wenjie, Yumei Zheng, and Yiqiong Xie. 2016. "The Future of Baby Hatches in China." *Women and Birth: Journal of the Australian College of Midwives* 29 (3): e58.

Tan, Shen Wu. 2021. "China Is One of Few Countries Not to Resume International Adoption, Experts Say." *Washington Times*, August 31, 2021. https://www.washingtontimes.com/news/2021/aug/30/china-only-country-not-resume-international-adopti/.

Tatlow, Didi Kirsten. 2012. "China's 'Left-Behind' Children." *New York Times*, June 1, 2012. https://rendezvous.blogs.nytimes.com/2012/06/01/chinas-left-behind-children/.

Taylor, Janelle S., Linda S. Layne, and Danielle F. Wozniak, eds. 2004. *Consuming Motherhood*. New Brunswick, NJ: Rutgers University Press.

Tobin, Joseph J., David Y. H. Wu, and Dana H. Davidson. 1991. *Preschool in Three Cultures: Japan, China, and the United States*. Chicago: University of Chicago Press.

Tronto, Joan C. 1993. *Moral Boundaries: A Political Argument for the Ethic of Care.* New York: Routledge.

Tu Wei-ming. 1978. *Humanity and Self-Cultivation: Essays in Confucian Thought.* Boston: Asian Humanities.

———. 1985. *Confucian Thought: Selfhood as Creative Transformation.* Albany: State University of New York Press.

Vanderklippe, Nathan. 2014. "The Tragic Tale of China's Orphanage's: 98% of Abandoned Children Have Disabilities." *Globe and Mail*, March 21, 2014. https://www.theglobeandmail .com/news/world/the-tragic-tale-of-chinas-orphanages-98-of-abandoned-children-have -disabilities/article17625887/.

Waltner, Ann. 1990. *Getting an Heir: Adoption and the Construction of Kinship in Late Imperial China.* Honolulu, HI: University of Hawai'i Press.

Wang, Leslie K. 2010a. "Children on the Margins: The Global Politics of Orphanage Care in Contemporary China." PhD diss., University of California–Berkeley.

———. 2010b. "Importing Western Childhoods into a Chinese State-Run Orphanage." *Qualitative Sociology* 33 (2): 137–159.

———. 2015. "Producing Global Adoptability of Special Needs Children in China." *Positions: East Asia Culture Critique* 24 (1): 129–154.

———. 2016. *Outsourced Children: Orphanage Care and Adoption in Globalizing China.* Stanford, CA: Stanford University Press.

Wang, Wen-chi, Robert B. McCall, Junlei Li, Christina J. Groark, Fanlin Zeng, and Xiaolin Hu. 2017. "Chinese Collective Foster Care Model: Description and Evaluation." *International Social Work* 60 (2): 435–451.

Watson, James L. 1975. "Agnates and Outsiders: Adoption in a Chinese Lineage." *Man* 10 (2): 298–299.

Weismantel, Mary J. 1989. *Food, Gender, and Poverty in the Ecuadorian Andes.* Philadelphia: University of Pennsylvania Press.

Weston, Kath. 1991. *Families We Choose: Lesbians, Gays, Kinship.* New York: Columbia University Press.

———. 2005. "Families in Queer States: The Rule of Law and the Politics of Recognition." *Radical History Review*, no. 93, 122–141.

Whetten, Kathryn, Jan Ostermann, Brian W. Pence, Rachel A. Whetten, Lynne C. Messer, Sumedha Ariely, Karen O'Donnell, Augustine I. Wasonga, Vanroth Vann, Dafrosa Itemba, Misganaw Eticha, Ira Madan, and Nathan M. Thielman, Positive Outcomes for Orphans (POFO) Research Team. 2014. "Three-Year Change in the Wellbeing of Orphaned and Separated Children in Institutional and Family-Based Care Settings in Five Low-and Middle-Income Countries." *PLoS ONE* 9 (8): e104872.

Whetten, Kathryn, Jan Ostermann, Rachel A. Whetten, Brian W. Pence, Karen O'Donnell, Lynne C. Messer, and Nathan M. Thielman, Positive Outcomes for Orphans (POFO) Research Team. 2009. "A Comparison of the Wellbeing of Orphans and Abandoned Children Ages 6–12 in Institutional and Community-Based Care Settings in 5 Less Wealthy Nations." *PLoS ONE* 4 (12): e8169.

Whyte, Martin, ed. 2010. *One Country, Two Societies: Rural-Urban Inequality in Contemporary China.* Cambridge, MA: Harvard University Press.

Williams, Fiona. 2001. "In and beyond New Labour: Towards a New Political Ethics of Care." *Critical Social Policy* 21 (4): 467–493.

Wolf, Arthur P and Chieh-shan Huang. 1980. *Marriage and Adoption in China, 1845–1945.* Stanford, CA: Stanford University Press.

Wolf, Margery. 1968. *House of Lim.* New York: Random House.

———. 1970. "Child Training and the Chinese Family." In *Family and Kinship in Chinese Society*, edited by Maurice Freedman, 37–62. Stanford, CA: Stanford University Press.

———. 1972. "Uterine Families and the Women's Community." In *Women and the Family in Rural Taiwan*, 32–41. Stanford, CA: Stanford University Press.

Wozniak, Danielle. 2002. *They're All My Children: Foster Mothering in America.* New York: New York University Press.

Wu, David Y. H. 1996. "Parental Control: Psychocultural Interpretations of Chinese Patterns of Socialization." In *Growing Up the Chinese Way: Chinese Child and Adolescent Development*, edited by Sing Lau, 1–28. Hong Kong: Chinese University Press.

Wu Yuping, Han Xiaoyu, and Gao Qin. 2005. *Jiating Jiyang: Dongji yu Jixiao* [Family fostering: Motivation and effect]. Beijing: Social Sciences Academic Press.

Xinran. 2011. *Message from an Unknown Chinese Mother: Stories of Loss and Love.* New York: Scribner.

Xu, Jing. 2017. *The Good Child: Moral Development in a Chinese Preschool.* Stanford, CA: Stanford University Press.

Xu, Yanfeng, Xiaoou Man, Lixia Zhang, and Bruce DeForge. 2020. "Family Foster Care and Children's Outcomes in China: Evidence from a Scoping Review." *Children and Youth Services Review*, no. 108, 1–13.

Yan, Yunxiang. 2003. *Private Life under Socialism: Love, Intimacy, and Family Change in a Chinese Village, 1949–1999.* Stanford, CA: Stanford University Press.

———. 2011a. "The Changing Moral Landscape." In Arthur Kleinman, Yunxiang Yan, Jing Jun, Sing Lee, Everett Zhang, Pan Tianshu, Wu Fei, and Guo Jinhua, *Deep China: The Moral Life of the Person; What Anthropology and Psychiatry Tell Us about China Today*, 36–77. Berkeley: University of California Press.

———. 2011b. "The Individualization of the Family in Rural China." *Boundary 2* 38 (1): 203–229.

———. 2018. "Neo-Familism and the State in China." *Urban Anthropology* 47 (3–4): 1–44.

Yan, Zhang. 2011. "Cross-border Human Trafficking Cases Rising." *People's Daily*, August 12, 2011. http://en.people.cn/90882/7567577.html.

Yang, Mayfair Mei-hui. 2013. "Foucault and China Studies." Paper presented at the panel "Foucault and China Studies," American Anthropological Association Annual Meeting, Chicago, November 20–24, 2013.

Ye Jingzhong. 2011. "Left-Behind Children: The Social Price of China's Economic Boom." *Journal of Peasant Studies* 38 (3): 613–650.

Ye Jingzhong and James Murray. 2005. *Left Behind Children in Rural China: Impact Study of Rural Labor Migration on Left-Behind Children in Mid-west China.* Beijing: Social Science Academic Press.

Ye Jingzhong and Pan Lu. 2011. "Differentiated Childhoods: Impacts of Rural Labor Migration on Left-Behind Children in China." *Journal of Peasant Studies* 38 (2): 355–377.

Yngvesson, Barbara. 2004. "'Going Home': Adoption, Loss of Bearings, and the Mythology of Roots." In *Consuming Motherhood*, edited by Janelle S. Taylor, Linda S. Layne, and Danielle F. Wozniak, 168–186. New Brunswick, NJ: Rutgers University Press.

———. 2010. *Belonging in an Adopted World: Race, Identity, and Transnational Adoption.* Chicago: University of Chicago Press.

Zai Liang. 2011. "Migration and Development in Rural China." *Modern China Studies* 18 (1): 73–100.

Zelizer, Viviana. 1994. *Pricing the Priceless Child: The Changing Social Value of Children.* Princeton, NJ: Princeton University Press.

Zhang, Everett, Arthur Kleinman, and Weiming Tu, eds. 2011. *Governance of Life in Chinese Moral Experience: The Quest for an Adequate Life.* London: Routledge.

Zhang, Hong. 2004. "'Living Alone' and the Rural Elderly: Strategy and Agency in Post-Mao Rural China." In *Filial Piety: Practice and Discourse in Contemporary East Asia*, edited by Charlotte Ikels, 63–87. Stanford, CA: Stanford University Press.

———. 2005. "Bracing for an Uncertain Future: A Case Study of New Coping Strategies of Rural Parents under China's Birth Control Policy." *China Journal*, no. 54, 53–76.

Zhang, Li. 2002. *Strangers in the City: Reconfigurations of Space, Power, and Social Networks within China's Floating Population*. Stanford, CA: Stanford University Press.

Zhang, Weiguo. 2006. "Who Adopts Girls and Why? Domestic Adoption of Female Children in Contemporary China." *China Journal*, no. 56, 63–82.

Zhao, Beige. 2012. "Foreword." In *Early Child Development in China*, edited by Kin Bing Wu, Mary Eming Young, and Jianhua Cai, xv–xvi. Washington, D.C.: World Bank.

Zhao, Xintong, and Chao Zhang. 2018. "From Isolated Fence to Inclusive Society: The Transformational Disability Policy in China." *Disability and Society* 33 (1): 132–137.

INDEX

abandonment: baby hatches, 10, 32, 59–60; children, 13, 74–75; children's stories, 32, 35–43, 44–46, 72–73, 79, 90, 99, 121, 132; Chinese culture, 21–22, 47–49, 117; disabled children, 5, 47, 52, 59, 61, 112; elders, 34–35, 50–51, 81–83, 131; girls, 7–8, 57; increasing rates for disabled children, 11–12, 28, 46, 58–59, 62–63, 67; relationship to inter-country adoption (ICA), 33, 55, 64–65, 67–69, 135, 149n2, 154–155n1; social, 27–28, 34, 38–39, 43, 49–53, 83–84, 137, 150n3, 151n7, 153n1; by state government, 41, 43–44, 69, 126; threats of, 91
ableism, 23, 29, 55–56, 65, 67–68, 70, 103, 116–117, 154–155n1
abnormality, 70–71, 117; familism, 50, 58, 107–109, 112–113; foster families, 100; with respect to disability, 98, 103; social roles, 52
adoption: ableism, 154–155n1; abroad, 3, 5, 19, 37–38, 52; agencies, 11–12, 63, 149n4, 150n11, 153n4; *chuxian*, 41–43; domestic, 8, 32–33, 39, 58; to "forever" families, 4; global politics, 47; intercountry adoption (ICA), 4, 53, 62–69, 79, 88, 103, 128, 135; kin, 7, 30–31; Meili, 38–39; Mercy Care, 49; in Nanning, 13; relationship to foster care, 14–15, 21, 34, 138–140; relationship to incarceration, 40; relationship to kinship, 21–29; suppression of domestic adoption, 5, 7–11, 25, 55–58, 60–61, 64–65, 151n9; wanting me to adopt, 54
advocacy, 25, 47–48, 124, 144
affection: effected through play, 76, 78, 151n10; encouraged by foster monitors, 46, 99, 152n13; within foster families, 25, 28–29, 39, 69, 72, 88, 118, 129; lacking, 91, 122, 136, 140
affinity, 27, 30
agency, 74, 153n2
alliances, 28, 50, 70, 88, 90, 137
ambivalence: attachment, 76; attitudes toward abandoned children, 150n1;

intergenerational, 25, 28–29, 84–85, 95–99; toward me, 79; motherhood, 90; neofamilism, 135; between orphanage and Mercy Care, 18
Anhui, 4
anthropology, 27, 94, 134, 138
appearances, 10, 97; *chuxian*, 41, 79; with respect to abnormality, 70–71, 73, 107–108, 119
Ariès, Philippe, 92
Asia, 7, 33
authority, 73, 76, 78–79, 93, 97–98, 120, 128, 131, 153n2
autism, 3, 14, 63, 93, 115

baby hatches, 10, 32, 59–60, 69
backward: foster parents, 17, 59, 66, 94, 124, 138; rural, 2, 59, 64
bad habits, 88, 110. *See also* backward
baihua, 2, 4, 94, 101, 114
baomu, 83, 97
Beijing, 2, 9, 82, 124
belonging: desire for, 27, 90, 140; to family, 50; in foster families, 72–74, 78–81, 86, 103, 124, 127, 153n3, 155n3; not belonging, 39, 49, 113. *See also* obligation
Bernstein, Robin, 92
birth defects, 59, 150n10
birth planning, 4–11, 16, 25, 32, 38–39, 57–58, 60–61, 64, 68. *See also* one-child policy
bonds: affective, 53, 99; between Auntie Li and Pei Pei, 126–127; with disabled children, 19; emotional, 129, 137–138; in extended family, 50; extrafamilial, 53; between father and son, 31; foster care, 17, 25, 30, 46, 72–74, 79–81, 84, 136; *guoji*, 31; kinship, 25, 136, 151n10; obligation, 79; social, 86, 153n1; transformative, 121
Briggs, Jean L., 76, 78, 152n12
Briggs, Lisa, 65

caifangren, 48. *See also* Kohrman, Matthew
capitalism, 71

cerebral palsy (CP), 3, 11, 14, 60, 63, 84, 90, 111;
    Dengrong, 44–45, 122; *naotan de haizi*, 48;
    Ren Ren, 71–72
Cheney, Kristen, 22, 66–67
child-rearing, 16–17, 73–75, 81, 83, 85, 91–95,
    129, 153n2. See also *guanjiao*; parenting
"child saving" discourse, 56, 66–67. *See also*
    Cheney, Kristen
child trafficking, 41, 151n9, 153n5
child training. *See* child-rearing
Child Welfare Institutes (CWIs), 5, 12, 56, 70
China Center of Adoption Affairs, 66
Chinese Census, 5, 33
Chinese Children's Day, 10, 92
Chinese Communist Party, 9, 14
choices: children's, 78–79; limited, 37, 57;
    secrecy in adoption, 31–32; as related to
    kinship, 23–24, 26, 139–140
Christians, 18–19, 21–22, 67, 143
chuxian, 41–43, 154n1 (chap. 4)
class, 16–17, 21, 55, 86, 88–95, 99–100, 134;
    middle-class, 25, 27, 67, 75, 123, 131–132, 136.
    See also status
cleft palate, 11, 40, 43–44, 63, 70, 113, 126
Colen, Shellee, 92
communism, 5, 15–16
contracts: excess emotion, 24, 29, 121–122, 129,
    131, 134; intergenerational, 83, 152n16; with
    respect to foster families, 9, 12, 28, 93, 99,
    127, 135, 138, 141; temporary, 25, 98
countryside, 1–3, 16–17, 31, 33, 35, 57, 95, 109, 123
COVID-19, 63, 143
Cultural Revolution, 16, 33, 35, 47, 83, 88,
    94–95, 151n6, 154n4
cure, 115–119, 121, 127

Daling, 1, 4, 14, 18, 19–21, 44–46, 72, 84, 149n6;
    resistance in, 130–132, 154–155n1; rural class
    differences, 90–93, 97–99; "special"
    character, 101–113, 117, 122–125
death: of children, 7–8, 60, 123, 142; father, 38,
    99; kinship, 153n3; social, 33, 80
Death by Default, 7
Deng, Pufang, 47
Deng, Xiaoping, 22, 47
Dengrong, 27, 44–46, 51–53, 55, 72, 91, 98–99,
    102, 121–125, 132
desire: to adopt, 8, 64; for belonging, 27; for
    children of both genders, 7, 57; for

intimacy, 28, 90, 99, 137; mine, 134, 147;
    orphanage, 128; prove class value, 16; with
    respect to foster families, 24, 29, 46, 63, 77,
    82, 119; Western, 23, 56, 67–69, 103, 115–117
diagnosis, 114–116, 154n1 (chap. 5)
disability: abnormality, 100, 112; cultural
    interpretations, 12, 21–22, 46, 49–53, 58–59,
    107, 135, 151n7; in Daling, 19; defined,
    149n2; disobedience, 109; explanation for,
    71; increased abandonment, 61, 154–155n1;
    monitoring of language, 43; none, 35, 153n1;
    policy, 47–48; relationship to ICA, 66–68,
    103, 116–117; relationship to impairment,
    152n5; social stigma, 88, 135; type of, 35, 115,
    126; undiagnosed, 14
disability studies, 22, 55–56, 74, 135, 149n2,
    154–155n1. *See also* ableism; disability
discipline, 73–75, 80, 88, 91–92, 96, 115, 119, 135
discrimination: disability, 12, 47–49, 53, 58–59,
    61, 112, 116, 126, 149n2, 152n5; divorce, 38;
    orphans, 44
disruption: Auntie Ma, 128–129; family line,
    31; foster families, 27, 29, 56, 79, 84, 117–118,
    122, 133, 136–140; Jiaqi, 104, 107; kinship, 22,
    26, 140; need, 86; parent-child order, 58–59,
    107
divorce, 38, 47, 53, 58, 89, 140, 153n1
Down syndrome, 3, 11, 14, 60, 63, 104, 111, 135
Dying Rooms, The, 7

education, 7, 9, 11, 16, 74, 132; for disabled
    people, 47, 59, 111–113; as related to
    morality, 83, 88, 90–95, 124, 135
emotion: abandonment, 81, 83; with respect
    to child-rearing, 75–76; class, 92, 99–100;
    envy, 90; excess, 24–25, 29, 69, 120–122,
    125–129, 131, 133–138; family making, 27, 46,
    91, 97–98, 153n1; in fieldwork, 21; motiva-
    tions, 82, 113
encouragement: child-rearing in foster
    families, 45, 53, 87, 122; Chinese government
    toward ICAs, 8–9, 61–64; Mercy Care, 13,
    18; to take another foster child, 119; from
    therapist, 114
Eng, David, 22, 67
envy: toward foster families, 17, 28, 90, 135;
    intergenerational, 95, 97–99, 137, 152n13,
    154n2 (chap. 4); kinship, 87
Ethiopia, 65

ethnography: mine, 22–25, 27, 29, 69, 130, 136, 138–141; other's, 57, 75, 89, 107–108

familism, 16, 39, 57, 102, 107–108, 112–113, 117; neofamilism, 51, 95, 99, 135
family making, 34, 86, 132–133; global, 14, 69; modern, 23, 55, 140, 143, 150n1; moral, 84; politics of, 27, 141
farmers, 2, 33
fate: bad, 48; children, 4, 32, 38, 41, 43, 68, 102, 113, 127, 132; elders, 136; families, 29, 50, 121
Fei, Xiaotong, 2, 23, 58, 107
fetishization, 68
fieldwork, 30, 143–144; abandonment, 32; adoption, 61, 63, 115–116; anthropological, 134; appearances, 71; Auntie Ma, 35; Briggs, Jean L., 76; disability, 48, 154–155n1; emotional intensity, 21–22; foster care, 14, 74, 82, 102, 130, 155n3; Guangxi, 6, 81, 151n5; intergenerational ambivalence, 88–89, 99; Mercy Care, 12, 18–20, 65; Nanning, 13, 54, 101; note-taking, 20; Wang, Leslie, 20, 59
filial piety, 5, 33, 51, 59, 107–108, 136, 152n16; children, 75; unfilial, 89, 94, 123
"forever" families, 4, 26, 100, 102, 115–116, 138, 149n4
foster care, 5, 9–10, 12, 149n3, 149n6, 153n1, 154nn1–2 (chap. 6); affinity in relationships, 50, 153n6; child-rearing, 91–92, 151n10, 152n12, 153nn2–4; of disabled children, 62, 109–114; families, 36–43, 44–46, 94–97, 101–103, 115–116, 119–122; government-sponsored, 4, 12–16, 22, 33, 137; relationship to ICA, 7, 34, 55–56, 63–69, 149n2, 149n4, 150n1, 150n11; informal, 8; kinship, 22–31, 58, 134–140, 150n13; marginality of, 53; Mercy Care, 149n7; monitors, 17–21, 48, 84, 99–100, 104, 152n13; parents, 35, 52, 71–76, 81–89, 107–109, 123–133

gift: child as, 128–129
Ginsburg, Faye, 92
gongxian, 83
Goody, Esther, 24
grandchildren, 15, 33, 78, 82, 136
grandparents, 31, 57, 78, 96, 147
Great Leap Forward, 35
Guangxi: fieldwork, 4, 10, 12–16, 18, 25, 55, 149n7; kinship, 31–32, 34, 38, 151n5;

minorities, 6; Nanning, 1, 64, 130–131; other cities in, 20, 42; out-of-the-way character, 2, 64, 81, 88, 94–95, 109, 115, 136, 149nn1–2, 151n9, 151–152n11
Guangzhou, 60, 66
guanjiao, 74
guardianship, 14, 40–41, 126, 132, 136
Guatemala, 65
Guilin, 42
Guo, Jinhua, 43, 49, 51, 58. See also Kleinman, Arthur
guoji, 31–33. See also adoption

Hague Convention, 11, 65–66
Hays, Sharon, 92
healthcare, 47, 59
Hengwei, 111–113
hepatitis B, 11, 135
heteronormativity, 23, 26, 56, 67–68, 103, 117
hierarchy: Chinese adults and children, 73, 79, 107; class, 90, 123, 129; disability policy, 48; family, 23, 25–26, 88, 100, 115–117, 138–139, 141; moral, 56, 67; social, 7, 108
high-quality, 7, 10, 25, 52. See also population quality
Holt International, 13, 89
Honghuan, 43, 80, 117
Hong Kong, 21, 31, 58, 94, 107
Hongmei, 3, 110–112
household: Daling, 109; extended family, 58; foster, 15, 43, 45, 48, 70, 97–98, 118, 125–127; heads of, 50, 57; registration, 32, 44, 113, 132; single-parent, 140. See also hukou
Hu, Mrs., 96–98
Huang, Auntie, 16, 27, 44–46, 50, 53, 91, 121–125
Hubei, 4, 48, 52
Huilan, 1, 3; in Daling, 111–113; with Dengrong, 53, 72, 122–125, 144–146; with foster parents, 84–85; intergenerational tension, 89–100, 136, 140; with Jiaqi, 104–109; relationship to orphanage, 17–18, 20; promotion, 131–132
hukou, 6, 16, 32, 43, 132

illness, 36; mental, 47, 49
impairment, 11, 41, 48–49, 51–52, 113, 123, 149n2, 152n15, 153n1
incarceration, 40–41, 43, 51, 126, 132, 151n7

inequality, 22–23, 53, 75, 92, 123, 128, 133; global, 55–56, 64–67, 79, 86, 143, 154–155n1

international non-governmental organization (INGO): care workers, 73–74, 103, 110, 115; care workers' intergenerational ambivalence, 27–28, 83–101, 125, 131–140, 152n13, 153–154n6; Chinese staff, 54; cooperation with ICA, 62, 68–69; foster care, 9, 13, 40; inquisitions, 36; Mercy Care, 4, 17–19, 149n7; other than foster care, 40, 57; resistance to, 121–123, 127–129; solicit money, 63; suspicion of, 21–22

intimacy: desire for, 28, 90, 100, 137, 140; foster families, 98, 135; neofamilism, 16, 95, 99; "outsourced," 62, 66–67, 116. See also Wang, Leslie

Inuit, 76

invisibility, 26, 127

isolation, 50, 52, 76, 79, 80, 82, 108

jiang daoli, 96. See also discipline

Jiaqi, 21, 102–109, 117

Johnson, Kay Ann: abandonment of infant girls, 7–9, 150n3; Chinese government's suppression of domestic adoption, 22, 55–61, 64–65, 150n1, 151n9, 151–152n11; domestic adoption, 31–32; ICA, 150n12; research, 149n9

Joyce, Kathryn, 65, 67

Kaili, 96–97, 118

Kasnitz, Devva, 53

Keyser, Catherine, 40

kindergarten, 13, 110–112. See also education; school

kinship, 4, 34, 136–140, 151n7; adoption, 7, 30–32, 38, 150n13; biological, 78, 135, 151n8, 153n3; Chinese, 52; gay, 24, 26; hierarchies, 118; ICA, 55–58, 103–104; making, 73–74, 83, 119, 151n10, 155n3; need, 86, 122, 141; patrilineal, 39; paucity, 129; temporary, 23–29

Kleinman, Arthur, 43, 49, 51, 58, 151n6. See also Guo, Jinhua

Kohrman, Matthew, 52, 152n14

Kuan, Teresa, 17, 75, 154n4

Lareau, Annette, 92

Law on the Protection of Disabled Persons, 47, 151–152n11

laziness, 44, 72, 98, 122

Leinaweaver, Jessaca, 65

Li, Auntie, 15–16, 20, 27, 39–41, 96–98, 118–127, 138

Lili, 103, 105–107

limbo, 41, 43, 53, 64, 113, 126

Liu, Teacher, 4, 10, 42, 87, 143; family boundaries, 99, 131, 136, 140; intergenerational tension, 85, 89–92, 94–95; relationship to Mercy Care, 13, 17

Longzhou, 35

loss, 27, 50, 96, 119, 128–129, 133, 142, 144

love: as if their own, 39, 101, 109–110; contingent, 95, 132; foster families, 27, 42, 44–46, 72–73, 82, 98, 120–121, 127; for God, 67; receiving love from society, 113; special, 116, 142–144

low-quality, 62. See also backward

Luli, 30–31, 33

Luo, Auntie, 71–72, 78

Ma, Auntie, 16, 20, 34–35, 138; with Meili, 27, 36–39, 44, 50, 54, 70, 89, 119–121, 128–129, 132; motivations to foster, 81–84; with Wei Wei, 77–78, 80

Mandarin, 2, 21, 88, 90, 93–94, 97, 114

maodun, 75

marginality: care, 67; Chinese government, 69; complexity, 5, 17, 24–25; disabled children, 102–103, 149n2; foster families, 127, 135–136; relationship to biology, 53; relationship to ICA, 55–56, 115; relationship to need, 50, 133, 144; retirees, 153–154n6; social, 22, 28–29, 81, 86

Marre, Dianne, 65

Mauss, Marcel, 128

medicine, 1–2, 123–125; children with medical conditions, 10–11, 18, 48–49, 63–68, 88, 142; insurance, 132; medical model of disability, 47; Western expertise, 103, 114–117

Meili, 20, 27, 41, 43, 46, 55, 102, 143; abandonment, 35–39, 44, 51–52, 153n1; adoption, 117, 132; with Auntie Ma, 34, 50, 70, 77, 82, 89, 119–121, 128–129; non-disabled, 13, 14, 28

mental illness, 47, 49

Mercy Care: defined, 4–5, 149n7; foster care in China, 12–21, 65, 91, 130, 143, 145; staff members, 28, 30, 35, 41–42, 85, 87, 89, 111–114, 119–122, 128; travel with, 10, 48–49

Ministry of Civil Affairs, 10

Mo, Older Sister, 1, 3, 91, 93–94, 111; with Dengrong, 44–46, 53, 72, 98, 122; with Jiaqi, 104–106; relationship to orphanage, 18, 20

Modell, Judith, 24–25, 128, 138–139, 150n13

modern. *See* family making

modernity, 16, 29, 53, 137–138, 153–154n6

morality, 16–17, 31, 49, 51, 71, 74–75, 81, 84, 120; in Daling, 107–108; as related to education, 83, 88, 90–95, 124, 135; hierarchies, 56, 67–68, 116

motherhood, 17, 81, 84, 86, 90, 92, 155n2

motivations: to foster, 15, 73–75, 81–83, 85–86, 88, 127, 130, 154n2 (chap. 6); to have children, 136; to keep adoption secret, 32; Mercy Care, 18; play in child-rearing, 78

Naftali, Orna, 136

Nanning, 1–2, 12–16, 20–22, 91, 105–106, 109, 113, 118, 132, 145

Nanning Municipal Orphanage, 3–4, 18, 93, 101, 115, 119, 125, 130, 131

Nanning Social Welfare Institute (SWI), 12–14, 18, 84. *See also* Nanning Municipal Orphanage

National Children's Day. *See* Chinese Children's Day

neediness: advocates for, 62; alliances, 153n6; children, 3; disabled children, 58, 69–70, 154n2 (chap. 4); foster families, 5, 21, 73, 75, 82, 90, 98, 127–136; infant girls, 8; kinship, 22, 26–30, 86, 100, 122, 137–141; medical, 66–68, 88, 124; mine, 143–144; older adults, 59, 89, 92; for personhood, 50; Western desire, 23

neglect, 7, 33, 59, 96–97, 108, 114

nengli, 52

neoliberal, 67

1991 adoption law, 39, 60, 151–152n11

obligation: Chinese personhood, 49, 53, 137; to family, 44, 51, 77, 95; foster families, 79, 82–83, 98; fulfilled, 58; legal, 127, 152n16; mutual, 73; social, 39, 52, 81, 107. *See also* belonging

one-child policy, 6, 57–58, 68, 136

orphanages, 2, 19–21, 36–37, 52, 59–60, 114–116, 143; baby hatches, 59–60; history of, 5,

7–11, 66–67; Jiaqi's return to, 104–109; monitors, 1, 4, 48–49, 65, 103, 109–112, 117–124, 126–136; monitors encourage affection, 72–74; monitors' intergenerational ambivalence, 17–18, 23–25, 27–29, 64, 75, 87–100, 139–140; monitors' perception of rural, 102; relationship to foster care, 13–16, 26, 39–46, 54–55, 61–63, 70–71, 79, 82–83. *See also* adoption; Nanning Municipal Orphanage; Nanning Social Welfare Institute (SWI)

orphans, 31–34, 38, 51, 107, 151n7; disabled, 112–113, 137; number of, 12–13. *See also* abandonment

out-of-plan children. *See* overquota children

overquota children, 8, 31–32, 40

parenting, 13, 78, 95; foster, 17, 20–21, 73–74, 88, 90, 92, 99, 101, 109, 115, 124

patrilineal, 16, 39. *See also* patrilocal

patrilocal, 34, 38–39, 151n5

Pei Pei, 55, 102; abandonment, 39–41, 43–44, 46, 51–53; with Auntie Li, 20, 27, 96–97, 118–119, 121, 125–127, 129, 132

Pengfei, 103, 113–117

pension, 6, 14, 16, 33–35, 88, 130

People's Republic of China (PRC): adoption, 150n1, 151–152n11; birth planning, 6–8; child-rearing, 75; child welfare, 10–15, 32–33, 62–63, 66; older adults, 47, 59, 149n5; vulnerability, 53

permanence, 37, 43, 63, 72, 80, 126, 132; in Daling, 19, 109, 117; domestic adoption, 9, 32; kinship, 24–27, 103, 113, 116, 122, 138–140

personhood, 22, 58–59, 107, 135, 137; for children, 153n2; disabled people, 107, 152n15; legal, 127; nonpersonhood, 51; orphans, 31–34, 151n7; relationship to abandonment, 46–48; social, 49–50, 66–68, 117, 124, 153n1

philanthropy, 50, 70, 108, 112–113

play: acts of, 74–75, 151n10, 153nn3–4; in childhood, 92; dialogues, 79; social roles, 107, 132; teasing, 43, 96, 102, 155n3; techniques, 124; threats, 80–81, 86, 91, 152n12; for Wei Wei, 78

plurality, 26, 88, 139

population quality, 16, 153–154n6. *See also* high-quality; low-quality

Potter, Jack and Sulamith Heins, 23, 49, 57–58, 81, 103, 107
poverty: abandonment, 7; adoption, 31; Auntie Li, 97–98, 126–127; Auntie Ma, 35; behavior, 108; cleft palate repair, 40; discourse, 90; families, 131–132, 140–141; foster mothers, 22, 25, 44, 46, 52–53, 66–67, 73, 83, 85–86, 92, 123, 137, 153n1, 153n6; Guangxi, 88, 151n9; implementation of disability rights, 47; Mandarin, 97; motivated to foster, 84; older people, 136; orphanage facilities, 20; oversight of foster care, 64; social, 23; social welfare, 61
pride: Director Wang, 101, 109; foster children, 3, 110; foster mothers, 82, 85, 93, 104, 126; Hulian, 124; village head, 112

Qian, Linliang, 22, 39, 50, 58, 70–71, 102–103, 107–108, 112–113, 117
Qin, Auntie, 77–78, 153n4
queerness, 67

race, 55, 92. See also white
Rapp, Rayna, 92
receiving and sending countries, 55. See also adoption
reform and opening up of the 1980s, 6, 22, 33, 59, 154n4
rehabilitation: center for, 13; laws, 47; medical, 114–116, 124; social, 22, 82–86, 137
relinquishment, 10, 25, 53. See also abandonment; orphans
Ren Ren, 71–72
replaceability: foster children, 126, 129; foster families, 4, 25, 28–29, 100, 103, 117, 127, 137–138, 140
resistance: to birth planning policies, 6; everyday acts of, 136; by foster families, 5, 24–27, 53, 56, 117, 130, 133, 137; by foster mothers, 127; mine, 79; by need, 22; unselfconscious, 25, 29, 121, 128, 137, 150n3
retirement, early, 5; lack of funds, 50, 81–82, 88, 126; mandatory, 33, 52; marginality, 153–154n6; women's, 15–16, 149n5
rights, 25, 144; children's, 136; disability, 47–48, 59, 65; education, 111–112; foster parents, 64, 66; legal, 151n11, 152n16; personhood, 49, 58

roles: ableism, 55, 65; children's, 58, 76, 78–80, 107–109; demand, 56; Dengrong, 46; familial, 39, 46; foster families, 63, 66, 71, 86, 132, 138–140; Meili, 39; observatory, 20; social, 25, 49–50, 52, 83, 99, 102, 153n1; societal, 27; state, 53
rural, 4–8, 15–16, 38, 43, 59, 112, 152n16, 154n2 (chap. 6); character, 102; Daling, 18–19, 90, 107, 109, 124–125, 130; Fei Xiaotong, 149n1; seniors, 33

Save the Child Fund, 9
Schneider, David, 23, 151n8
school, 15, 36, 95–96, 154n4; countryside, 57; disabled children, 12, 110–113; hukou, 6, 16; orphanage, 14, 40–41, 43–44, 114, 116, 126; preschool, 74–75; public, 59
secrecy, 89, 90; adoption, 23, 31–32, 150n1; Mercy Care, 19
seniors: child-rearing, 94, 96, 153n2; citizens, 13; defined, 15, 149n4; financial motivations to foster, 97; retirement, 33; vulnerability, 35, 50, 52–53, 152n16
shame, 78, 91, 122
Shang, Xiaoyuan: child welfare, 10, 15, 32, 38; disability, 58–59, 112; kin fosterage, 43; social welfare, 50
Shanghai, 2, 9, 126
shishi shouyang, 32
Shuttleworth, Russell, 53
Social Welfare Institutes (SWIs), 60. See also Child Welfare Institutes (CWIs)
special needs, 11–12, 44, 48, 55–56, 63, 65, 88, 154–155n1
status: moral, 49; orphan, 40, 43–44, 65; social, 33–35, 50, 64, 82, 85, 88, 90–92, 94, 103, 124. See also class
stigma: abandonment, 33, 150n1; Chinese personhood, 49, 51, 68; disability, 48, 67, 88, 108, 137; incarceration, 41; orphans, 43
Strathern, Marilyn, 34
stratification, 6, 43, 90, 92, 139
stress: child-rearing, 75; fieldwork, 19; motherhood, 17, 85; one-child policy, 57; to SWIs, 5
subjectivity, 74, 124, 153n3
Suling: with Dengrong, 122; generational disputes, 89, 94, 131; with Hongmei, 110–112; with Meili, 35–36; with Pei Pei,

39–40, 125, 127; relationship to Mercy Care, 17–20; with Xiaoyuan, 41–43
Sunshine Villages, 40
suzhi discourse, 6–7, 52, 153–154n6. *See also* high-quality

teasing, 43, 73–74, 76, 78
temporary: contracts, 98, 141; family forms, 24–26, 69, 140; foster families, 125, 143, 149n3; foster family bonds, 80, 121; kinship, 29, 137–138; life together, 4; parenting, 101; relationships, 127–128, 131, 133, 142. *See also* Temporary Policy on Foster Care
Temporary Policy on Foster Care, 9, 14
therapy, 3, 13–14, 72, 93, 124
trauma, 21, 73, 91, 106
Trump, Donald, 63

uncivilized, 2, 89, 90, 135. *See also* backward
United Nations Convention on the Rights of Persons with Disabilities (UNCRPD), 47
urban: Beijing, 82; definition for orphan, 36; education, 95; foster care, 4–5, 14–15, 19, 108, 110, 154n1–2 (chap. 6); reinstitutional-ization, 10; residency, 16; rural-urban divide, 6–7, 23, 149n1, 154n4; schools, 43

Vietnam, 35, 151n9
villagers, 2, 6, 108
vulnerability: costs to, 144; foster mothers, 85; for older adults, 33, 52; relationship to abandonment, 53; social, 27–28, 43, 48, 51, 73–74, 81–82, 86, 90, 137, 152n17, 153n3

wages, 14, 85, 98, 129–130, 135, 154n1 (chap. 6)
Waiting Child Program, 11, 56, 62–64, 69
Wang, Director: in Daling, 84, 91–94, 97, 101, 109, 124–125; with Pengfei, 114, 116–117; relationship to orphanage, 14, 18, 131

Wang, Leslie, 20, 22, 52, 59, 62, 65, 92, 112
Watson, James, 31
Wei Wei, 77–78, 153n4 (chap. 3)
welfare: child, 10–15, 32, 38, 40, 66, 69; institutions, 152n1; social, 5, 9, 19, 28, 47, 50–52, 58–59, 61–62, 127; state, 33
Western: adoptive families, 127, 137, 140, 150n12; countries, 26, 63, 65, 113, 153n6; demand, 22, 66–69; desire, 23, 56, 115–117; disability rights activists, 48; expertise, 90–92; families, 138; "forever" families, 100, 102–103, 149n4; INGOs, 19, 62; literature, 107; medicine, 123; my identity, 20–21; readers, 75
Weston, Kath, 24, 139
white: adoptive families, 26, 56, 67, 103, 117; Mercy Care, 5; my whiteness, 54
Wolf, Arthur, 23
Wolf, Margery, 23, 80
Wozniak, Danielle, 24, 26
Wu, Yuping, et al., 82, 124

Xiao, Wang, 30–31, 33
Xiaoyuan, 39, 42–43, 79–80, 102
Xu, Jing, 17, 74–75

Yan, Yunxiang, 15, 23, 50–51, 89, 94–95, 99, 107
Yang, Older Sister, 92–93, 104–106, 124
Yngvesson, Barbara, 22
Yulin, 20
Yunnan, 35, 151n9
Yuping, 13–14, 39, 96–97, 118, 125–126, 129

Zedong, Mao, 50, 57, 75, 130
Zelizer, Viviana, 92
Zhang, Hong, 50
Zhou, Director, 110
Zhuang: dialect, 2, 94, 101, 110; minority group, 6

ABOUT THE AUTHOR

ERIN RAFFETY is a research fellow at the Center for Theological Inquiry, an empirical research consultant at Princeton Theological Seminary, and an associate research scholar at Princeton Seminary's Institute for Youth Ministry. Raffety currently researches and writes on disability, congregational ministry, and church leadership and is an advocate for disabled people. She lives in Lambertville, New Jersey, with her husband and daughter.

Printed and bound by CPI Group (UK) Ltd, Croydon, CR0 4YY

09/06/2025

14685730-0001